D0531323

MIKE PARKER

C333997437

Published by AA Publishing (a trading name of AA Media Limited,
whose registered office is Fanum House, Basing View, Basingstoke RG21 4EA;
registered number 06112600).

First published in 2013. This edition published in 2016.
Copyright © Mike Parker 2013 and 2016

Contains Ordnance Survey data © Crown copyright 2014 Ordnance Survey 100021153

 © 2013 RoadPilot® Driving Technology

Extracts from Meera Syal's *Anita and Me* are reprinted by permission of HarperCollins
Publishers Ltd, © 1996 Meera Syal

A CIP catalogue record for this book is available from the British Library

ISBN: 978-0-7495-7823-7

A05414

Cover: Composite of illustrations by Mary Stella Edwards, taken from *Track to Highway
– A book of British Roads* by G Gibbard Jackson, published 1935 by Ivor Nicholson &
Watson Ltd. Copyright Ackland-Edwards Trust.

Printed and bound in China by 1010 Printing International

theAA.com/shop

Contents

SCOCIA : ULTRAMARINA
hec et albania dicta est
Sutherlande
Orkade Insule
Galeweia
Regio scotorum
Murus dividens scotos et pictos olim
WALLIA
Richemund
Duneline
Eboracum
Pons fret
Lincolnia
Legrecestr
Bedef
Dunestapl
cenobium sancti albani
london
Bathonia
Balnea badonis
Midelsex
Windlesor
Wintonia
Exsexe
Suset
Cantuar
Rouecest
NORTHFOLK
SUFOLK
DORSET
DEUONIA
CORNUBIA
ORIENS

History, as far as we were taught at school, is all about kings, queens, dates and battles. If we were lucky, we might have had the odd field trip to a castle, a stately home or a museum to prove it. Yet sometimes the most prosaic of features tell us even more about our past and our identity, how we came to be the people and the country that we are today.

Without doubt, roads and maps fall into the category of the strictly prosaic. They are both there in the background, doing their job with the minimum of fuss, and doing it so well that we barely give them a second glance. It is, however, well worth doing just that, even more so when we combine the two and gain a picture of Britain's development over thousands of years.

Roads are often compared with the arteries of the human body, and for good reason. They channel the lifeblood of a nation, moving people and goods around, shaping the development of our towns and cities and providing the framework on which all else is hung. From dirt tracks to Roman highways, turnpikes to motorways, every era has attempted to build a road network to suit its needs and priorities. Some have been more successful than others.

That story in itself is fascinating, for it goes to the heart of our governance, economy and identity – and also throws up some surprisingly juicy tales. It becomes even more intriguing when we look at the changing maps that depicted this growing road network, for, like the roads and indeed any other aspect of life, they too are always subject to the whims of fancy and fashion.

As cartography has undergone a revolution in the digital age, our take on its history and development has changed too. Not so long ago, mapping was a topic reserved for dusty corners of science and academia, off limits to most. Today, the sheer ubiquity of maps, on our computers and phones as much as our bookshelves, has brought a welcome reappraisal, and now we see them more readily in their wider context. Every mapmaker decides what goes on the map, and – sometimes more importantly – what stays off it. Such decisions tell us volumes about the politics inherent in any map, something that can range from benign emphasis for the sake of clarity right through to the very darkest forms of propaganda.

Opposite: Matthew Paris's 13th-century map of Britain, with the settlements on the road between Dover and Berwick-on-Tweed artificially aligned to emphasise its route as the backbone of the country

In Britain, we are fortunate to have a heritage of truly beautiful maps, and many of them appear within these pages. The appreciation of this has sharpened in the white heat of the digital revolution. For all its phenomenal usefulness, online and GPS-dependent mapping has yet to reach the stage where we generally find it an aesthetic joy. Not so with many of the old paper maps, whether painstakingly etched onto copper plates by men and women who had taken decades to learn their craft, or lovingly transcribed by the expert cartographers of great global companies such as Ordnance Survey and Bartholomew.

When I wrote my cartographic memoir, *Map Addict* (2009), I had a sneaking suspicion that the tale was one that might be of interest to more than just a few fellow diehard map nerds. So it proved; one man's inability to go to the end of the road without first consulting the map chimed with more fellow sufferers and sympathisers than I ever dared imagine, those who appreciated cartography not just for its practical utility but for its artistic, cultural and political qualities too. In recent years, mine was only one of many new books that took the topic and ran with it in all kinds of directions; added to that, there have been numerous superb exhibitions, articles, TV and radio programmes about maps. And websites, of course. They are the principal impetus for the trend, for now we can sit in our own front rooms and fly across the world, zooming in and out where we please, or peruse many of the world's great map libraries, or read any number of informed, entertaining and provocative blogs that put it all into context.

To a lesser extent, the same has happened with the history and development of roads; the internet has helped us find our inner geek, to be proud of it and to find those who share our enthusiasms. But there is always room for the more languid perusal offered by books and paper maps. Researching and writing *Mapping the Roads* has been an eye-opener for me. I've loved the way the story has ebbed and flowed through the centuries, but especially through the revolution brought about by the age of the car over the last 120 years. More than any other single factor, it is the car that has shaped our landscape and changed our maps, for better and for worse. It is a story full of intrigue and invention, ambition and hope – sometimes fulfilled, sometimes thwarted. It is a tale of Britain, told through its lifeblood.

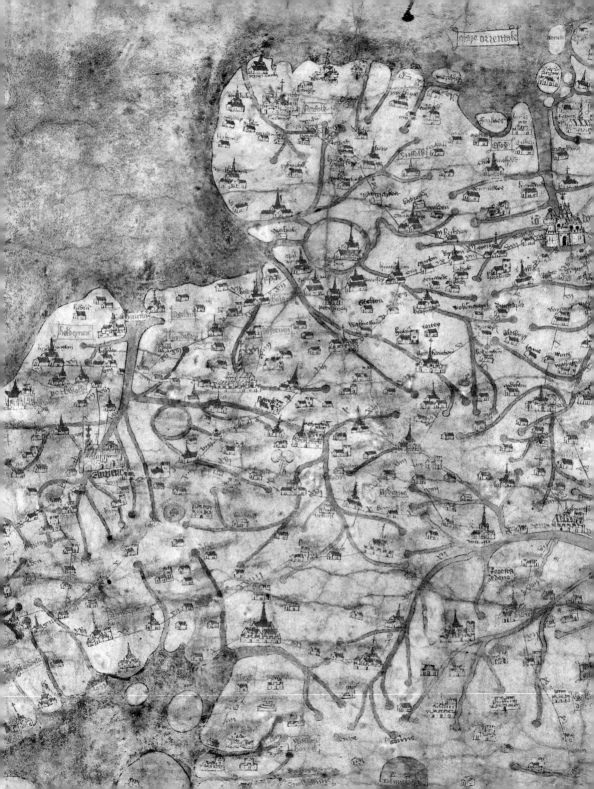

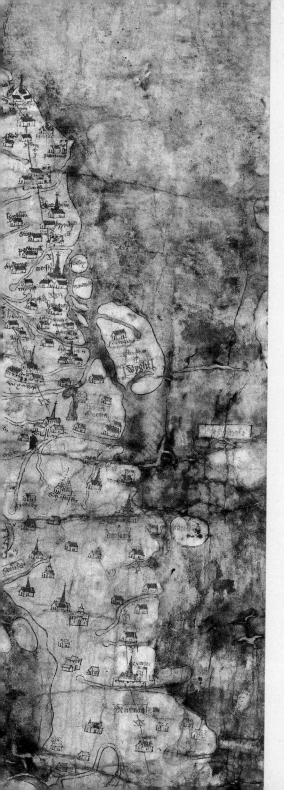

Chapter 1

ALL ROADS
LEAD TO ROME
(UP TO 1675)

What – and when – was Britain's first road map? It's impossible to say, though there were surely nomadic Neanderthals scratching maps in the dirt to show each other the route to their next stop, the safe track to a favoured hunting ground or to warn of possible ambushes ahead. We can only imagine their maps briefly scored into tree bark or honed from stones, sticks and mud.

But there are many permanent remnants of this distant age. From the tip of Cornwall to the outer reaches of the Shetland Islands, Britain has a wealth of standing stones, henges, dolmens, barrows and stone circles folded into its landscapes, some dating back as far as the Stone Age. These are places of fantastic mystery and excitement, offering us the chance to peel back the centuries and plug ourselves directly into the minds of our ancestors.

Although we can never be entirely certain why such monuments were built, many theories suggest a topographic or cosmographic basis for their design. Numerous ancient stone circles and alignments are known to point towards important sunrises and sunsets in the annual calendar: Stonehenge, on Salisbury Plain, is the most celebrated example, although evidence suggests it is a more significant marker of the winter solstice, rather than the summer equivalent that draws the crowds today. In truth, Stonehenge is so elaborately constructed that it can be used to pinpoint both solstices, and a whole raft of other important solar and lunar movements through the calendar. Many other stone circles and alignments, including Castlerigg in Cumbria, Callanish on the Outer Hebrides and Ballochroy in Argyll and Bute, were positioned with great precision to reflect the passage of the sun and moon, and often also used their place in the landscape as orientation towards significant nearby hills and rocky outcrops. Maps of a kind perhaps, but not as we know them.

Previous page: Detail from the Gough Map *(c.1360), which shows 3,000 miles of road as red lines between towns*

Some ancient stones were carved with designs that can be read more explicitly as maps. The best European examples lie in the valley of Valcamonica, part of the Italian Alps. The area is home to hundreds of thousands of carvings on its smooth rocks of sandstone and schist: human figures, animals, abstracts, wagons, even entire scenes of battles

Above left and right:
Fields, houses and roads
are depicted in the rock
petroglyphs of Bedolina,
Valcamonica, in the
Italian Alps (c.1500 BC)

and farming. Some have been identified as rudimentary maps; the finest dates from around 1500 BC and measures 14 by 8 feet. It shows one circular and more than 30 rectangular shapes thought to be fields, some six houses and an assortment of people and animals. Linking everything together is a network of carefully recorded tracks, including ones that suggest hillside hairpin bends. Some scholars insist that the map is only figurative, but many believe that the level of detail is such that it must have some literal basis in the local topography.

There is nothing so intricate, nor quite so explicitly map-like, in any of the ancient carvings found in Britain. The greatest concentration is in

Above: Carvings on the rocks at Old Bewick, Northumberland (c.3000 BC)

northern England and southern Scotland, and none are more impressive than those found on the magnificently bleak moors of Northumberland. The carved stones of Old Bewick, near the town of Wooler, contain a typical range of cup-marks, cup-and-ring patterns and concentric circles, and have been dated to between 3500 and 2000 BC. Linking the varied circular patterns are a number of deeply carved connecting grooves, paths perhaps, which have led to some theories that these – and others nearby – might be topographic maps. Some such rocks were placed in strategic locations commanding a number of valleys and ancient trackways, which lends further credence to the idea that they perhaps had some waymarking purpose. Even if not, the ancient rock art of Northumberland is intriguingly atmospheric, and well worth a squelch across the tussocky hills.

HOW ROADS SHAPE OUR SETTLEMENTS

The shifting pattern of roads over the centuries has had a demonstrable effect on the map of British towns. Settlements grew in the wake of new routes, often at bridging points or important crossroads. As a result, other nearby settlements would wane, or even disappear altogether.

A fine example of this can be found in the various incarnations of Salisbury. The original settlement at Old Sarum, a couple of miles north of the modern city, was an Iron Age hill fort built on a hill at a crossroads of two major trade routes, and just above the River Avon. The Romans fortified it and steered five important routes to meet there. The Vikings and Saxons came here too, as did the Normans, who walled the city and built a castle and cathedral within it.

The Saxons also placed an abbey and accompanying settlement in the more sheltered valley of the River Nadder, a tributary of the Avon, some three miles southwest of Old Sarum. As well as the shelter, Wilton was a good bridging point of the often boggy Nadder valley, and the town grew rapidly, with '12 paroche churches or more' by the time of the Norman conquest. By the ninth century, this part of the west Saxon kingdom had become a discrete unit of administration: Wiltshire, named after its capital, Wilton.

By the early 13th century, overcrowding and feuding in the tight confines of Old Sarum, together with its exposed site, resulted in the Church deciding to build a new cathedral down in the fertile river meadows to the south, and the modern city of Salisbury was born. Old Sarum famously deteriorated to the point where it became the most indefensible of all 'rotten boroughs'; by the time of the 1832 Reform Act, its 11 electors (none of whom lived there) were still sending two members to parliament.

Wilton too was quickly eclipsed by the new city. As the new cathedral rose on the meadows, a bridge over the Avon was built nearby, one that can still be seen in place today. Traffic diverted from Wilton over the new Harnham Bridge, roads in and around the new city grew and both Old Sarum and Wilton went into decline – the former absolutely, the latter in a rather more genteel fashion.

Above: A frosty winter morning on the Ridgeway long-distance path at Hackpen Hill, Wiltshire

Some of our oldest tracks and roads can still be identified. The Sweet Track, an elevated wooden walkway on the Somerset Levels near Glastonbury, has been precisely dated to 3807/6 BC, and is only one of many prehistoric tracks built to give hunters a dry route across the peat bogs and marshes. Running for approximately one and a quarter miles, it appears that the Sweet Track was only used for about a decade, probably up to the time that it was subsumed into the black sump itself. Similar fragments of ancient tracks regularly surface during archaeological digs: one even older than the Sweet Track, buried nearly 15 feet beneath today's ground surface, came to light during the construction of a new wing for Belmarsh Prison in 2009.

Of greater interest are the longer routes that can still be traced across the landscape. Identifying our oldest roads for certain is fraught with difficulty – the only substantial one we can be sure about is the Ridgeway, cutting along the chalk scarp that separates the southeast of England from the rest of the country. Some stretches, especially across the Berkshire Downs, are studded with Iron Age hill forts and camps, as well as many other telling nuggets of ancient history.

PILGRIM ROUTES AND TRADE ROUTES

Although rarely used solely for a single purpose, many early roads became known by a variety of names according to their primary function. Some were religious, such as the pilgrim routes to Walsingham in Norfolk, St David's and Ynys Enlli (Bardsey Island) in Wales, or the shrine of St Swithun at Winchester. The most celebrated was Thomas à Becket's shrine at Canterbury, which spawned an entire industry of inns, ostlers and guides along an assortment of routes. Most notable were the ancient track across the North Downs, known now as the Pilgrim's Way national trail, and the route from London, along the old Roman Watling Street, immortalised by Chaucer in *The Canterbury Tales* (*c.*1387). As Chaucer so happily demonstrates, a pilgrimage was usually far from a pious occasion, and so it remains.

Monastic trods are another set of religious routes that can often still be traced. These usually connected abbeys and outlying granges of particular religious orders, such as the Cistercians' route between their two abbeys of Cwmhir and Strata Florida in mid-Wales, the Benedictines' between Buckfast and Tavistock abbeys in Devon, and the spectacular Mastiles Lane in North Yorkshire, connecting a grange of the enormously wealthy Fountains Abbey at Kilnsey with distant estates of the abbey in the Lake District. As well as their monastic purpose, all of these tracks were much used as drovers' routes. The one category of religious track seldom used for any other purpose was the corpse road, which linked outlying parts of parishes with their mother church.

Drovers' roads can be found in most of northern and western Britain, heading southwards and eastwards towards markets in the wealthier areas. The practice of driving cattle long distances may have gone on way back into the pre-Roman era; it was big business by the Middle Ages, when the country's economy was largely based on the wool trade. Upon the creation of the turnpikes and the enclosure of land between the 16th and 19th centuries, many of the drovers' roads became the unofficial routes for all. Even with the arrival of the railways, which saw off most droving, some routes in Scotland and Wales were still being used for their ancient purpose in the first few years of the 20th century.

Other trades that readily gave their names to roads and tracks include the military herepaths, whose name indicates their Viking origins in our landscape, portways to market towns or ports, and the saltways that placed towns such as Droitwich in Worcestershire and the various –'wiches' of Cheshire (for example Nantwich, Middlewich and Northwich) firmly at the heart of the Roman and medieval road networks.

Medieval historians talked of four great pre-Roman roads across the country that, in the early Middle Ages, were accorded the status of royal highways; the 13th-century chronicler Matthew Paris mapped them in his *Scema Britannie* (c.1250). It's a very odd map, little more than a rough sketch, and far less accomplished than his others. According to Paris, three of these four great roads were Romanised (Ermine Street, Watling Street and Fosse Way), and the fourth, the Icknield Way, was not. We should take the idea with a pinch of salt, given that, on his map, Paris has the national crossroads, where all four roads meet, at Dunstable.

But there is growing evidence of a rudimentary pre-Roman network of roads, some of which may have been expertly engineered. The recent discovery of a metalled and cambered road in a Shrewsbury quarry has been dated as complete at least a century before the Roman invasion. There are many more. Look at any modern road map, where Roman roads still scorch straight across the countryside, and it's often the case that they cut through and even duplicate other ancient roads that were probably there first.

Above: The Roman road across Wheeldale Moor, near Goathland, North Yorkshire

When it comes to the first proper roads and their accompanying maps, we inevitably look to the Romans. Their road network has left a permanent stamp on the layout of the country, not least in the positioning of many towns. The road building, on a scale and to a standard never before seen in Britain, began as soon as the Romans invaded in AD 43, and for obvious reason: there is no swifter way of conquering territory than creating secure transport routes through it. After four years, the Roman province of Britannia encompassed all of the south and east of England (as far as a line drawn roughly between the Severn and the Trent). Within that, there were some thousand miles of road, including the mighty Fosse Way as a highway along the province's northwestern borderlands.

Oleū ĩfmox . Oleū siṁ . Oleū cū Balsamo .

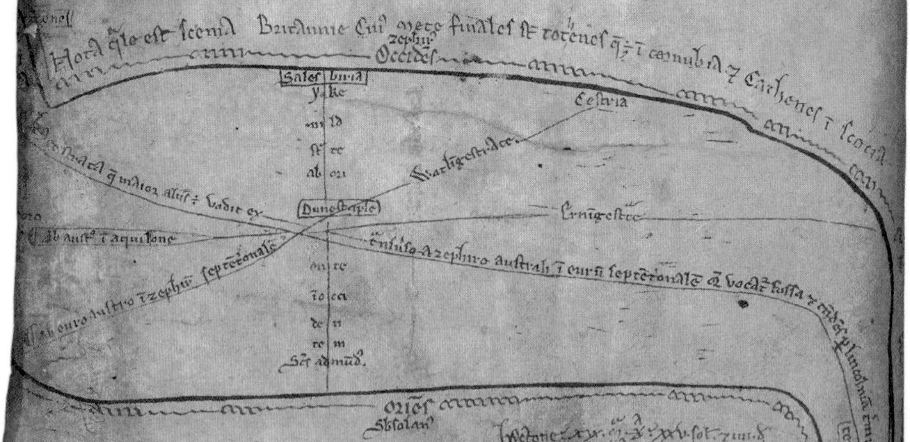

Occides

Zephir

Hoc ꝑ̄o est scemia Britannie cui̯ ꝣ̄ro finales sṫ totenes q̃. � cornubia 7 Carhenes ī scoceā

Sales bina

Cestria

Suartigestr̄ dcē

Dunestaple

Lmigestr̄e

ī aut̄ c̄ aquilone

ēsula ā zephiro austrah̄ ī curū septētonale q̄ vocat̄ fussa 7 vide plūcōnis fmiāt̄o

Sēt admūd

Orief

Subsolan̄

Hoctone . xv . q̃ . x x̄v. sol. 7 iiii d
Leimim̄ q̄ lix̄. x d. bignté
Ercelvine . q̄ iii. decim̄ x . iij
Brechime . c . iij s̄. decim̄ x . ij
Wareswe iiii. iij . x . vi . soʒ vi . ꝺ
Tirefeld xvi . iij. dec̄ i . iij . 7 xxxv d
Sū̄a om̄ fece de subue xlvi . q̄ . d̄ . xvi . sol

Sū̄a decime pensiom̄ ex diocesi
do ecc̄a de dachet . vi . iij . 7 dim̄ . x . ii . soʒ 7 viii . ꝺ
de Wuburne xv . soʒ . 7 c . xvii . ꝺ

Sū̄a decime elemosin̄ 7 ry
do ecc̄a de chiefꝫ 7 iii minutis decim̄

Sū̄a totat̄ supedc̄e . xlv . oi .

Sū̄a decime ecc̄ if . dioc̄ a ſ̄

Suma
pl. oj . lxxvi

RULER STRAIGHT ROMANS

The first wave of Roman roads culminated in the building of the Fosse Way, the 200-mile highway from Seaton in Devon (with a spur off towards Exeter) to Lincoln. In its entire length, the road never deviates further than six miles from a direct line drawn between its end points. This level of accuracy required very specific engineering, as well as considerable knowledge of the landscape. With no magnetic compasses, the ability to project the forthcoming direction of the road would have been achieved using astronomical and solar positioning, an elementary surveying instrument called the groma, and perhaps ways of establishing an aim point on the horizon such as fire, smoke or even homing pigeons.

There was good reason for such directness. These were invaders' roads, designed to speed troops and traders deep into the British hinterland from their initial bridgeheads in the south and east of England. Their well-drained stone surface provided the easiest passage for Roman vehicles, from the elaborate chariots of officials to the most basic of carts and wagons. Pulled by oxen, horses or mules, such vehicles did not turn easily, making a straight route far more practicable, even if that meant having to tackle considerable gradients, such as the Fosse Way's final 1:6 pull up into Lincoln.

The straightness of Roman roads is the first thing that we learn about them, often from the back of the car as children. Looking at a modern road map, the eye is still drawn to the lines of Roman roads, carving their way so efficiently through the patchwork maze of subsequent centuries. Our home-grown efforts at managing the landscape look so piecemeal and haphazard by comparison with the invaders' brutally methodical directness.

In many ways, the big Roman highways were the forerunner of the motorway, nearly 2,000 years later. They were built for speed and with no real sense or context of the countryside through which they cut. Forts, camps and wayside stops, like the service stations, distribution depots and retail parks of today, mushroomed alongside them. They created settlements, rather than connecting existing ones, and were flanked by wide, clear shoulders of land. As with so many other aspects of our modern existence, the Romans invented the prototype.

Opposite: Matthew Paris's Scema Britannie *map (c.1250), showing the 'four great roads' of Britain meeting at Dunstable. It has a curious orientation, with west at the top*

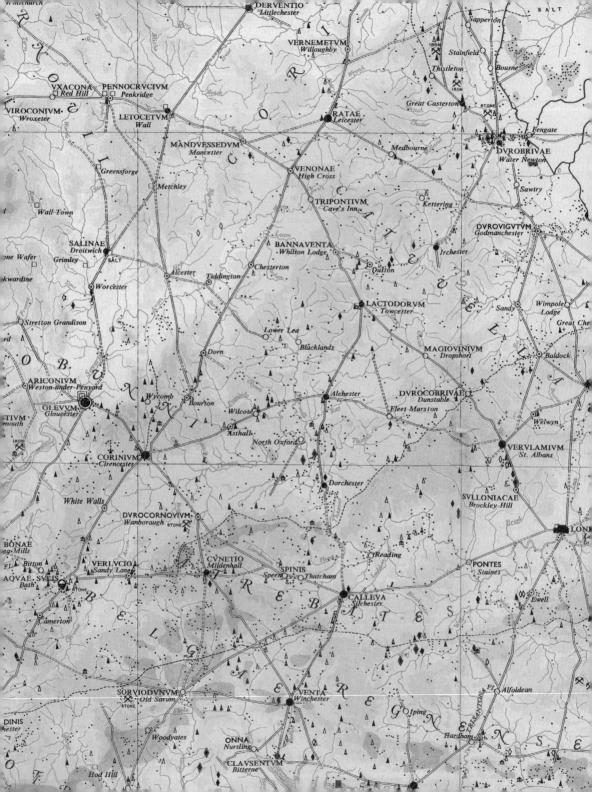

Over the ensuing decades after the Roman invasion, the road network spread. According to the venerable Ordnance Survey map of Roman Britain, a popular fixture in the company's repertoire since 1924, there is something over 2,000 miles of identifiable Roman road in Britain, though this is a very conservative estimate. Others put the figure at three, four and even five times as much, and include many lesser roads as well as the more celebrated highways.

The Romans knew all about the power of maps, as much for their swagger value as their utility. The sole surviving Roman map from the era itself is the supersized (60 by 43 feet) marble wall plan of Rome known as the *Forma Urbis Romæ*. It shows every street, courtyard, column and fountain of the Imperial City at a colossal 1:240 scale.

So many aspects of today's world originated in the Roman era, and that includes the road map. Although all we have now is a 13th-century copy of a third century original, the *Peutinger Map* is a forerunner of the kind of road atlas we know so well today. Roads are shown at the expense of nearly all other features, distances are annotated alongside each route and only the main towns, wayside rest stops and road junctions are given space; over 500 named places appear. Other detail, including any accurate sense of scale, shape and size of the landmasses represented, is entirely subsidiary. The map is believed to be an adjunct to the *Antonine Itinerary*, a long list of Roman roads that was compiled at about the same time as a manual for soldiers and couriers.

Like the *Forma Urbis Romæ*, the *Peutinger Map* was also designed for showy purposes. This map of the entire Roman Empire, from the Atlantic shore of Europe to the Indian Ocean, was fitted onto an elongated scroll, 1 foot wide and 22 feet long. It was evidently not created with marching centurions in mind. It is a statement of might, designed – as many maps have been since – to overawe the viewer by the sheer scale of the possessions portrayed. The old saying that all roads lead to Rome is given magnificent cartographic form, with the Imperial City shown in splendour as a seated female figure in a huge medallion, with the River Tiber flowing at her feet, and 12 named highways radiating out like the spokes of a wheel. Rome is unquestionably the hub of the world.

Opposite: An extract from the Ordnance Survey's Roman Britain map (1956)

Overleaf: The westernmost section of the Tabula Peutingeriana, *or* Peutinger Map *(c.AD 250), showing the* cursus publicus, *the road network built by the Romans. Britain appears in the top left corner; the main landmass shown here is France and the Low Countries, with Algeria across the Mediterranean to the south*

The westernmost section of the *Peutinger Map* is missing, so the only part of Britain shown is a sliver of the south and east coasts, from Lemavio (Lympne) and Dubris (Dover) up to Sinomagi (perhaps Saxmundham or Ixworth in Suffolk). There is a road marked along each of the south and east coasts, and either side of the Thames estuary, and further roads are seen heading inland towards Londinium (London) – but for that and the rest of the country, we have to depend on a Victorian reconstruction of the absent fragment.

THE GHOST TOWNS AT ROMAN JUNCTIONS

Once the Roman road network had penetrated deep into Britain, forts and settlements inevitably grew at its major junctions. This gave birth to many modern towns, most of which have the telltale suffix of –chester, -cester or –caster in their name, including Manchester, Cirencester, Dorchester, Colchester, Leicester, Lancaster, Towcester, Chichester, Worcester, Gloucester, Winchester and Chester itself.

A few of the Roman towns did not survive their departure. Perhaps the most mysterious is Silchester in Hampshire, the Roman Calleva Atrebatum, itself built on an earlier Iron Age settlement. This was a major garrison town, covering 100 acres, and the hub of six significant Roman roads, including the main road west from London. It features in four of the fifteen British routes in the *Antonine Itinerary*, three of which have it as that route's terminus. The modern village of Silchester lies a mile to the west, but there is almost nothing, save for the ruined Roman city walls and the present-day parish church, on the site of Calleva Atrebatum. Excavations have so far failed to find the answer to its sudden abandonment.

Sometimes, the expected town just never happened. Where two of Roman Britain's biggest roads – Watling Street and the Fosse Way – meet, the resultant settlement of Venonis grew up on what is now the Warwickshire–Leicestershire border. This spot was seen by the Romans as the very centre of England, both geographically and cosmically, yet the town never amounted to much. Known today as High Cross, after the 18th-century column erected there to mark its omphalic status (and whose ruins are set for restoration), it is even less impressive today: a cheerless former coaching inn now just yards from a noisy dual carriageway, a couple of farms, a roadside caravan churning out bacon butties and – using the same advantage of its place atop a gentle hill as did the Romans – a gargantuan mobile phone mast.

Following the Romans' departure in the early fifth century, there were no substantial improvements in road building for more than a thousand years. The stone roads left by the Romans were much used, although frequently parts were abandoned, neglected or plundered for building materials. The stretches that remained, however, were still impressive many centuries later. Eighteenth-century antiquarian William Stukeley marvelled at the state of the Fosse Way near Ilchester in Somerset, remarking that its flat, quarried stones laid edgeways remained firmly intact, and resembled 'the side of a wall fallen down'.

When it comes to the next maps, we have to march forward into the 13th century to find anything. We've already encountered the St Albans monk Matthew Paris and his strange *Scema Britannie* sketch map of the four great roads of Britain colliding at Dunstable. Paris left other, considerably more impressive maps that shed some light on two important roads. His exquisite plan of Britain of *c.*1250 was the first European map to have north at the top, and it is the line of the Great North Road that provides its spine and focus. The road is shown by a series of 17 settlements, from Dover to Hadrian's Wall, rising in a near straight line up the map, a line that if continued from its northern terminus at Newcastle points directly at Edinburgh. In reality, of course, the route from Dover to Newcastle via London, St Albans, Stamford, Newark and Doncaster is far from straight, but the prominence given to it on this map demonstrates its status and importance.

Paris also left us our first road strip map, in the shape of his *Chronica Majora*, showing pilgrimage routes from London to Rome and Jerusalem. In many ways this was a strikingly modern map, practical in cartographic terms as well as woven through with the customary allegorical detail of the early medieval *mappae mundi*. The walled capital of London is

Right: Another version of Matthew Paris's Chronica Majora *strip map of the pilgrimage to Jerusalem, from his* Historia Anglorum. *The left-hand panel shows the journey from London to Dover, via Rochester and Canterbury*

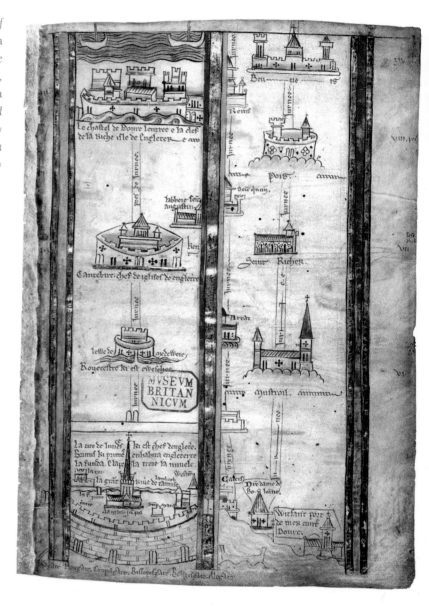

represented by a central image of St Paul's, flanked on either side by 'la Tur' (the Tower of London) and Westminster Abbey. From London Bridge, two alternative routes are depicted, with the text that describes them forming the representation of the road itself. It's a straight choice: 'le chemin ver la costere et la mer' (the road by the coast and sea) or 'le chemin a Rouescestre' (the road to Rochester), shown astride a lively River Medway, before heading to Canterbury and Dover. Even the time taken to travel is neatly annotated alongside: both are marked as 'Jurnee', or a day. Later pages of the *Chronica*, particularly in Italy, use the very modern approach of showing alternative routes on fold-out flaps. These two maps confirm that, at this point, our two main roads were from London to Edinburgh and London to Dover – the A1 and the A2, as they were to become many centuries later.

The great-grandfather of all British road maps came soon after Paris' exquisite efforts. What became known as the *Gough Map*, after the 18th-century topographer who donated it to Oxford's Bodleian Library, is a definitive break from the religious iconography and allegory of early medieval mapping. This was a purely geographic exercise, a recognisable map of the whole of Britain with as much precision and detail in it as could possibly be mustered, even if the detail and accuracy fade the further north and west you go. Cornwall, Wales and Scotland, all largely *terra incognita* to the royal clerks who probably drew it, are especially shapeless.

Thanks to the inclusion of various features that make dating the *Gough Map* quite precise, the edition that survives now was created within five years either side of 1360, although it is believed to be a revision of a previous map from as early as 1280. Central to it are some 600 towns and cities, and a 3,000-mile network of roads connecting them. The roads are shown as red lines, most of them annotated by Roman numerals showing the distances between settlements – a commonplace feature of cartography to us, but one that was not then repeated until 1671, when Thomas Jenner produced his map of Britain.

Other surviving contemporary manuscripts largely confirm the network of routes shown by the *Gough Map*. The Premonstratensian order of monks had some 30 abbeys spread around the country; an

Overleaf: The Gough Map *(c.1360). Britain lies on its side, and shows phenomenal accuracy in the south and east, but much less so the further north and west you go*

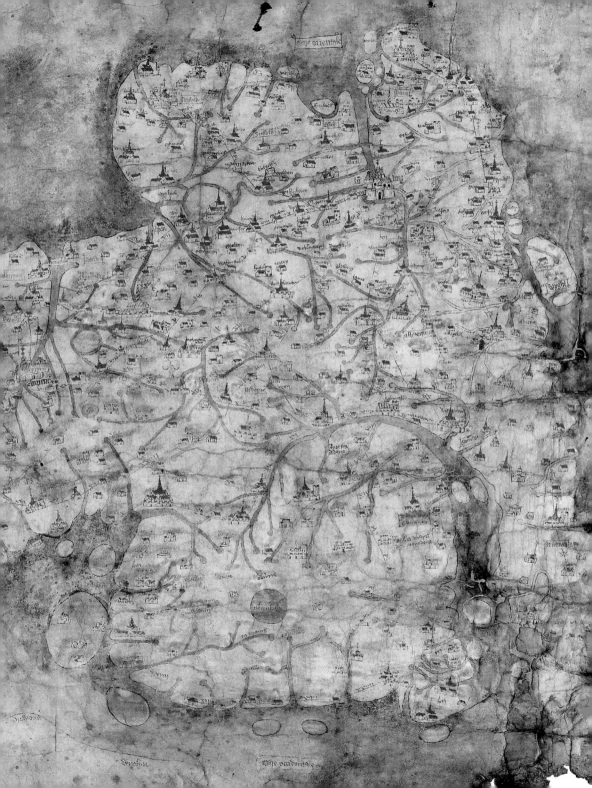

itinerary from 1400 survives at Titchfield Abbey, between Southampton and Portsmouth on the Hampshire coast. This details routes to the other outposts of the order, from Titchfield itself in the south to Alnwick in Northumberland, 276 miles away, and from Norwich and Leiston, Suffolk in the east to Torre, Devon in the west. Most of the routes correspond with those on the *Gough Map*.

But is every red line an actual road? There is some doubt. While some of the lines certainly correspond with known routes, many do not. Furthermore, although some 40 per cent of the lines equate with surviving Roman roads, many of the best-known – such as the Fosse Way, Icknield Way and large sections of Watling Street – are not shown; neither is any road between London and Dover nor York and Newcastle (indeed, there are no red lines at all around Newcastle and Durham, despite the latter city's careful depiction on an exaggerated loop of the River Wear). The red lines may in some cases be just graphic depictions of marked distances, or even something a little more politically charged. There is a red line shown hugging the north and west Wales coast as far south as Cardigan, connecting the newly constructed 'iron ring' of castles of Edward I, but such a road has never really existed and its portrayal is perhaps more propaganda than reality.

There are no red lines at all shown in Scotland. Indeed, the geography of the northern section of Britain on the *Gough Map* is hopelessly vague: there is no attempt to delineate with any accuracy the shape of the Scottish coastline, the whole landmass is wildly out of scale, estuaries, rivers and settlements are marked in the wrong place, and there is more annotation of local earldoms than of towns and cities. This all points to the substantial part of the research and surveying work having been done before Edward I began his Scottish campaigns in 1291.

Some parts of the *Gough Map* show particular accuracy. The shape of the southeast of England and East Anglia is instantly recognisable to us now, and contains a profusion of red lines, most corresponding to known roads. In such a congested part of the country, the scribes of the map have done well to pack in rivers, settlements and roads. Unsurprisingly, most of the roads emanate from London – the impregnable fortress – shown as a grand and elaborate vignette on the map.

The most intriguing area of the map is that depicting the region to the south and east of York. It's often been assumed that one of the map's scribes must have come from this part of the world, or that this version of the map came from hereabouts, for the detail is unsurpassed elsewhere, particularly in showing what we believe to be roads. It remains something of a mystery, however. York itself, grand enough to be the only city outside London worthy of gold lettering, is not shown on any great north–south route; a spur from the city connects up with the Great North Road at Leeming. This has followed its well-worn route all the way from London, but instead of continuing up towards Durham and Newcastle, soon veers west instead along what is now the A66, to Bowes, Brough, Appleby and Carlisle. To the east of York there are a number of roads: one down to Howden on the Ouse estuary, one up to Malton and, strangely, two running parallel to Market Weighton (one via Pocklington, the other not specified, but thought to cross the Derwent at Stamford Bridge) before joining forces en route to Beverley and Hull.

ROADS ON EARLY SCOTTISH MAPS

That there are no roads at all marked in Scotland on the *Gough Map* tells us a number of things. First and foremost, this was to the mapmakers a strange and foreign land, as shown by the rather plaintive label *Hic habundant lupi* ('Here dwell wolves') up in the far northwest. The reality of geography – the country's shape, size and distribution of towns – is at its absolute sketchiest in Scotland; instead, we get a distinctly vague landmass carved up and labelled with the names of local earldoms. The mapmakers, probably in the royal court in London, evidently knew little about the place, except who owned it.

That said, home-grown early Scottish maps show noticeably fewer roads than their English and Welsh counterparts. The Romans left a far less definite imprint north of Hadrian's Wall, and almost nothing beyond the Antonine Wall, between the Clyde and the Forth. Accounts of English royal campaigns in Scotland, particularly those of Edward I between 1291 and 1307, give us an idea of the road network, if with no real detail as to its quality.

*Opposite: Detail from the
Blaeu Atlas of Scotland
(c.1654), showing some
of the roads of Lothian*

The greatest name in early Scottish mapping is Timothy Pont (1565/6–1614), who produced a series of highly distinctive, and amazingly accurate, sketch maps of regions of the country. Although many bridges appear, and Pont's own notes refer to his routes, there is only one road marked on his original maps: the Causey Mounth, a stone causeway running inland through the bog between Stonehaven and Aberdeen, the route of which can still be traced today.

After his death, Pont's cartography was used as the basis for more detailed maps, most notably the magnificent *Blaeu Atlas* of the 1650s, which included a number of roads. The lovely map of Lothian, for instance, shows some seven roads converging on Edinburgh from all directions, while the Renfrewshire map takes considerable care to show the annotated 'Way to Glasgow' from the then much larger burgh of Paisley.

As regards the distance measurements on the *Gough Map*, there seems to have been a certain amount of rounding up or down going on, as nearly half of all the distances shown are in multiples of five, ending in a V or X. If the measurements are in miles, most come out at less than the recognised distance. The road from York to Howden, for example, is marked with the figure XVI, or 16; modern measurement has it at 20.9 miles. Most likely, the unit of measurement is the old French mile or the leuca, a Roman version of the league, both equivalent to approximately 1.3 modern miles.

The era of the *Gough Map* also gave rise to the first legislation on building and maintaining a road network. Edward I's Statute of Winchester (1285) decreed that 'highways leading from one market town to another shall be enlarged', and that all scrub and undergrowth 200 feet either side should be cleared, in order to leave no place 'whereby a man may lurk to do hurt'. Lords of the manor were held responsible for this, even if it meant cutting a swathe through their own parkland. The statute also enshrined the idea of the road as an easement, or absolute right of way, and introduced the notion of raising 'hue and cry' against felons. Road tolls made their debut too. In 1346, Edward III authorised one to be levied for the repair of a few streets in central London; 18 years later he added Highgate Hill to the list.

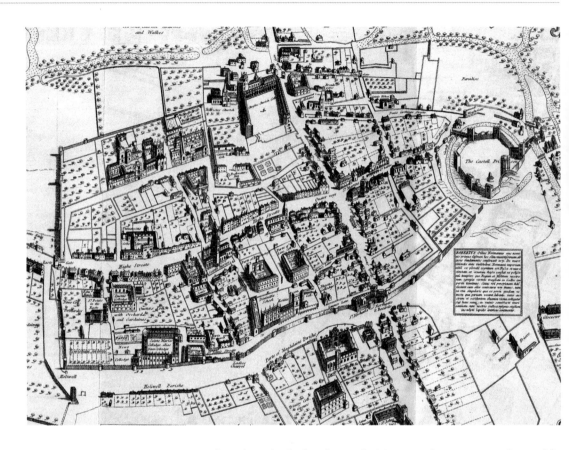

Above: Detail from an engraving of Ralph Agas's 1578 street plan of Oxford, a map that launched many cartographic conventions

In reality though, little changed. Most roads were rutted, muddy cart-tracks, often impassable for months at a time, and this remained the case for the next few hundred years. In 1216, King John famously lost his crown jewels around the Wash when the royal baggage train fell victim to flooded, muddy roads, but things had barely improved, even for royalty, over 300 years later. In 1568, Queen Elizabeth I gave an audience to the French ambassador and complained to him, as he later relayed in a letter, of 'the aching pains she was suffering in consequence of having been knocked about in a coach'.

If anything, it appears that the roads deteriorated in the Elizabethan age. The 1555 Highways Act had decreed that they become the responsibility of their parishes, and that all parishioners were to undertake four days of forced labour on their repair and maintenance; a subsequent Act of 1562 upped this to six days. It was widely flouted. Writing in *Holinshed's Chronicles* in 1577, William Harrison said of the new laws that 'the rich do so cancel their portions, and the poor so loiter in their labours' that instead of effecting an improvement 'the streets do grow to be much more gulled than before, and thereby very noisome for such as travel of the common highways'.

Previously, many of the monasteries had taken care of local roads, but this had abruptly ended on their enforced dissolution from 1536. Furthermore, the deterioration of the roads can also be blamed on a reason with which we are all too familiar: the booming Tudor age had seen a massive rise in traffic using them, and they just couldn't cope. One big growth area was the postal service, operating through a large network of fast horses along five designated routes going out in spokes from London to Berwick/Edinburgh, Dover, Cornwall, Bristol/Milford Haven and Holyhead – almost exactly the routes of the A1, A2, A3, A4 and A5 of centuries later.

Throughout the Middle Ages the roads stagnated, and there was little evolution in cartography either. The *Gough Map*, and the shape and detail of Britain that it depicted, was the base for all national mapping well into the 16th century. The first big breakthrough came in printed large-scale street mapping of cities, in which many of the common features of modern mapping were first created. The earliest survivor is William Cuningham's fairly rudimentary bird's-eye plan of Norwich (1558), though this was swiftly improved upon by Ralph Agas, whose 1578 map of Oxford looks very much more familiar. Street names are scribed along their length, buildings are accurately depicted and annotated and, as on a modern Ordnance Survey map, trees are used as pictograms for orchards and greens. Agas later produced similarly detailed street maps of Cambridge and London, the latter over six feet long and printed from wooden blocks.

Of all the 16th-century plans of the English capital, John Norden's of 1593 is perhaps the most ground-breaking. Although still ostensibly a bird's-eye view, the angle is less oblique, giving it a far more familiar

cartographic look. It has an index at the bottom of some streets, churches and prominent buildings, referring to letters and numbers annotated on the map itself. In the northwestern corner there is the first example of an off-map direction indicator in the form of the label 'The Way to Hampstead'. After Norden's death, bookseller Peter Stent reissued the map, together with a further 76 street names. He also added 'The Way to Ware' on the road to the north out through Bishopsgate.

Norden had intended to publish detailed maps of every English county, as part of his ongoing *Speculum Britanniae*, a 'mirror of Britain': the

the London map was first seen in his Middlesex survey. County tableaux had been the predominant map of Tudor society since Christopher Saxton's 1579 atlas of English and Welsh counties, although he included neither roads nor city street plans. John Speed, whose own county atlas came out just over 30 years later, used some of Saxton's mapping and embellished it greatly, including the addition of bird's-eye view street plans of county towns and cathedral cities on each of the individual county maps. Only one road appeared on any of the general county maps, however: a depiction of the Great North Road as it passed through Huntingdonshire.

THE GREAT NORTH ROAD

John Speed's Tudor county atlas of Britain (1611) is one of our loveliest icons of cartography. Yet within its 70 lavish maps, most depicting the individual counties of England and Wales, only one road is ever shown: the Great North Road, as it slices through the middle of Huntingdonshire. This solitary appearance confirms the road's status as the backbone of the land.

In the millennia of its existence, the Great North Road has undergone many mutations. It largely corresponds to the Roman Ermine Street, the great legionary highway to the north, although that name comes from the Saxon Earningas Stræt, after the Earninga tribe of the Royston district, through which the original route passed. Long after the fast cobbles of the Romans had disintegrated, creating a mud-bound slog on the country's still busiest road, the route was established as England's first turnpike in 1663.

In the early years of the turnpike, a journey from London to York by stagecoach took four days and cost 25 shillings inside, or 18 shillings outside. It was a boisterous run. In 1675, a clerk at Trinity College in Cambridge by the name of Thomas Mace published a tract detailing how bad the road was, and how coachmen and travellers were fighting to the death over the most lucrative and easiest bits to travel. There are, he said, 'innumerable controversies, quarrellings and disturbances, daily committed by uncivil, refractory and rude Russian-like rake-shames in contesting for the way, too often proved mortal, and certainly were of very bad consequences to many.' With the coming of the

Opposite: The first British appearance of the triangular distance table between towns, in John Norden's England, an Intended Guyde for English Travailers *(1625)*

turnpike, and the first stirrings of road rage, the modern Great North Road was born, a thread of endeavour stretched long over the flat countryside. When it came to numbering the road network after World War I, what other contender could there possibly have been for the moniker of A1?

Nearly a century on, the A1 remains the longest numbered road in Britain, running 410 miles from London to Edinburgh. Notable for its flatness, it has never been the most dazzling of drives – frequent traveller Sir Walter Scott called it 'the dullest road in the world' – but that is almost part of its charm and status. This has never been a road agog with holiday excitement or designated viewpoints. It is perhaps the ultimate in workaday routes, the hard highway of commerce and governance between two ancient capital cities.

To dismiss it so loftily is to miss the undeniable romance in the prosaic. The country's backbone is perhaps better imagined as our main artery, through which the lifeblood of evolving nations has flowed. It is the route of Dick Whittington and Dick Turpin, Robert Louis Stevenson and Charles Dickens, greasy spoons and Stilton cheese, Holy Island and the Angel of the North, of belligerent marching armies and poet John Clare's demented northward stumble. The Great North Road is truly the only real British rival to Route 66.

Unlike Saxton or Speed, John Norden never managed to publish his full county atlas. Apart from Middlesex and London, the only other map and study to appear in his lifetime was Hertfordshire in 1598. His study of Cornwall, surveyed in 1605, was not finally published until 1728, and Essex not until 1840. The extraordinary level of detail in his maps and accompanying gazetteers partly explains why so little was ever finished; certainly, later mapmakers far preferred to use his work, where it existed, over Saxton's or even Speed's. Details included some distinctly modern touches. His were the first maps to use an alphanumeric grid in the margins, so that mentions in an index could be swiftly located on the map itself. Norden also included a key to explain the symbols used and pioneered the triangular distance table that we still find in road atlases today. For the first time, maps were being prised from the hands of rulers and the gentry, and made useful for ordinary travellers.

Midlesex, with some confining Townes.	London	Brentford	Vxbridge	Edgeworth	Hendon	Fincheley	High-gate	Hamsted	Hackney	Acton	Stratford Bowe	Stanes	Hampton Court	Kingsbery	Hounslowe	Gerneforde	Harrow	Canons	Watford. Hert	Bernet. Hert	Theobald. Hert	Colbrooke. Bucke	Edmonton	S. Myms	Riflip	Harlington
Lalam.	14	7	8	12	12	14	14	12	18	9	18	2	5	11	5	8	9	11	12	17	22	5	18	17	10	4
Harlington.	12	6	5	8	9	10	12	10	15	7	16	4	7	8	4	4	11	7	8	14	19	3	16	14	6	
Riflip.	13	9	4	5	8	9	11	10	16	8	16	8	12	6	7	4	11	4	3	10	15	6	14	10		
S. Myms.	12	13	13	6	6	5	7	7	12	10	13	17	17	7	13	9	8	7	8	3	6	15	6			
Edmonton.	7	12	16	9	7	5	4	5	5	9	7	18	16	8	13	11	11	10	12	4	5	17				
Colbrook. Buck.	15	6	3	9	11	12	15	14	17	9	18	3	11	9	5	6	7	8	9	15	21					
Theobald. Hert.	12	16	18	11	9	8	8	9	10	13	11	21	20	11	17	15	14	12	14	6						
Bernet. Hert.	10	10	13	6	4	2½	6	5	8	8	10	16	15	5	11	9	8	6	9							
Watforde. Hert.	15	9	5	5	7	8	10	9	15	9	16	10	13	5	9	5	4	3								
Canons.	10	7	6	½	2½	4	7	6	12	6	13	10	12	2½	7	3	2									
Harrowe.	10	6	5	2½	5	6	8	7	14	5	14	8	10	3	6	1										
Gerneforde.	9	5	5	3½	5	6	8	7	12	5	14	7	9	3½	4											
Hounslowe.	10	2	7	7	8	9	9	8	12	4	13	5	4	6												
Kingsberye.	7	6	8	2	2	3	5	4	9	4	11	10	10													
Hampton Court.	10	4	10	12	11	12	12	11	12	7	14	7														
Stanes.	15	7	6	10	13	15	14	13	17	9	18															
Stratford Bowe.	3	11	18	12	8	9	6	7	1½	9																
Acton.	5	2	9	5	4	5	5	4	8																	
Hackney.	2½	10	17	11	8	7	4	5																		
Hamsted.	4	6	12	6	3	3	1½																			
High-gate.	4	8	13	7	3	3																				
Finchley.	7	7	11	4	1½																					
Hendon.	7	6	10	3																						
Edgeworth.	10	7	7																							
Vxbridge.	14	8																								
Brentforde.	7																									

The vse of this Table.

THe Townes or places betweene which you desire to know the distance, you may finde in the names of the Townes in the vper part and in the side, and bring them into a square as the lines will guide you: and in the square you shall finde the figures which declare the distance.

And if you finde any place in the side which will not extend to make a square with that aboue, then seeke that aboue which will not extend to make a square, and see that in the vpper, and the other in the side, and it will showe you the distance. It is familiar and easie.

Beare with defectes the vse is necessarie.

Inuented by IOHN NORDEN.

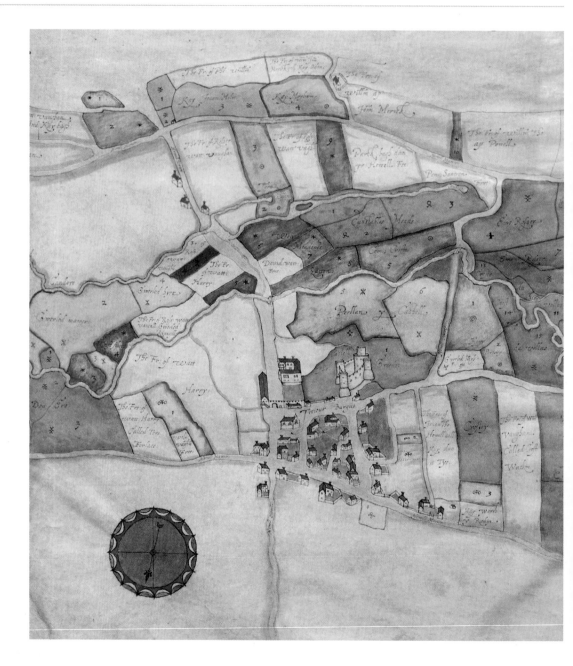

Roads are shown on Norden's Middlesex, Hertfordshire and Essex maps, their first appearance since the *Gough Map* of over two centuries earlier. His Middlesex has the roads delineated in dotted lines, some from Roman days, such as Ermine Street (now the A10/A1010) up through Hoxton, (Stoke) Newington, Edmonton, Ponders End and out of Middlesex at Waltham Cross, and Watling Street (the A5), passing through Kilburn, Brent Street and Edgware. Some of the early non-Roman main roads make their cartographic debut. What became the A40 edges out along the northern edge of Hyde Park and through Acton, Hanwell, Dormers Wells and Hillingdon, leaving the county at Uxbridge. On the other side of Hyde Park, the modern A4 goes through Kensington, Hammersmith, Brentford, Syon (marked with the symbol for 'Houses & Palaces of Qu:Eliz.') and Hounslow, where the road splits – as it does still – into the A4 Bath Road past Cranford, Harlington and Sipson, and the A30 to Staines, where it crosses the Thames, then Egham and the boundary of Windsor Great Park.

Other county maps showed a definite move away from the lumpy molehills and seemingly disconnected villages of Saxton, and towards a far more pragmatic aesthetic. Philip Symonson's 1596 map of Kent is arguably the finest. It is a beautiful map, and manifestly modern in its ambition and scope. Rivers, woods, mills, great houses, castles and boundaries (of counties, lathes, bailiwicks and hundreds) are shown. Like a modern Ordnance Survey map, individual churches are shown accurately with a tower or spire, or even double-spired as at Reculver on the north Kent coast. There are numerous roads on the map. Six converge on Canterbury, all easily recognisable today as the main A roads fanning out from the city.

By the time the 17th century was well under way, the Tudor explosion in cartography had solidified into consistently more accurate and detailed mapping, whether of counties, towns or estates, and roads were appearing on nearly all of them. Early estate maps are some of the loveliest. The 1635 estate map of Laxton in Nottinghamshire shows the area's roads in fine detail, and demonstrates to us how little they have changed over the ensuing centuries. The road map was here to stay, and was soon to take on a radical new form.

Opposite: An Elizabethan estate map of lands belonging to Duke of Beaufort, c.1587. The layout of the village of Tretower, Breconshire, has changed little, while the bucolic lanes across the top and bottom of the map have become the A40 and A479 respectively

Overleaf: Detail of the 1635 map of Laxton, Nottinghamshire, commissioned by the new estate owner to see the extent of his property. The village's road network has barely changed since

Chapter 2

TRANSPORT
REVOLUTIONS
(1675–1895)

R oads are the dominant feature of most of our maps, and that has been the case since September 1675, when John Ogilby's *Britannia* was published. The first European road atlas, using for the first time the regular scale of 1 inch to 1 mile (1:63,360), *Britannia* set many of the standards by which we still operate today.

Ogilby's atlas is a beautiful monster of a book. It contains 73 routes throughout England and Wales (with one brief incursion into Scotland) showing a total of 7,500 miles of road. Each road is followed in strip form, with six or seven strips to the page, in a style that harks back to the itineraries of Matthew Paris, but at a whole new level of exquisite detail. It is by far the best snapshot of Britain in the 17th century.

The maps are gorgeous, although a few (for example London–Rye) are distinctly substandard in comparison with the others. Every mile of road is depicted and faithfully annotated at its side; dots down its middle record the eight furlongs into which each mile is divided. Distances were calculated using a hand-pushed 'way-wiser', basically a wheel on a handle that measures distance as it turns, displaying it on a dial. Much attention is paid to the waterways en route – essential information in an age when flooding and impassable fords could necessitate massive detours. Similarly, significant hills are marked using a pictogram of a mountain the right way up for the ascent, and upside down for the descent. Where a road dips into a valley, thus going down before it goes back up, it appears on the map like a full pair of lips. The road to Portsmouth, now largely the A3, twists through a major convolution of hills at Hindhead, and it is strange to think that this obstacle has only recently been overcome with the opening, in July 2011, of a 1.2-mile tunnel.

In order to maintain every route within the strict confines of its strips, upon each one Ogilby places a compass wheel showing the direction of north. This often varies within a route, and sometimes even within a single strip, something that Ogilby demonstrates using a thick black line across its width where the angle changes, and another compass wheel showing that we have moved on to a different bearing. Woods, commons and furzes have their own depictions, useful navigational features such as church towers, large houses, inns, beacons and even gibbets appear,

Previous page: 'Illustration of the Kingdom of England and Dominion of Wales' – the index map for John Ogilby's Britannia *(1675), showing the routes to be found in detail within his massive atlas*

bridges are labelled with the material of their construction and, often, how many arches they contain, county boundaries are fastidiously recorded, and the roads themselves are clearly depicted as either enclosed by hedge or wall, or open.

THE DANCING MAP MAN

Cartographers, for all their many attributes, are seldom the big hit of the office party. John Ogilby (1600–1676) was a glorious exception. A man of infinite ability to spin fantastical schemes out of thin air, he managed numerous strange careers in swift succession, only finally alighting on mapmaking in his late sixties.

Left: John Ogilby presenting his subscription list for Britannia *to the King and Queen, detail from* Morgan's map of London, *1682*

His unconventional ways of making money began at the tender age of 12, and out of brutal necessity. His father was in the debtors' prison, and young John scratched a living for his family by selling trinkets. The derring-do that characterised his entire life soon showed itself, for he ploughed his savings into a lottery scheme aiming to advance the colonization of Virginia, and duly won a handsome prize. This paid off his father's debts and afforded young Ogilby the chance to train as a dancer.

A beautiful and elegant youth, Ogilby soon caught the eye of the Duke of Buckingham, King James I's probable lover. The ever-ambitious Ogilby became a fixture of royal balls and masques, until he fell and injured himself at one held to celebrate James giving Buckingham the estate of Burley-on-the-Hill in Rutland. He could not dance again, and limped for the rest of his life.

As ever, Ogilby seemed little deterred. Although injured, he secured a position as dancing instructor in the household of Thomas Wentworth, later the first Earl of Strafford, and one of Charles I's closest ministers. When Wentworth was sent to Ireland as Lord Deputy, Ogilby went too and became the Master of the Revels and impresario behind Dublin's first theatre. When the Irish rebellion broke out in 1641 it all came swiftly to an end, and Ogilby only narrowly avoided assassination. As he returned penniless to London, his ship was wrecked and his patron Strafford executed. It was time for the next career change: translation and publishing of the classics.

Ogilby managed to rekindle relations with some of his erstwhile noble friends, a considerable boost to his new business, even during the dark years of Oliver Cromwell's protectorate. Marrying a rich widow helped too. On the Restoration of the Monarchy in 1660, Ogilby burst back into the limelight, as a trusted stalwart of the new king. Charles II had Ogilby deliver the poetical content of his coronation, and his business, in producing fine books for wealthy subscribers, boomed.

Disaster struck once again, when the 1666 Great Fire of London wiped out nearly all of Ogilby's stock. Yet it also sowed the seeds of his final career, cartography, for he was one of those commissioned to survey the ravaged capital and draw up the massively detailed maps, on a scale of 100 feet to 1 inch, of what had been lost and who owned it. With his publishing background, he appreciated the fine art of good cartography and knew well the terrific upsurge in interest in maps, especially among the new mercantile classes.

Ogilby obtained foreign original maps and atlases, and made them his own for a wealthy English audience, who lapped them up. Charles II appointed him 'His Majesty's Cosmographer and Geographick Printer'. He drew up elaborate plans for a set of new atlases and gazetteers of Britain, of which *Britannia*, depicting the roads, was to be just one volume. It was, however, the only one that appeared before his death. It is sobering to imagine what potential was lost, but even with just the one volume, Ogilby left a magnificent legacy of a full life very well lived.

The picture of Britain from Ogilby's atlas is of an emerging modern nation with an apparently excellent road network. The reality was very different. Although there are plentiful exhortations against taking 'ye worst route' to somewhere, and occasional notes warn of the likes of 'a very dirty way' near Soham or 'a Stream of water runing in the way' near Bury St Edmunds, the clear, confident depiction of the roads was very much at odds with the selection of wide, muddy tracks, old drovers' routes and boggy ruts down which the traveller was directed. In some instances, most notably across the nine-mile stretch of treacherous tidal sands off the north Wales coast towards Anglesey, the road depicted with such confidence did not really exist at all.

Above: The introductory cartouche for Ogilby's Britannia, *intriguingly showing the mapmaker (centre right, with his trusty wheel measurer) diverting away from the obvious main road*

Of the 73 routes, the longest depicts the Great North Road from London to the Scottish border at Berwick: 339 miles, spread over five pages of maps. This is one of the first 13 direct post routes from the capital to all corners of the kingdom; a further 18 'Direct Dependants' extend them to other destinations. Distances for these routes are all calculated from 'ye Standard in Cornhill, London', and account for 54 of the 100 pages of maps. Then there is the category of 'Cross Independants', 30 cross-country routes, of which five start from Bristol and five from Oxford. The atlas concludes with 10 pages of 'Accidentals', a series of mop-up connecting routes, some of which from their appearance seem to have been created in rather a hurry.

For all its apparent clarity, *Britannia* is full of mystery. There are numerous notes and annotations that raise some intriguing questions. Why is 'Esq. Cook's house', between Gloucester and Newent, marked

Overleaf: Part of the route to Holyhead as seen in Ogilby's Britannia, *showing the 'road' across the sands to Beaumaris on Anglesey – but only 'when ye tide is out'*

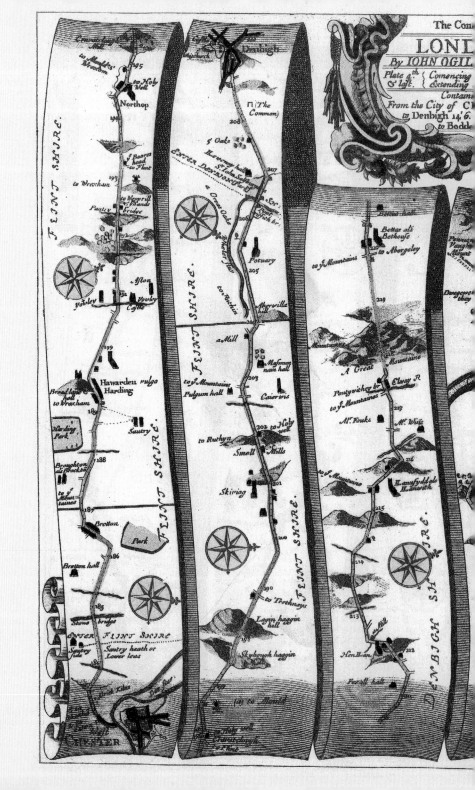

The Con
LONl
By IOHN OGIL
Plate 9th
& last.
Comencing
Extending
Contain
From the City of Cl
to Denbigh 14 6.
to Bodde

Crewickshy
to Mostly Brumin
to Holy Well
195
Northop
196

FLINT SHIRE

to Wrexham
193
f Boores head to Flint
to Wepprill Sands
Pantry bridge
192

Aston
191
Yowley
Yowley Castle

190
199
Hawarden vulgo Harding
Broad Lane hall
to Wrexham
189
Harding Park
Sautry
188
Broughton als Brockton
to f Mountaines
187
Bretton
Park
186
Bretton hall
185
ENTER FLINT SHIRE
Stone bridge
Sautry field
Sautry heath or Lower leas
184
Dee River
CHESTER

FLINT SHIRE

ENTER FLINT SHIRE

Denbigh
(The Common)
208
5 Oaks
207
Hawerny hall St John Saffary
to Bathin
Great Oaks
Phaler fach br
Potuary
205
to Bathin
Abervilla hall
204
a Mill
Masrmeynam hall
203
Fulgum hall
to f Mountaines
Caierwis
202 to Holy well
to Ruthyn
Smell Mills
201
Skiriog
200
to Trethneys
190
Lagin haggin hall
198
Skybough haggin
to Holy well Cherwirkeynigh
to Mould

FLINT SHIRE

FLINT SHIRE

DENBIGH SH

Bettws hall
Bettws als Bethowse
210
to Abergeley
to f Mountaines
219
A Great Mountaine
Pontywichey br
Elway R
to f Mountaines
Mr Fouks
Mr Wise
217
216
Llanwfydd als Llansmith
to f Mountaines
215
Penmore Vaughn Mount
Dungepere they

214
213
a Mill
HenBlan
222
Foxall hall

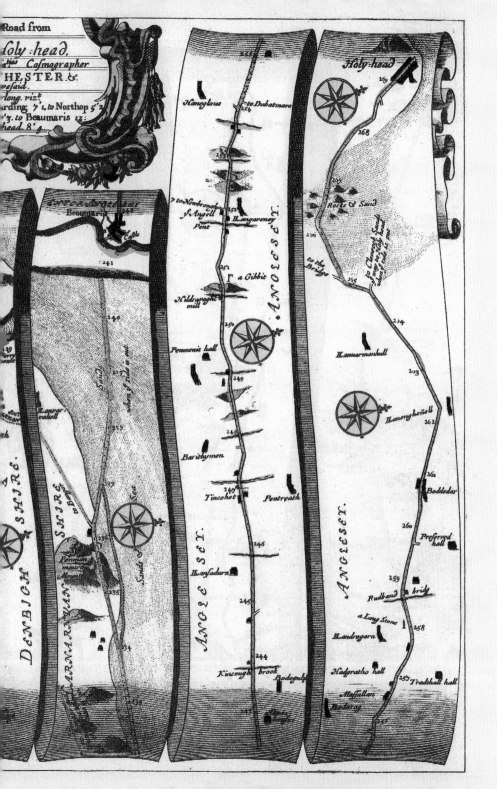

Road from

Holy-head.

the Cosmographer

HESTER &c.

aforesaid

*long. riz*t.

arding 7'½, to Northop 5'½,

'z. to Beaumaris 12:

head. 8'4.

Holy=head.

269

268

Rocks & Sand

267

266

to the Bridge

265

to Chequet Sand you may safely ford when it is set out

264

263

Llannarmanhull

Llanonghevell

262

261

Boddedar

260

Preserved hall

259

Rudland bridg

a Long Stone

258

Llandrygarn

Hadgratho hall

257 Tyddhall hall

Maffallan

Bodorgg

256

255

Llaneglous

to Dubatmare

254

253

to Newbrough

St Angell Pont

Llangavoney

251

r a Gibbit

250

Holdraraght mill

Pennenis hall

249

248

Barithymen

247

Tincohet

Pentreath

246

Llansadurn

245

244

Kincough brook

Bodgulp

ANGLESEY

ANGLESEY

ANGLESEY

ANGLESEY

the Beaumaris

Castle

241

240

239

Llanyr

vakell

238

237

236

235

234

DENBIGH SHIRE

CARNARVAN SHIRE to Bangor

Pennon Marsh Moor

Sands of Lavan Sea

Sea

Sands when *ye* Tide is out

larger than anything else on the London to St David's map? Who is the unnamed Gentleman whose house is marked off to the right of the route from St Albans to Oakham? And who was Tom the Trumpeter, and why is his place marked on the Dartmouth to Minehead route just north of Newton Bushel (Newton Abbot)?

There are far larger questions lurking too. A 2008 BBC television series, *Terry Jones' Great Map Mystery*, posited the view that *Britannia* was a carefully coded blueprint for a French invasion of Britain, one which would have had the full, if entirely covert, support of King Charles II. The evidence is compelling. Ogilby began the volume, with considerable government support, shortly after Charles had signed the 1670 Treaty of Dover with Louis XIV of France – a treaty so secret that knowledge of it didn't come into the public domain until 1830. Charles had grown up in France, and much admired (and desired) the absolute monarchy, rooted in Catholicism, enjoyed by the Sun King; such authority was in stark contrast to his piecemeal Restoration powers in England. The Treaty of Dover laid plans for Charles to declare publicly his Catholicism and for French troops to help back this with a swift invasion.

According to Terry Jones and his historian writer and producer Alan Ereira, this is why such prominence is given in *Britannia* to routes in Wales, the Marches and the West Country, paving the way for a back-door invasion. It's noticeable that this is the case right from the outset: the index map of all the routes in the atlas is thick with routes in these sparsely populated parts of the country, while there is a comparative paucity shown in the southeast. Tiny Presteigne, for example, the county town of Radnorshire slap on the England–Wales border, is depicted on three maps, one of which even has Presteigne as its ultimate destination; Hastings, Eastbourne and the Isle of Thanet appear on none. Although it can be excused by alphabetical order, the very first route in *Britannia* is from London to Aberystwyth, which at the time was a remote fishing hamlet of fewer than a hundred houses, and not even the most significant port on Cardigan Bay, let alone beyond. Was this a pointer to a suggested landing place for an invading army? Furthermore, metal mines, useful for armaments, are prominent in a way that no other industrial sites are, and some old Catholic pilgrimage routes (at a time when anti-Catholic

Left: 'Lancaster' from the
Pocket Book of Counties
of England & Wales *by*
Robert Morden, 1680

sentiment was at its raging height) are included too. In the course of the series, Terry Jones interviewed Professor Ronald Hutton, eminent historian of this era, who agreed that this interpretation was significant and highly plausible, saying that *Britannia* 'has dirty political fingerprints all over it'.

Even if *Britannia* never fulfilled its secret political purpose, it most certainly fulfilled its cartographic one. Ogilby's atlas was an instant success: following initial publication in the autumn of 1675, two further impressions appeared within a year. By April 1676, individual maps from the collection were being sold separately, much like the AA and RAC route plans of 250 years later. Other cartographers happily ripped off Ogilby's work as their own. Pocket-sized editions were launched, including series that were shamelessly marketed as *Ogilby Improv'd*, which they rarely were. Publishers of county maps, still the dominant cartography of the day, rushed to shoehorn Ogilby's information about the road network onto their products. Perhaps the most striking was Robert Morden's playing card set of English and Welsh counties, onto which he squeezed the roads. The depiction of counties on a set of playing cards had been a popular theme since Tudor times, thanks mainly to the fact that there were 52 of them, the precise number needed for a full set of cards.

The glorious and (quite literally) revolutionary cartography aside, a major factor in the success of Ogilby's atlas was that the country was opening up for increasing numbers of people, even if travelling conditions were still far from easy – even in the capital. As late as 1736, courtier Lord Hervey, writing from his home in Kensington, complained that 'the road between this place and London is grown so infamously bad that we live here in the same solitude as we would do if cast on a rock in the middle of the ocean; and all the Londoners tell us that there is between them and us an impassable gulf of mud.'

Despite such trying conditions, the age of the stagecoach had arrived. The first public coach service had begun in 1657, running the 190 miles between London and Chester in four days, at a cost of 35 shillings. Weekly runs from the capital to York and Exeter were also launched, each able to take six paying passengers. In 1700, York was

a week's journey from London; coaches left simultaneously from the Black Swan in Holborn, London, and the Black Swan in Coney Street, York, every Thursday at 5am. Thanks to the execrable state of the road, the service could run only during the summer months, but even then passengers frequently had to walk stretches that were impassable or be forced into unexpected overnight stays while waiting for the route to dry out. Although it was the same story on every road, stagecoach routes proliferated: London to Exeter in five days, Dover in three and Tunbridge Wells, Salisbury and Oxford all in two.

The state of the roads was not the only concern to travellers. Highwaymen were a real threat, as were extortion by coachmen and innkeepers, arguments and even fights amongst the passengers themselves. The decision as to which inns the coach would stop at was nominally made by the passengers, who would often appoint a chairman at the beginning of the journey and take votes on the matter.

Above: The London to Birmingham Stage Coach *(1801) by John Cordrey, who specialised in painting coaching scenes. Roundels on the side tell us that the coach stopped at Coventry and Dunchurch. The lively group of passengers includes a wedding party*

The coachmen, with a probable financial interest in steering them to particular hostelries, frequently ignored such democracy. In 1760 a court case was brought before the King's Bench on behalf of a group of stagecoach passengers who had disagreed with their coachman as to his chosen inn, and had walked on to another a little further along the road. Awaiting the driver, they watched him speed past imperiously, leaving them to find their own way to London. The jury found in their favour and awarded damages of £20.

Efforts to speed up the laborious journeys were constant. New designs of coach were patented and put into practice, but the horrendous state of the roads precluded any real improvement. Even if the actual service was little better, there was always room to make people believe that it was, with some canny marketing. In May 1734, the *Caledonian Mercury* contained an advertisement for a new weekly service between London and Edinburgh, which promised 'Gentlemen and ladies will be carried to their entire satisfaction' and that they were to do the journey in 'three days sooner than any coach that travels the road' – no small promise on a route that generally took a fortnight, and one that they were unable to keep. In 1754, a company of flash Manchester merchants advertised their new 'Flying Coach', breathlessly promising 'however incredible it may appear, this coach will actually (barring accidents) arrive in London in four days and a half after leaving Manchester'. Competition was hotting up.

So too was the political pressure to sort out the sorry state of the road network. Toll roads, or turnpikes, were thought of as one answer. The first had been successfully established in 1663 on the Old North Road, though it was not until 1695 that the next Turnpike Act was put through parliament, and only six others were passed in the next 10 years. From then, things began to accelerate. Turnpike trustees were to co-ordinate income and labour from the various parishes along the highway's route, and add to that tolls from the road users. This combined income, together with preferable rates of interest on borrowing, was applied to the upkeep of the highway, and covered not just better drained and surfaced roads but also new features such as the statutory provision of milestones along the way.

With the better conditions of the roads, and much more traffic on them, came the practice of driving on the left. Historically, this had been the preferred side of the highway for horsemen and marching armies, as most people are right-handed and were free on that side to greet oncomers or – if needs be – draw their sword at them. The practice became enshrined in law in 1722, in an effort to deal with the congestion on London Bridge. The Lord Mayor decreed that 'all carts, coaches and other carriages coming out of Southwark into this City do keep all along the west side of the said bridge: and all carts and coaches going out of the City do keep along the east side of the said bridge'. The convention spread, and stuck.

WILLIAM ROY'S MILITARY SURVEY OF THE SCOTTISH HIGHLANDS

As the Romans had demonstrated 17 centuries earlier, the swiftest way to tame hostile territories was to build good roads straight into their heartlands. Mapping the new roads, and thus 'proving' the conquest, only consolidated the strategy.

In the 1700s, Scotland was bubbling with agitation. Jacobite uprisings, in support of the claims to the throne by the exiled Stuarts, were especially strong in the Highlands. The response of the Hanoverian government under George I in London was to send Field Marshal George Wade to the far north in order to appraise the situation there. At the time, the Highlands lacked any infrastructure, including roads. Wade proposed and built a series of barracks and military forts at strategic points, with new roads connecting them. Following the greatest Jacobite rebellion in 1745, which only ultimately failed a year later on the battlefield at Culloden, it was decided that Wade's Highland network of roads and forts should be mapped in detail. Chosen for the task was a team that included a young Lanarkshire man, William Roy (1726–90), and an even younger draughtsman, Paul Sandby (1731–1809), who went on to become one of the most celebrated watercolour landscape artists of the age. Roy quickly became the party's leader.

They surveyed and mapped the Highlands between 1747 and 1752, carting an impressive array of heavy machinery around the mountains. Speed

Overleaf: Detail of Perth area from William Roy's Military Survey of Scotland (c.1750), which mapped many Scottish roads for the first time

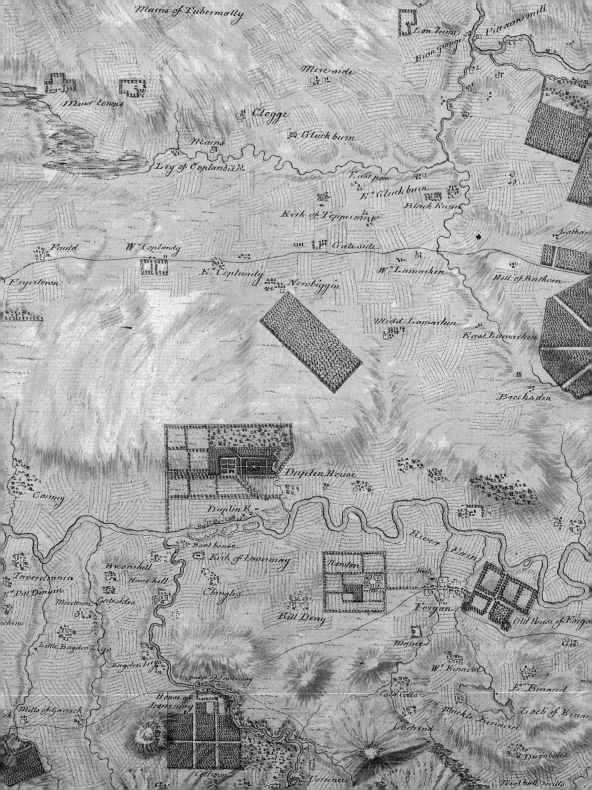

was of the essence, meaning that topographical features of no great military significance were not always incorporated. Roads, forts and settlements were carefully measured and mapped, however, and the resultant plans were published at a scale of 1 inch to 1,000 yards. With evident artistic input from Sandby, the maps are beautiful, 'rather a magnificent military sketch, than a very accurate map of a country', as Roy put it many years later, towards the twilight of his career. Not only do they show us the roads of large parts of Scotland mapped for the first time, but the Military Survey also provided the genesis for William Roy's subsequent battles with the exchequer to expand and improve the experiment across the whole of Britain. Eventually he was successful, and as a result the Ordnance Survey was born.

By 1770 there were some 15,000 miles of turnpike roads, and stagecoach travelling times had begun to drop sharply. This was further improved from 1784 by the introduction of fast-track mail coaches, complete with their own guards. These could take up to six paying passengers and had special privileges on the road, including the right to speed through the turnpike gates. By 1797 this reduced the mail coach journey between Manchester and London to 28 hours; cheaper commercial coaches did it in 36. In 1750 the coach journey from London to Cambridge took two days. By 1820 this had dropped to seven hours, thanks largely to the new surface of road – crushed stone under a drainable surface – pioneered by John McAdam. The process became known as 'macadamisation'.

The mapmaker for this early golden age of coaching was the enterprising John Cary, who produced a steady stream of maps for different audiences from his workshop in the Strand in London. Following the success of a county map of Middlesex, he produced in June 1786 the *Actual Survey of the country fifteen miles around London*, in many ways the first recognisable road atlas. There are 50 pages of maps, and for the first time they are preceded by a general grid map of the entire area covered within, marked into squares that tell the reader upon which page he will find the relevant section. Cary goes to great lengths to explain this new feature to the reader in his foreword, of which this is but a short extract:

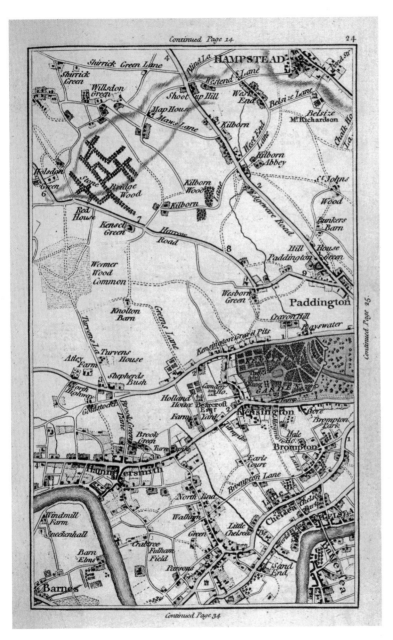

Left: A page from John Cary's Actual Survey *of the country fifteen miles around London (1786), in many ways, the capital's first road atlas*

Above: James Craig's initial plan in 1765 for the New Town of Edinburgh to be constructed in a grid shape suggestive of the British flag

Suppose you want the Road from London which is in page 25, to Epsom; refer to the Squares in the General Map that lead to it, which is 25–35–36 and 43, apply them to the corresponding pages in the Book, and you will find the road lain down as follows. From London page 25, you go to Newington Butts, from thence to Clapham, and Upper Tooting in page 35, to Tooting and Morden in page 36, to Ewel and Epsom in page 43.

Backing this system up is another common feature of road atlases making its cartographic debut, in the text written at the side of each map telling you upon which page the continuation can be found. As for the mapping itself, it is crisp and lovely, and like Ogilby's over a century before, adheres to the scale of 1 inch to 1 mile. Roads are clearly marked in two categories: lesser and side roads are narrow, the main turnpike routes wider and engraved thicker to one side.

Immediately, Cary turned his attention to mapping the entire country; the result a year later was his *New and Correct English Atlas*, in which maps of 'South Britain', as he had it, were organised by county, as in earlier national atlases. Unlike predecessors such as Saxton, Speed and Morden, however, Cary's maps were stripped of lavish ornamentation; they were pitched at the new travelling classes, with the best roads clearly delineated, together with sections at the end listing 52 specific routes from London to all parts of the country, and detailed lists of market and post towns.

PUTTING BRITAIN ON THE MAP

John Cary was far from alone in preferring to refer to Scotland and England as 'North Britain' and 'South Britain'. Throughout the 18th century (and well into the 19th) these terms were often used, and had been ever since the 1707 Act of Union. While the term of 'South Britain' never really took off for England (and nominally Wales), there was a concerted effort to nail the 'North Britain' label onto the Scots, and with some success.

In 1765 a public competition was held to design the planned new town of Edinburgh. The winning entry, by a young architect named James Craig, took the notion of Britishness to new levels, for his plan was to build the streets of the new town in the shape of the Union Flag. This was ultimately deemed impractical, and a more sober street grid was constructed instead. It would not, however, have been the only example of the British flag appearing on the map: in much the same spirit as Edinburgh in 1765, the Union Flag's ghostly shape can still be seen via Google Maps in the late Victorian street layout of former colonial outposts Khartoum in Sudan and Faisalabad in Pakistan.

Although the *New and Correct English Atlas* is both lovely and fascinating, there's a sense that it doesn't quite know what it is doing, or whom it is for. The old style of map, with its deference to the gentry, has not disappeared; Cary's accompanying essay on each county focuses hugely on them, and each is finished with a long list of that area's 'Principal Gentlemen's seats'. The essays are full of information, some useful and some quite bizarre. In the former category, he details the number of parliamentary seats per county: he is as staggered as we are that Cornwall 'sends 44 members to parliament...which is more than any county in England, and within one as many as the whole Kingdom of Scotland', while Durham, Leicestershire and Huntingdonshire have four apiece, and even Middlesex, including London, sends 'but 8'. At the more bizarre end, he states that the Lincolnshire air is 'thick and foggy, yet wholesome', that Cambridge University was founded in the year 531, that Berkshire 'has about 671 villages' and that both The Peak in Derbyshire and Nettlebed Hill in Oxfordshire are reckoned to be 'the highest in England'.

The mapping can't quite make up its mind either. On many of the major roads, he shoehorns distances every mile onto their course, evidently influenced by Ogilby and his many plagiarists, but it's not a tactic that works well on already cluttered county maps, especially those on smaller scales. While some – diminutive Rutland the obvious example – are beautifully clear, larger counties, such as Devon, Essex, Shropshire, Wiltshire and Lincolnshire, or those with cartographically awkward shapes like Northamptonshire and Sussex, look messy. (The perennial problem of mighty Yorkshire is solved by having five different maps: one of the whole county, and then separate ones of each Riding.

Opposite: John Cary's New and Correct English Atlas (1787) reverted to the old-fashioned county map (Warwickshire seen here), but had a modern take for travellers, with its clear depiction of roads and distances

Overleaf: Cary's 1790 map in the Survey of the High Roads from London, *showing the various turnpike trusts operating on the roads out of London*

The West Riding is the only division in the whole atlas to be afforded two maps.) That said, on the larger number of occasions when the map works, it works a treat, and Cary's strong eye for good, clear design is very much the genesis of the type of cartography just about to become the norm with the birth of the Ordnance Survey.

Neither is the *New and Correct English Atlas* ever very clear as to where the growing number of new turnpike roads will be found. You might suppose that the seemingly random roads appended with distances every mile are the turnpike routes, and so they often are, but by no means always. In the 52 detailed route itineraries (all of them from London) plotted from town to town, only one turnpike is mentioned, just north of Kidderminster on one of the three proffered London to Holyhead routes.

Cary soon realised that clear depiction of the turnpike roads was the key to selling his wares to the new map-hungry travelling classes. His next major publication was the 1790 *Survey of the High Roads from London*, a set of strip maps of the routes from the capital to towns around it, which stated on the title page that it included the 'different TURNPIKE GATES'. The first map in the book is a colour-coded plan of London to show which trusts ran which turnpikes, thus informing the traveller which gates could be passed on the one ticket and thus, as Cary puts it in his preamble, 'preventing unpleasant altercation'. To back this up, on the maps themselves each turnpike gate is labelled with the name of the trust operating it.

Even more prominent on the title page was the proud boast that the atlas also included 'Every Gentleman's Seat, situate on, or seen from, the ROAD (however distant)' which tells us much about Cary's target market. Older maps often portrayed the houses and estates of the landed gentry, in deference but also in the hope that flattery might generate custom; Cary includes not only them but also hundreds of houses owned by the new mercantile middle class. This was the first time new money had been mapped alongside the old. To press the point home further, Cary's key of symbols at the beginning largely consists of an explanation of his elaborate system for depicting sightlines towards these houses from the road. Even houses that were visible, yet too far away to be included

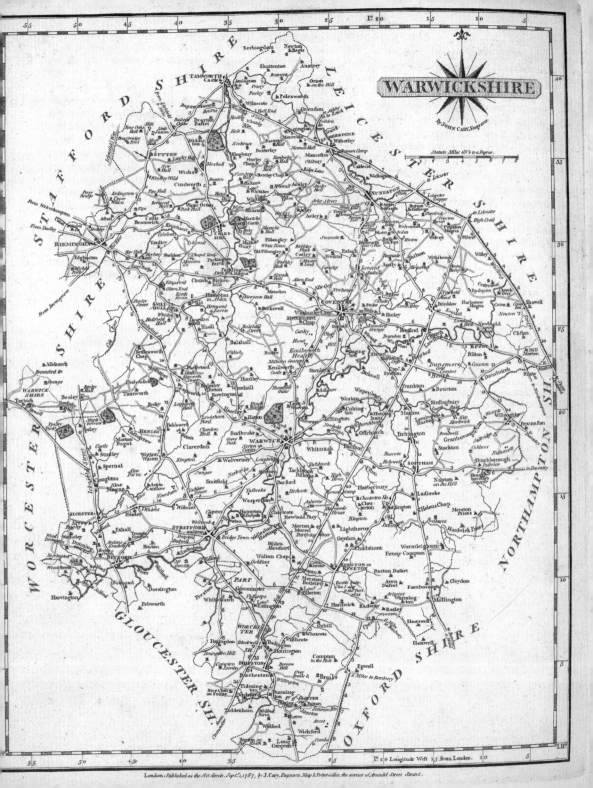

WARWICKSHIRE

By JOHN CARY, Engraver.

Statute Miles 69½ to a Degree.

London, Published as the Act directs, Sept. 1, 1787, by J. Cary, Engraver, Map & Printseller, the corner of Arundel Street Strand.

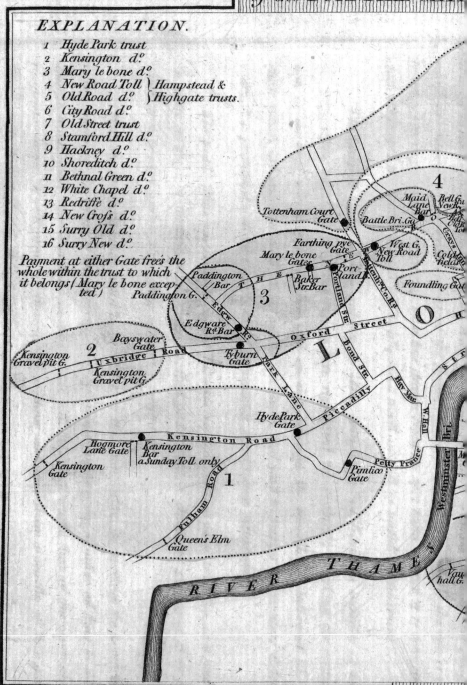

EXPLANATION.

1 Hyde Park trust
2 Kensington d.º
3 Mary le bone d.º
4 New Road Toll ⎫ Hampstead &
5 Old Road d.º ⎬ Highgate trusts.
6 City Road d.º
7 Old Street trust
8 Stamford Hill d.º
9 Hackney d.º
10 Shoreditch d.º
11 Bethnal Green d.º
12 White Chapel d.º
13 Redriffe d.º
14 New Cross d.º
15 Surry Old d.º
16 Surry New d.º

Payment at either Gate frees the whole within the trust to which it belongs (Mary le bone excepted)

Published

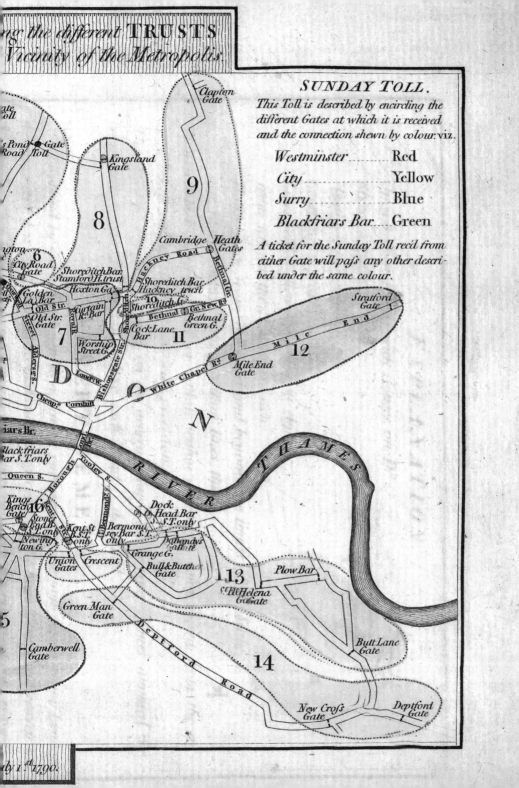

SUNDAY TOLL.

This Toll is described by encircling the
different Gates at which it is received
and the connection shewn by colour: viz.

Westminster .... Red

City .... Yellow

Surry .... Blue

Blackfriars Bar ... Green

A ticket for the Sunday Toll rec'd from
either Gate will pass any other described under the same colour.

Clapton Gate

Kingsland Gate

9

ate Toll

s Pond Road Toll

Gate

8

Cambridge Heath Gates

Hackney Road

Bethnal G.

ington

6

City Road Gate

Shoreditch Bar Stamford H. trust

Shoreditch Bar Hackney trust

Golden La. Bar

Old Str.

Hoxton Ga.

Curtain Rd. Bar

Shoreditch G.

Gr. New Rd.

Bethnal G.

10

Old Str. Gate

Kingsland Str.

Cock Lane Bar

Bethnal Green G.

11

7

Worship Street G.

Stratford Gate

Mile End

12

D

London

Bishopsgate Str.

Cheaps

Cornhill

White Chapel Rd.

Mile End Gate

N

O

Friars Br.

RIVER

THAMES

Blackfriars Bar S.T. only

Queen S.

Tooley S.

Dock Head Bar S.T. only

Kings Bench Gate

16

Stones End B. S.T. only

Kent St B S.T. only

Bermondsey bar S.T only

Dohandys Gate R.

Newington G.

Union Gates

Crescent

Grange G.

Bull & Butcher Gate

13

Plow Bar

St. Helena Gate

Green Man Gate

Deptford Road

14

Butt Lane Gate

5

Camberwell Gate

New Cross Gate

Deptford Gate

Right: Detail of the road from Colnbrook to Maidenhead (via Salt Hill) from John Cary's 1790 Survey of the High Roads from London. Cary mapped the sightlines to big houses along and near by the road, including those of the 'new money' mercantile class

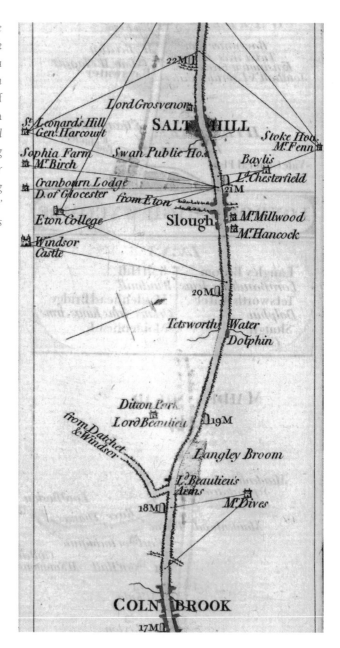

at the one inch scale, are lined from the road to the margin. There is a navigational impetus in this, of course, but with every householder's name carefully etched on the map, there's a definite dose of flashy one-upmanship going on here too.

Cary honed his maps of both London and the country beyond into a wide range of styles and formats; with his *Traveller's Companion* of 1790, he returned to the county atlas format, but made it into a series of fold-out maps cased in a leather wallet, a product expressly aimed at travellers. The turnpikes were more prominent too, both in the guide's subtitle (*or a Delineation of the Turnpike ROADS of England and Wales*) and on the maps themselves, where post routes and other turnpikes were shown distinctly. Again, though, being hidebound by the county map format gave some rather patchy results, and in some of his later national maps and atlases, he wisely jettisoned it in favour of equal scale maps chopped into a grid, as he'd done with the map of the environs of London at the start of his career.

THE REBECCA RIOTS

Although the turnpike trusts undeniably improved the shocking roads of Britain, they also provided plenty of cover for unscrupulous gentry and some get-rich-quick schemes. To qualify as a trustee, a man needed either land worth a minimum of £2,000 or a yearly rental income of at least £80, keeping the operation firmly in the clutches of the already wealthy classes. Many took their responsibilities seriously, but many did not, diverting revenues away from their intended usage and leaving the roads as rutted and impassable as before, while still charging for their use.

In some parts of the country, the number of toll gates proliferated wildly, causing much local outrage, particularly among small tenant farmers who were obliged to use the roads regularly for the transportation of animals and grain. Early turnpikes had allowed the free passage of lime carts in parts of the country where it was needed to neutralise acidic soils, but this was dropped in the early years of the 19th century, sowing the seeds of yet more resentment.

Above: Engraving of John Leech's 1843 Punch *cartoon, entitled 'Rebecca and her Daughters'*

The most famous fightback against the turnpikes erupted during the lime-carting season (May) of 1839 at Efail Wen, near the Carmarthenshire–Pembrokeshire border in west Wales. A small group appeared one night and attacked the week-old toll gate. It was quickly restored, but the protestors returned a month later, much boosted in number, to destroy the gate and burn down the accompanying toll house. Many of the protesters were disguised in women's clothing, and called themselves *Merched Beca*, the daughters of Rebecca, after a verse in the Bible (Genesis 24:60) stating that Rebecca and her descendants should 'possess the gate of those which hate them'.

The Rebecca Riots spread across south, mid and west Wales like wildfire. Toll gates became the focal point for numerous rural grievances, some not related to transport at all. The sheer number of riots, and their evident deep roots within rural communities, provoked the authorities to act, and not just in swift and sometimes bloody retribution. Many toll rates dropped, as did some agricultural rents, and a Royal Commission was established to examine the very justified complaints around toll roads, the result of which was the 1844 Turnpikes Act that curbed some of the worst excesses.

Perhaps the zenith of Cary's exuberant career was his mammoth *New Itinerary*, first published in 1798. By then he had undertaken the job of surveying the nation's post roads for the Postmaster General, so had much new first-hand information. Naturally, he also used the position as a marketing tool, plastering his 'official' credentials over everything. The book contained fold-out maps of England, Wales and southern Scotland, with the turnpike and mail routes carefully identified and reference numbers alongside the roads to take the reader to the relevant section. After those, there were 460 dense pages of lists, for the *New Itinerary* was an earlier coaching version of George Bradshaw's famous railway timetables. There were lists of routes and all the towns they served, including their populations, markets, inns, a brief guide, mileages from each other and from London and a comprehensive catalogue of local gentry; a full list of all coaching services organised according to the inns from which they departed; lists of canals, rivers and packet routes and, to help make sense of it all, an assortment of lengthy indexes.

Cary's new work quickly drew the attention of many, including the editors of what had become known as *Paterson's Roads*, a directory of British roads first published by army officer Daniel Paterson in 1771. This listed routes from London and cross-routes in exhaustive detail, and concluded with a supersized version of John Norden's triangular distance table, which gave every mileage possible between 300 different towns in long lists of numbers that went on for more than 170 pages. In

Opposite: The road that never was – and never could be: detail from Kitchin's 1769 New Map of the Counties of Cumberland and Westmorland *showing a non-existent road between Hawkshead and Ennerdale*

the preface to the 12th edition of *Paterson's Roads*, published in 1799, a year after the first edition of Cary's *New Itinerary*, the editors lambasted Cary, claiming that his book 'is made up almost entirely from *Paterson*, and the Plagiarism is so manifest that…the Piracy may be traced Page after Page.'

There may have been some truth in the claim, but their occupation of the moral high ground was not helped by the fact that this 12th edition of *Paterson* was a massive expansion on the previous 11, and that all of the extra material had been lifted from Cary's book. Quite literally so: in the subsequent court case, a man who had worked on the *Paterson* admitted that he had been told to scissor whole sections directly out of Cary into the new work – proof that cut-and-paste plagiarism is no modern phenomenon. He also admitted that he was encouraged to slip in the odd mistake or difference to Cary's text, thus hoping to make it look original. Cary won the case, and added a seven-page addendum to his next edition of the *New Itinerary* detailing every twist and turn of the court proceedings, topped with an indignant rebuttal of the *Paterson* team's impudence.

Plagiarism has always been a major problem in cartography, and in this age perhaps more than in any other. As so much of the best and most accurate mapping was being done locally at county level, helped in part by financial prizes offered by the Society of Arts, many London-based publishers thought nothing of passing such works off as their own. Where no such mapping existed, old maps were often used instead, with no effort made to check their veracity. As a result, mistakes crept in and were then repeated in many subsequent maps and itineraries. Bowen and Kitchin's 1769 *New Map of the Counties of Cumberland and Westmorland*, produced far away in the capital, included a road from Hawkshead to Ennerdale that has never existed, and never could, for it would have to traverse the highest mountains in England. This potentially catastrophic mistake was nonetheless faithfully repeated in a number of later maps and itineraries, including some by both Paterson and Cary.

Despite these occasional slip-ups, no one at the end of the 18th century came close to mapping the road network, as well as textually

detailing it in the most laborious fashion, better than Cary. Boosted by its 'official' credentials, the *New Itinerary* was revised and republished on a regular basis, growing every time. By the time the final, 11th edition came out in 1828, the book was a whopping 785 pages. The fold-out index maps were exquisite, and over the years they were joined by strip maps of main routes and additional large-scale maps of popular areas. These show that Cary was tilting his business towards the new tourist trade, particularly those travelling to take the waters at spas and seaside resorts, rather than to the travelling merchants that had initially caught his attention. The first four extra maps were of the environs of London, Bath, Margate and chic, expanding Brighton (already a long way from the tiny fishing village of Brighthelmstone that had appeared on Cary's earliest maps). Later maps included the Lake District, the Isle of Wight, the Malverns, Cheltenham and the whole of Scotland, the latter particularly mapped for tourists; fishing grounds were mapped as thoroughly as the roads.

The greatest road scheme of the Georgian age makes its cartographic debut in the ninth edition of Cary's *New Itinerary*, published in 1821. He gives over 13 pages to an exhaustive account, complete with a large outline map, of Thomas Telford's new trunk road to Holyhead and the packet to Dublin. The highlight of the route was the new Menai Bridge connecting the mainland and Anglesey, the replacement for John Ogilby's treacherous nine-mile trek across the shifting sands of Traeth Lafan (and indeed a replacement for Cary's own early portrait of this same gossamer route as an unlikely turnpike road). 'Mr Telford,' states Cary, 'conceived the Bold design of passing the Road over this awful Chasm and rapid Tideway by Means of a Bridge of Suspension, which promises to form a new Æra in Bridge Building.' And so it did.

THE COLOSSUS OF ROADS

The coaching age produced legendary road builders. The most remarkable was perhaps John Metcalf (1717–1810), completely blind from childhood, who surveyed and built 200 miles of new road in the north of England. There's a statue of 'Blind Jack', as he was known, sitting on a bench with his trusty measuring wheel in the market place of his native Knaresborough; opposite is a very fine pub named in his honour.

Thomas Telford (1757–1834) has a few pubs named after him too, as well as an entire 1960s new town that's by far the biggest sprawl in Shropshire (it only just escaped being called Dawelloak, a hybrid of the names of its three original settlements). It's fitting that our greatest Georgian engineer should be remembered in the county in which he first gained prominence, as the Shropshire Surveyor of Public Works. As well as canals, churches and the prison in Shrewsbury, Telford designed and constructed some 40 bridges in the county. Nearby, he was also responsible for the vertiginous Pontcysyllte canal aqueduct over the River Dee.

His engineering talent and growing fame took him all over Britain, building not only bridges but also new roads. In these early days of the new United Kingdom, political impetus was on the side of bringing the distant parts closer to London; £50,000 was provided by the exchequer to enable Telford to rebuild the notoriously poor road between Carlisle and Glasgow. He also improved the roads to Edinburgh.

In 1801 the parliaments of Britain and Ireland were united, and improving the arduous three-day journey to Dublin became the most urgent need. Many packets to the Irish capital left from Liverpool, but this was a perilous crossing. To minimize time at sea, the solution had to be getting a route across the rugged mountains of north Wales. Local landowner William Maddocks had his eye on the prize, and was already busy building an embankment and road across the massive sea marsh of Traeth Mawr. He wanted to develop the tiny port of Porthdinllaen, on the Llŷn Peninsula, as the departure point for Dublin, and built the new towns of Porthmadog and Tremadog en route (the latter's main street is still named London Road for its eastern half and Dublin Road the western). However, a parliamentary vote in 1810 favoured Holyhead instead, and charged Telford with the construction of the route.

There were not too many improvements needed to the road between London and Shrewsbury, along the old Roman Watling Street. West of Shrewsbury and into the inhospitable contours of Wales, it was a different story. Telford needed to build numerous bridges and embankments, blast away rocks and precipices, and take his new road through the very heart of

Snowdonia, the loftiest mountain range south of the Scottish Highlands. Most challenging of all was the need to span the turbulent waters of the Menai Strait between the mainland and Anglesey; this he achieved with the then longest suspension bridge in the world. That he managed to do all this, while keeping his road (now the A5) on a gradient that never exceeded 1:20, is undoubtedly the greatest legacy of the man nicknamed by poet Robert Southey 'the Colossus of Roads'.

John Cary's precise style of cartography was a considerable influence on the nascent Ordnance Survey, officially born in 1791. Their first 1 inch to 1 mile maps, of the southern and eastern coasts of England, share a similar look in their typography, symbology and the delineation of different landscapes such as heaths, commons, parkland, woods and waterways. Ordnance Survey also adopted Cary's technique of showing height by hachuring, a far better way of depicting the shape, size and scope of hills and mountains than the crude molehills of earlier cartography. Similar also to Cary was the practice of showing a turnpike road by a thicker line on one side of its depiction on the map, though this was not always entirely accurate, nor consistent.

The 19th century in British cartography was something of a lawless Wild West. While the eminently respectable Ordnance Survey worked gradually to survey the kingdom in detail, they had no interest in aiming their maps at anyone other than the government and military. Commercial companies were left to rip off Ordnance Survey's surveying and repackage their maps for the wider public, and this they did with gusto, always proclaiming loudly on their packaging that their map was based on – or indeed *improved* upon – the Ordnance map. As so little actual surveying was going on (for the first half of the century, Ordnance Survey had to focus much of its resources in Ireland), the new wave of road building by the turnpike trusts often went unmapped for years.

Many of the old routes had climbed up along ridgeways and dropped sharply back down to the towns and villages en route. Macadamisation and improved drainage techniques meant that new, far flatter roads could finally be built along river valleys. Even when Ordnance Survey got around to adding the new roads, the necessary updating work was not always done by their commercial counterparts, as this necessitated laborious work in re-engraving precious copper plates. If there is a theme to many of the route maps of the 19th century, it is that they were often considerably out of date.

This was not helped by the fact that the roads themselves were soon seen as a thing of the past. First came the canals, and then the growing network of railways, the accurate and speedy portrayal of which was of far greater concern to cartographers and their customers. For a decade or two, the old and new worlds collided on the maps: Pigot & Company's 1840 *New Map of England & Wales*, for instance, gave its readers the headache of trying to differentiate on a small scale between the similar depiction of mail roads, turnpike roads, (unturnpiked) cross-roads, rail roads, rivers and navigable canals.

Maps for leisure – again, a section of cartography pioneered by John Cary with his New Itinerary maps of fashionable resorts and picturesque

Overleaf: Pigot & Co's New Map of Wales (1840), showing a detailed 'explanation' and Thomas Telford's new coach road to Holyhead and the Dublin boat, but as yet no 'rail roads' in the region

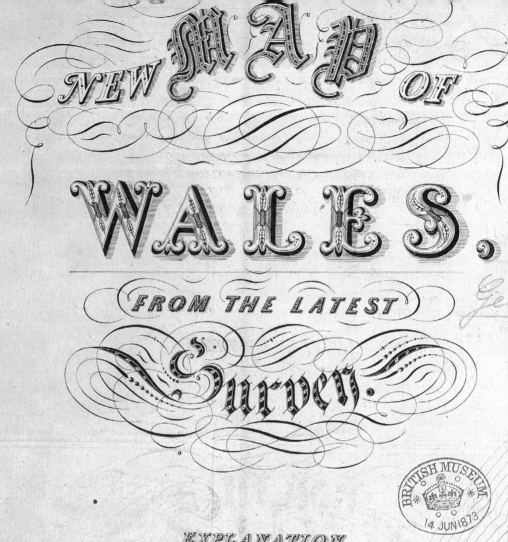

NEW MAP OF WALES,

FROM THE LATEST Survey.

EXPLANATION.

Mail Roads _ thus

Turnpike Roads

Cross Roads

Rail Roads

Rivers

Navigable Canals

Market & Borough Towns in Capitals, with
    their distances from London _ as   171 BRECON

Borough Towns are described by Stars, which
    denote the number of Members returned _ as FLINT ⁎

Large Hills, with their height above the level
    of the Sea _ as   Snowdon
    3571 Feet.

Porth

Nant Ho...

Braich y P...

Trwyn y ...
    Po...
    Maenb...

BARDS
ISLAN...

LIII°

40

HOLYHEAD

ANGLESEY

BEAUMARIS

LLANGEFNI

ABERFFRAW

NEWBOROUGH

CARNARVON

BANGOR

Llanberis

Snowdon 3571 ft

CARNARVON

BAY

NEVIN

PWLLHELI

CRICKEITH

BEDDGELERT

HARLECH

MERIONETH

BARMOUTH
or Bermo

DOLGELLY

PORTHNIULL BAY

St Tudwals Is

landscapes – were a growing sector throughout the 19th century. Companies such as Cassell, George Cruchley, Joshua Archer, Chapman & Hall and George Philip all produced and marketed maps aimed at those using the new steam beasts to get out into the countryside for walks and exploration. They were not always great, nor indeed terribly accurate, maps, as the railways and their stations were often clumsily grafted on to much older cartographic plates. This can be seen in the massively undersized representation of industrial boom towns like Birmingham, Bolton, Bradford and Cardiff, and the absence of new settlements such as Stourport-on-Severn, Leamington, Blackpool and Bournemouth.

As railway mania spread into every corner of Britain, the coaching industry withered and collapsed, and with it the impetus for either new roads or the upkeep of the old ones. There was a new transport revolution around the corner, however, and it arrived from France at the very end of the 1860s: the mass-produced bicycle. All developments in transport had thus far been in ways that were communal and dependent on prescribed routes; cycling opened up all the bits in between. More to the point, it opened up the road network to the ordinary man (and it was nearly all men at first), who was determined to make the most of his new bank holidays and half-holidays.

There were revolutions afoot in the world of cartography too. Steel plates gradually replaced softer copper ones throughout the 19th century; they were tougher and could thus withstand multiple use and adaptation (a copper plate could be worn beyond utility after just a few hundred prints had been taken from it). Better still for a fast-changing landscape, the development of lithographic techniques meant that it was possible to create a map with no need for elaborate engraving or painstaking hand-colouring. The price of paper dropped enormously in the second half of the century, opening up the floodgates for cheap, popular maps and atlases to slake the thirst of an increasingly geographically minded public.

As the 19th century entered its final decade, there were half a million bicycles on the roads of Britain, 10 times the number of just 15 years earlier. There was an explosion of cheap road maps, packaged towards cyclists, though many of these were printed from worn or old plates, some nearly a century old. Cosmetic changes, such as the colouring of roads to indicate their quality or the addition of symbols for steep hills and the offices of the Cyclists' Touring Club, were hastily added. The very first map expressly aimed at cyclists seems to have been one of all of England and Wales, together with a small tranche of southern Scotland, that was produced by publishers Tinsley Brothers, of the Strand, in 1876. It was, it claimed, 'especially prepared for the use of bicyclists', although essentially it was just a reproduction of a John Cary map of 1796, with 30 suggested cycling routes overprinted in red, and on a scale of little practicable use.

The cycling craze gave mapmakers plenty of chance to repackage existing maps, but with a little new emphasis. Not all were quite as antique as the Tinsley Brothers' offering. Bartholomew's quarter-inch plan of southeast England, for instance, was bought in and repackaged as a cyclists' map by at least four other publishers. One, reprinted in 1895, was renamed Henry Grube's *The Cyclist's Map – The Country Fifty Miles Round London*. Concentric circles every five miles were added, radiating out from St Paul's Cathedral, and, according to the key, 'good roads' were shaded green, while 'dangerous hills' were represented by a red line across the road and a red dot on the steeper side (brakes were still something of an added bonus). That this was not originally a cycling map is rather given away by the inclusion of offshore shoals, sandbars, bathymetric fathom lines and shipping routes. There is even a prospective Channel Tunnel mapped, arcing out under the sea from the Dover–Folkestone railway line at Shakespeare Cliff. This dates the original map quite specifically, as this was a project begun in 1881, but forcibly abandoned only a year later.

Most commercial mapmakers tried hard to woo potential customers by picturing and naming them on their covers; cyclists were swiftly incorporated. Perhaps the ultimate in this trend was the Letts county map series of the 1880s, which managed to portray in four different roundels in the corners of the cover its four target markets: a train crossing a viaduct to represent railway travellers, someone on horseback for the riding brigade, a knapsacked hiker in the mountains and a gentleman proudly riding his penny farthing past a country church. Later versions even included a vignette of people in hot air balloons.

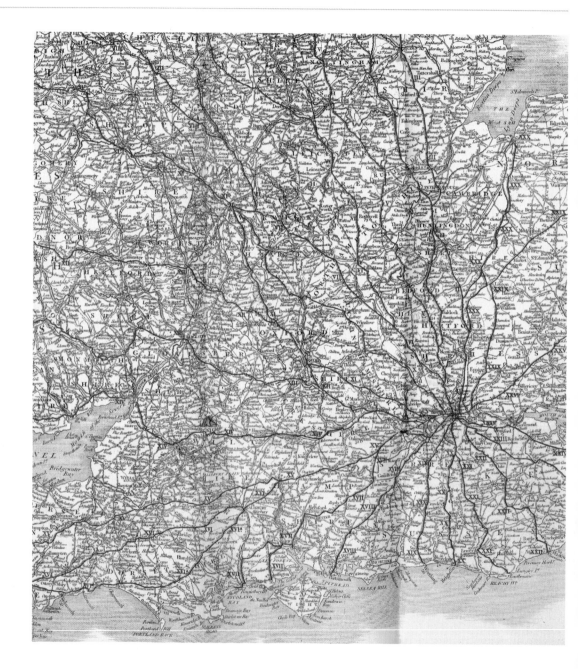

As ever, you got what you paid for. The best bet for a pioneer cyclist was to use the original maps of one of the two companies whose work provided the basis of nearly everyone else's: John Bartholomew & Son Ltd and Ordnance Survey, but these were pricier. Ordnance Survey were largely as reliable as ever, although many cyclists considered their one-inch scale too large and the only alternative, the quarter-inch to the mile, too small. In the early years of the next century, Ordnance Survey introduced a half-inch series, but by that time the far better known, and in truth far better quality, Bartholomew's half-inch series had cornered the market and was not giving it up. Bartholomew's had a real ace up their sleeve, in the shape of their pioneering colour shading of height, from the green of the valley floor, up through ever darkening shades of brown, and then purple and white, for the hills and mountains. Ordnance Survey had introduced contours in the second series of their one-inch maps, from 1847, but it was Bartholomew that brought the idea of the contour to life with their precise and alluring use of colour. The inexact hachuring, and one-size-fits-all symbol for a steep hill (how steep? And for how long?), looked quite literally very pale in comparison.

But ssshhhh...what's that distant dust cloud heading towards us? And what's that *noise*?

Opposite: The Tinsley Brothers' 1876 cyclists' map of England, Wales and southern Scotland was one of many cheap old maps hastily updated for the new cycling craze

NORTH BERWICK
Harb
Link House
Rhodes
North Berwick Law
613
Ferrygate
Newhouse
Dirleton
Cas
Collegehead
Muirfield
Gullane Point
Gullane
Saltcoats
Queenstonbank
Links
Highfield
DIRLETON STA
Kingston
Tower
Rockville
Balgone
Sydserf
Fenton Barns
East Fenton
Castle
Aberlady Bay
Chapel
Stonelaws
Brownrigg
Waughton
Peffer Burn
Muirton
Whitehill
Prora
Aberlady
Drem
Merryhatton
EAST FORTUNE STA
East Fortune
Boar Stone
W Fortune
Ballincrieff Mains
Mungoswells
Muir houses
Ballincrieff
Athelstaneford
Kilduff
Mains
Spittal
Byres
Garleton
Barney Mains
Summit
Garleton Hills
Beanston
Setonhill
Coates
Amisfield Mains
Tyne
Hailes Castle
Redcoll
Huntington
Ugston
Abbey
Stevenson Ho
Traprain Law
Southfield
Trabroun
Cairndinnis
Stevenson Mains
Standingstone
Gladsmuir
Ugstonrigg
Nungate
HADDINGTON
Hopefield
Clerkington
Morham Ch
West Mains
Lennoxlove
Pencaitland
Samuelston Loanhead
Westfield
Morham
Whitelaw
584
West Morham
Begbie
Samuelston
Coalstoun Ho
Chesters
Bolton
Myreside
Baro
Herdmanston
Kirkland
Carfrae
Spilmersford
Blance
Up Bolton
Middle Mains
Townhead
Tyneholm

Chapter 3

Poop Poop! – The Motor Car's Arrival (1895–1918)

Although one school of thought has the 20th century beginning for real with the death of Queen Victoria in January 1901, it could equally be said that the mood of the new century crept in a little earlier, with the arrival on British shores of the automobile. More than any single invention before or since, the car was destined to shape the landscape in its own image.

Dating the precise arrival of the car is hotly disputed. Frederick Bremer built his own vehicle out of bits of bicycles in the back yard of his parents' Walthamstow home, and is said to have driven it on the streets of London's East End in 1892. It's still there now, the prize exhibit in Walthamstow's Vestry House Museum. While young Brits were knocking up a car in the yard, the Germans, of course, were taking the whole thing far more seriously; another school of thought has it that the first 'proper' motor car to run on British roads was a Benz Velo, imported by Henry Hewetson in 1894. After a trip to Benz headquarters in Mannheim, Hewetson was so impressed that he and Walter Arnold began construction of their own cars, incorporating an engine supplied by Benz. Arnold's Motor Carriage Company opened up a showroom near the Tower of London in 1896 and showcased their vehicles at the city's first Motor Show, held in August of that year at the Imperial Institute. This wasn't the first such show in Britain, however. A year earlier, the Mayor of Tunbridge Wells, David Salomons, had held a Horseless Carriage Exhibition with a grand total of five exhibits: two cars, a fire engine, a steam carriage and a tricycle.

Previous page: An East Lothian example from the Gall & Inglis Graded Road Maps of Scotland (1903) for cyclists and motorists, with colour coding of different grades of road and the addition of triangles to denote steep hills

There are others who might claim the title of Britain's first motorist. In the early 1890s, the Honourable Evelyn Ellis had been stationed in the British Embassy in Brussels, from where he'd watched with interest the developing French and German automobile industries. To his mind, the absurd British law introduced in the Locomotive Act of 1865 – stating that steam traction engines (and thus any horseless carriage) travelling at over 4mph should be preceded by a man with a red flag – was killing at birth any tentative automotive stirrings at home, so he took it upon himself to challenge it. To that end, in June 1895 he arranged for a bespoke car to be built by the Parisian firm of Panhard

& Levassor, including a Daimler engine, and for it to be shipped to Southampton. It arrived on 3 July and was taken by train to Micheldever station in Hampshire. From there it was collected by Ellis, accompanied by engineer Frederick Simms, and driven, at considerably over the speed limit, to his home at Datchet in Buckinghamshire, 56 miles away. Much to their annoyance, the police failed to stop them anywhere en route, though they caused plenty of other people to gawp incredulously, as Simms wrote in the following weekend's *Saturday Review*:

> In every place we passed through we were not unnaturally the objects of a great deal of curiosity. Whole villages turned out to behold, open mouthed, the new marvel of locomotion. The departure of coaches was delayed to enable their passengers to have a look at our horseless vehicle, while cyclists would stop to gaze enviously at us as we surmounted with ease some long hill.

By the end of 1895, following further imports, there were estimated to be 14 or 15 cars on Britain's roads, a figure that had ballooned by the turn of the 20th century to around 700–800. The domestic car industry had finally spluttered into life too. Frederick Simms bought the British rights to the Daimler engine, which he sold on to Harry Lawson, the pioneer of the 'safety' bicycle. In January 1896, Lawson launched the Daimler Motor Company. A friend of Lawson's had an empty cotton mill in Coventry for sale, which Lawson, looking for manufacturing premises, promptly snapped up, thus establishing the long tradition of the car industry in the West Midlands. It was to be a historic and powerful association with an area that was both steeped in the tradition of metal-bashing and ideally situated at the heart of the transport network.

The first cars cost upwards of £400 apiece (over £40,000 at today's prices), so the small coterie of early automobilists comprised only the rich and powerful. Evelyn Ellis took the Prince of Wales, soon to be Edward VII, out for a spin in his Panhard in February 1896, and he became a passionate convert to the cause. Such men of influence were determined – and able – to see legislation passed in the motorist's favour. In the same month as the prince's first drive, Frederick Simms, Harry

Lawson and others founded the Motor Car Club, two months after David Salomons, the go-getting Mayor of Tunbridge Wells, had established the Self-Propelled Traffic Association. Both groups had their sights set firmly on the abolition of the red flag rule and the 4mph speed limit. In their first couple of months, Salomons' group sent out 56,000 campaigning letters on the issue.

Despite opposition from the railway companies, which could already smell the threat, the Locomotives on Highways Act became law in November 1896, removing the requirement of the red flag and increasing the speed limit to a dizzy 14mph. The Motor Car Club celebrated with a gala dinner at the Metropole Hotel in Whitehall, before sending participants (probably none of them sober) off on the inaugural London to Brighton rally. To set the tone of what had been christened 'The Emancipation Run', Lord Winchelsea kicked off proceedings with a ceremonial tearing up of the red flag, before sending the 33 cars – around half the total in the country at the time – on their way. It was a foul, wet November Saturday, and considerably fewer than half made it to Brighton. A parade of cars through the seaside town was planned for the Sunday, but that was even wetter and the event had to be cancelled. Britain had entered the motor age in the only way it knew how: posh, bristling with belligerence and soaked.

Even with so few cars on the road, the first road accident fatality had already been recorded. Three months before the Emancipation Run, Mrs Bridget Driscoll of Croydon had been heading to a fête at Crystal Palace when she was mown down by a Roger-Benz Horseless Carriage, being demonstrated by the Anglo-French Motor Company and driven by an employee, Arthur Edsall. At the subsequent inquest, Edsall insisted that he had been doing no more than the statutory limit of 4mph, though a witness stated that the car had been going at a 'tremendous pace', and 'as fast as a good horse could gallop'. Finding Mrs Driscoll's death an accident, coroner Percy Morrison said he hoped 'such a thing would never happen again'.

DUST TO DUST, TAR TO TARMAC

For the vast majority of ordinary people, the first decade of the automobile craze literally passed them by. They had no chance of joining the wealthy enthusiasts chugging along the roads with such joy, and continued much as they had before, on the trains, on horseback, on bicycles and on foot. The only effect on their life was that it was suddenly enveloped in frequent, choking clouds of dust.

In *Cider With Rosie* (1959), Laurie Lee remembers the Gloucestershire village of his childhood, caught unknowingly in a freeze-frame just before the onslaught of the motor age. The 'villages like ships in an empty landscape' were connected by an intricate network of 'white narrow roads, rutted by hooves and cartwheels, innocent of oil and petrol'. When those automotive pioneers came hurtling by in their Daimlers and Oldsmobiles, the innocence Lee had described evaporated in an instant, and it was all down to the dust coating their washing, their children and their hedges, and that flew into their eyes, teeth and open windows.

Even the finest roads of the coaching age were built only of crushed stone bound together with mortar and clay; the suction effect produced by the passing of pneumatic car tyres pulled out the mortar, making the road surface progressively collapse and become ever dustier. That early enthusiast for the car, Toad of Toad Hall in Kenneth Grahame's *The Wind in the Willows* (1908), is often seen hurtling through the countryside, poop-pooping his horn in reckless joy, and utterly oblivious to the 'enveloping cloud of dust that blinded and enwrapped them [Rat and Mole] utterly'.

The Roads Improvement Association (RIA) had been founded by cyclists back in 1886, and was at the forefront of campaigning on behalf of the new motorised road users too, for the poor quality of the road surfaces was a regular concern for both. In 1901 the Nottinghamshire County Surveyor, Edgar Hooley, was passing an ironworks and noticed that a black stretch of the road was free of ruts and not giving off any dust. He asked what had happened, and was told that barrels of tar had fallen from a dray and burst open. To cover up the mess, waste slag from the ironworks had been poured onto the tar, and this has solidified into a smooth, hard surface. It was just what Hooley had been looking for.

By 1902 Hooley had perfected the process of heating tar, then adding slag and broken stones to the mix, which was then steamrollered into place. This he

Above: Poop! Poop! *(1998) by Jonathan Barry: Toad of Toad Hall was the archetype of the early motoring enthusiast, engulfing all behind him in a cloud of dust*

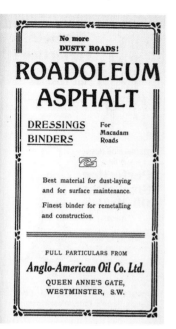

Above: An advertisement for asphalt in Pratt's Road Atlas of England and Wales *(1905)*

called 'tarmacadam', later patented under the trade name Tarmac. To prove the worth of his experiment, Hooley tarmacked a five-mile stretch of the Radcliffe Road (now the A52) out of Nottingham, and it was an immediate success. The RIA organised trials of the new surface in Kent that same year, and by 1907 were testing ways of spreading Tarmac with specialist new machines throughout Middlesex and Berkshire. So successful were the trials that the entire Bath Road through Berkshire was tarmacked, with thousands of miles of British highway following soon.

The Motor Car Club and the Self-Propelled Traffic Association were not the only lobbying groups set up to fight for motorists' rights. There was also the British Autocar Committee, which published a weekly periodical, *The Autocar*, from November 1895, despite the fact that the number of petrol-driven vehicles on the road at the time was only just edging out of single figures; it continues today as *Autocar* magazine. In there too were the Road Motor Association and the British Motor Syndicate; it was all getting a little chaotic, and cluttered by vested commercial interests.

In May 1897, Henry Sturmey, first editor of *The Autocar*, wrote in the magazine, 'We wish we had a really independent autocar organisation in this country to which the autocar world could look for guidance'. As did many other pioneering motorists, he cast a wistful eye across the Channel to the far more car-friendly milieu of France, which included the already venerable and respected Automobile Club de France. The energetic Frederick Simms responded to the call, and on 11 December 1897, the Automobile Club of Great Britain was formally inaugurated.

Evelyn Ellis's attempts at provoking the police into action had failed back in 1895, but as the number of cars increased on British roads, so did the number of cases brought by the police against speeding and reckless motorists. Dark suspicions grew that the constabulary were resorting to disguises and trap tactics in order to snare unsuspecting motorists for often trivial infringements of old laws from the pre-petrol age – suspicions that were soon confirmed in various courtrooms. Some, including car companies themselves, paid cyclists to patrol a few key roads, looking out for speed traps and warning any approaching motorists.

The response of the Automobile Club was tentative. They occasionally offered support and legal advice, but it was becoming increasingly clear that they saw themselves principally as an exclusive gentlemen's club rather than a campaigning group, and it was left to individuals, and their own offshoot, the Motor Union, to get stuck in to the dirty work. When the Motor Car Act, bringing in driving licences (but no test as yet), registration plates and a higher speed limit of 20mph, was going through parliament in 1903, MPs active in the Automobile Club failed to speak up, and significant rifts developed in their ranks. In June 1905, in order to take on the police traps, yet another new organisation was set up. Unlike the Automobile Club, it neither vetted potential members nor barred women. They named themselves the Motorists' Mutual Association, but changed it twice more in the first few weeks, first to the Automobilists' Mutual Association and then finally to the Automobile Association. Rivals the Automobile Club soon gained the new king, Edward VII, as their patron and with it, the 'Royal' prefix to their title. The AA and RAC were here.

Left: A 1905 Punch cartoon depicting a policeman leaping out to entrap a motorist who has been going over the 20mph speed limit

SALUTING THE WAY

The AA and the RAC were both born as reactions to the indifference – even outright hostility – of the legal establishment towards the motoring craze. Not only did they have to fight the battles of motorists, but it was left to them as well to shape the new landscape into which the car so readily slotted.

Both organisations opened offices throughout the country, proffered insurance and advice, placed emergency telephones by the roadside, developed a network of approved garages, mechanics and hotels, and employed patrols. These, initially on bicycle and then motorbike, were the backbone of the organisations; members were encouraged to look to them for any motoring query, as well as to be tipped off wherever police speed traps were operating. This gave rise to the famous phenomenon of the saluting AA man. So as not to break the law by receiving a direct warning, members were told that if they passed an AA patrol and he didn't salute, they were to stop and ask him the reason. More often than not, that would be because of an imminent speed trap. Inevitably, this policy was challenged in a court case, but the case was dismissed, and it survived as part of the AA's repertoire of services until 1962.

Above left and right: Early AA patrols went by bike; The traditional salute from AA patrolmen to members grew from a coded warning of speed traps ahead

It was even left up to the motoring organisations, the AA especially, to provide signage on the roads. Some of these early signs can still be found in situ today, especially the enamel roundels that give the name of the town or village being entered in a band across the centre, and with an assortment of distances to other destinations above and below. Each one concluded at the bottom with the distance to London (always unbelievably precise: 263¼ miles from St Mawes in Cornwall, a not-quite-round 299¾ miles from Low Lorton in Cumbria) and the slogan 'SAFETY FIRST'. The AA also erected many distance fingerposts on the road, and signs warning of steep hills, dangerous corners and schools. In their distinctive yellow and black livery, and always including their name and logo, they were also a highly effective advertisement and recruiting tool. Maps and bespoke route plans soon followed. From 1912, handwritten personalised itineraries were provided for members, along with town plans and detailed routes for suggested 'day drives'.

It should be remembered, though, that for many years yet, those on bikes were a far more significant target market for mapmakers than were motorists – an eye witness at the launch of the 1896 Emancipation Run from London to Brighton estimated that some 10,000 cyclists had accompanied the 33 cars down Whitehall. Cheap maps, usually mass reprints from older originals, were little more than advertising tools for cycle shops, specialist clothes suppliers or local newspapers. Some offered gimmicks, such as miniaturising the maps into 'pocket size' or printing them on Pegamoid, the trade name for the application of a nitrocellulose varnish onto muslin. This gave sellers the chance to market their maps as waterproof; W H Smith & Son soon produced

Above: The Complete
Safety Cycling Map of
England *(1900) by*
Gall & Inglis

such a series where even the cover was embossed Pegamoid, giving it the appearance of cheap leather.

Publications for cyclists had mushroomed in the last few years of the 19th century, and they often published maps under their own banner. At the end of the 1890s, *Cycling* magazine (still going strong today as *Cycling Weekly*) gave its readers a national map of England and Wales, produced by cartographers Gall & Inglis, that promised on its cover to show 'the quality of 28,000 miles of road and marking of 1,700 dangerous hills'. In 1908 they gave readers a Bartholomew map under the same banner; the maps are different enough, but most striking is the difference in the covers. The first has a picture of two rakish cyclists standing in the middle of an empty crossroads as they consult the map, their bikes casually left on the verge under a fingerpost. It is a picture of rural tranquility at its most benign. A decade later, and the scene has changed entirely. A grim-faced cyclist has been pushed to the side of the illustration, and to the side of the road, by a car thundering past and filling almost the entire vignette. In the vehicle, the two men in the front stare resolutely ahead, while the two high-hatted ladies in the back peer haughtily at the poor cyclist as they speed by.

Gall & Inglis were one of the most regular names in maps for pioneer cyclists and motorists. They had been established as a religious publisher in Edinburgh in 1810; the Gall in the name refers to one of their founders, Reverend James Gall, progenitor of a cartographic 'equal area' world projection almost identical to the one launched as wholly new by Arno Peters with such a fanfare in the 1970s. The projection, beloved of developing world charities and campaigners for the way it 'corrects' the over-emphasis of Europe and North America in other world views, is now more properly known as the Gall–Peters projection.

The company itself was never ashamed to recycle other maps, and much of the Gall & Inglis catalogue at the turn of the 20th century was reprinted from a full national set of half-inch scale copper plates that dated back to John Cary in the 1790s. They produced regional and county maps from these, with the better roads picked out in a sandy red colour, but their first real coup harked back not just to the actual cartography of Cary, but to one of his favourite thematic styles too – and

*Left: Driving the Great
North Road: Gall &
Inglis's* The Motor Strip
Route Map London
to York *(1908), with
diversions to Leeds
and Harrogate*

*Overleaf: Detail of the
mapping and height cross-
section plan from* The
Motor Strip Route Map
London to York

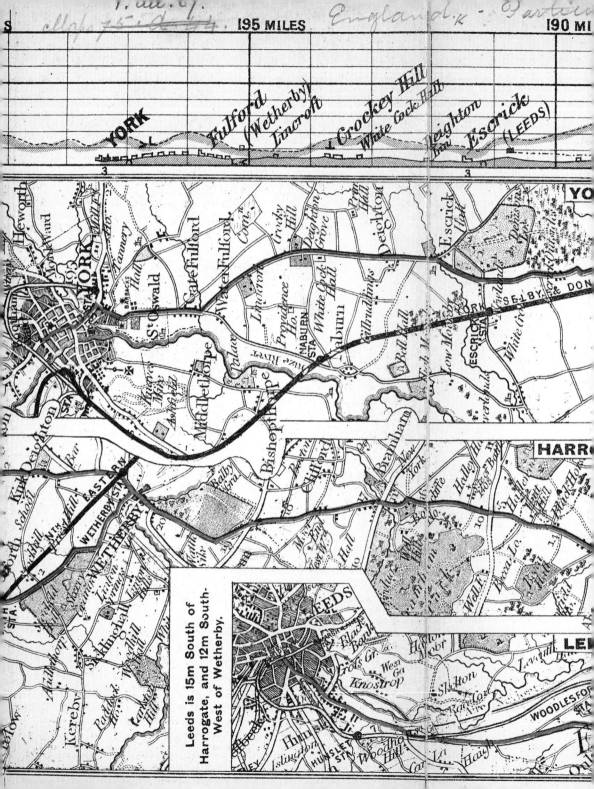

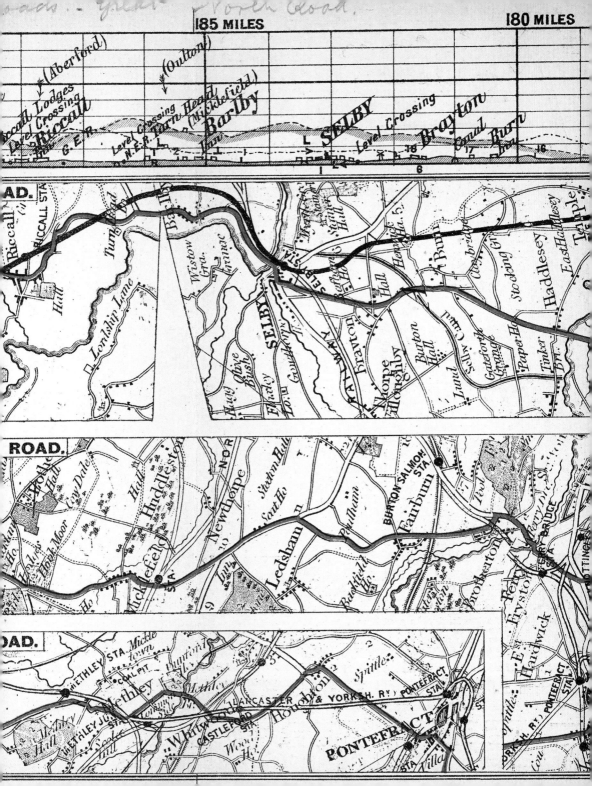

indeed that of Ogilby before him. This was in the shape of a series of strip maps of long cross-country routes for the ambitious cyclist. Covering entire lengths of route such as the Great North Road, Telford's Holyhead road, the Bath Road, the Exeter Road and even a Land's End to John o'Groats route in three sections, they combined a half-inch scale map, with the designated route picked out in red, alongside a corresponding mile-by-mile, foot-by-foot gradient profile.

Alternative routes were picked out in red hatching, while railways and stations (pretty much the only substantive additions to Cary's original plates) were prominently marked too. On the gradient profile plan, there was a raft of letters and symbols for different kinds of fork in the road, junctions, crossroads, sharp turns and bridges. When the routes passed through towns, the cluster of letters and symbols was nigh on impenetrable, but this was a popular series, if only because it seemed that the user was getting such good value for money. Retailing at a shilling for the paper version, and two shillings for a cloth-backed version wrapped in a 'waterproof' cover, the maps, if unfolded to their full length, were anything between four and sixteen feet long. Not that you were encouraged to do so, for that was the whole point: you could follow a route, even of a few hundred miles, and as their advertisements had it, 'the Map turns over page after page JUST LIKE A BOOK And never requires to be unfolded'. The arrival of the car gave these lengthy route maps even greater impetus, and it says all you need to know about the road network at the turn of the 20th century that it was entirely possible to navigate around it using maps little changed since the 1790s.

The strip maps were justly popular, but restrictive if the adventurous cyclist fancied a ride away from the designated main routes. For that, Gall & Inglis encouraged their public towards other reprints of the half-inch maps at county and regional level, but in order to get the same level of information about the all-important topography, each map contained a legend tersely stating that 'For Elevation Plans and Descriptions of the roads, see the *Contour Road Book*', another of their publications. Cyclists especially needed one single map that gave as much information as possible; having to cross-reference it with an accompanying book of tables and charts was enough to dissuade many from using them at all.

That said, their *Contour Road Book* (first published in 1897) was a useful addition to any cyclist's kit bag, and was popular too with early motorists, who were almost equally as wary of steep hills as those who had to get up them under their own steam. Each map took a large section of the country and gave detailed gradient profiles of the main routes within. Accompanying notes were suitably sombre, such as here, describing the 32-mile route from Brighton to Chichester:

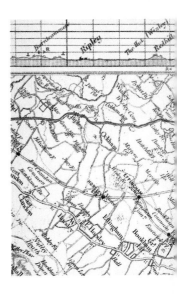

> *Good surface to Hove, then very bumpy to Shoreham, whence good to Arundel; hereafter an up and down road, but with good surface to Chichester. Bad hill at 21m.*

The holy grail for these Edwardian cartographers was to produce a map that combined a good plan on a decent, useful scale with information about topography – hills especially – and quality of the road surfaces. Thanks to their maps' popularity, and judicious collaboration with the likes of the Cycling Touring Club, Gall & Inglis had at their disposal an army of willing volunteers to help provide them with information to update and enhance their maps.

Above: Detail from the Gall & Inglis 'Ripley Road' Map (1899), on the back of the strip map of the road to Brighton

THE RIPLEY ROAD

The arrival of the pneumatic tyre in the 1880s gave cycling a massive shot in the arm (and, more pertinently, a lack of jolting to the bottom), and the pastime soon spread into all sections of the population. This was not just a way to get out of the smoky cities for a gasp of country air, it was the chance to dress up, picnic, go to the pub, flirt and be free, even if only for a precious afternoon. For saddle-bound Londoners, there was no better day out than a turn down the Ripley Road.

Ripley lies on the London to Portsmouth turnpike road, now the A3, although the village has been bypassed by a roaring dual carriageway since the 1980s. It was an important stop on the Portsmouth coaching route, but the railways passed it by and the old road grew dusty and deserted. Then in the mid-1870s, a Mrs Dibble, the widowed licensee of the Anchor Inn, together with her pretty young daughters, started providing teas and accommodation aimed at the new devotees of cycling. Over the next few decades Ripley became the Home Counties cycling mecca, 23 miles from Westminster Bridge through a patchwork of England at its most gentle. The route took you out of London across Wimbledon Common or Richmond Park, along the Thames at Kingston, and into rural Surrey, skimming across commons, past woods, pleasure gardens and stately parkland, culminating in tea or something stronger at the Anchor or the Talbot, the village's old coaching inns. And all on a fairly good, and mostly flat, road that afforded plenty of chance for races and showing off.

Sherlock Holmes and Raffles the Gentleman Thief both let slip their knowledge of the Ripley Road. H G Wells included it in two novels, including *The War of the Worlds* (1898). A cycling-themed board game, at which you won by reaching the Anchor, was created in its honour. But not everyone approved. In his series of books in the 1890s about famous old roads, perennial nostalgist Charles G Harper wrote that 'the Ripley Road, now-a-days, is, in fact, the stalking-ground of self-advertising long-distance riders, of cliquey and boisterous club-men, and of the immodest women who wear breeches awheel'.

The sunshine of those three magic decades soon evaporated. Mrs Dibble died in 1887, her daughters in 1895 and 1896. Their brother sold the pub to hoteliers from Guildford. More importantly, the cyclists no longer had the road to themselves. The motoring fraternity were muscling in and shoving those on two wheels to the side. The traffic increased, turning Ripley from a pleasure park idyll into a bad-tempered bottleneck on a dust-choked road. In July 1904, a plaintive lament to the Ripley Road by Jessie Pope appeared in *Punch* magazine, containing the lines:

> *I drank the country breeze at first,*
> *Unsoiled by fetid fumes,*
> *But now I'm cursed with a constant thirst*
> *That parches and consumes.*
> *I am choked and hit with smoke and grit*
> *When I venture from my abode,*
> *My pets are maimed and my eyes inflamed,*
> *For I live on the Ripley Road.*

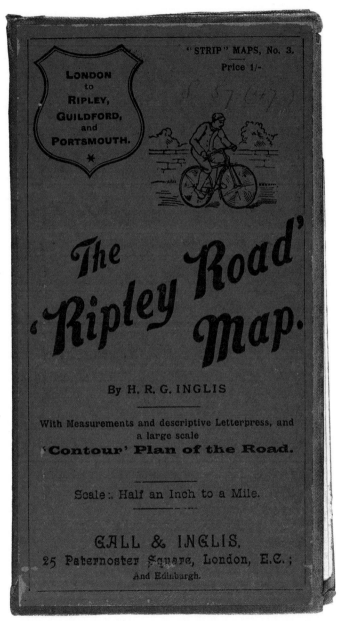

"STRIP" MAPS, No. 3.

Price 1/-

LONDON
to
RIPLEY,
GUILDFORD,
and
PORTSMOUTH.

The
'Ripley Road'
Map.

By H. R. G. INGLIS

With Measurements and descriptive Letterpress, and
a large scale
'Contour' Plan of the Road.

Scale: Half an Inch to a Mile.

GALL & INGLIS,
25 Paternoster Square, London, E.C.;
And Edinburgh.

*Left: The Gall & Inglis
'Ripley Road' Map
(1899) – the back cover of
their Brighton Road Map*

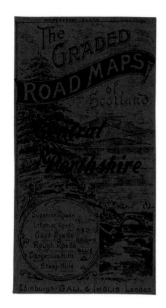

Above: The Graded
Road Maps of Scotland
*(1903): Gall & Inglis tried
a new series of Graded
Road Maps, designed
to show the quality of
different roads by use of
colour coding*

I pass my days in a yellow fog,
My nights in a yellow dream
Haunted by handlebar, clutch and cog
And eyes that goggle and gleam.
I am not robust, but I dine on dust
Gratuitously bestowed
And for twopence I'll sell my house in the dell
By the side of the Ripley Road.

This information from those on the ground was best employed in Gall & Inglis's half-inch Graded Road Map series. At last they set about engraving new plates in a more modern style, but this was a laborious process and the series never got beyond coverage of southern Scotland and northern England. As well as the clear new typography and updated industrial townscapes, the maps contained a whole new set of colours and symbols designed to appeal to both cyclist and early motorist.

Chief amongst these were the division of roads into different overpainted colours: 'Superior Roads' were daubed in yellow, 'Good Roads' in a brown produced by the (sometimes sloppy) overprinting of red on yellow, 'Inferior Roads' in red and 'Rough Roads' in blue. Strangely enough, the same colour range was used for roads, but in precisely the opposite order, by Ordnance Survey some 70 years later when they launched their metric 1:50,000 range, now known as the Landranger series. At least with the latter, the blue roads (i.e. motorways) were unlikely to be easily confused with similarly coloured waterways, but that was not so with the Gall & Inglis maps, for the blue 'rough' roads were usually those meandering across the landscape in a way that was all too readily muddled with the course of a river.

Gall & Inglis reasonably surmised that the two factors most important to road users were the quality of the route itself and the prevalence of steep hills en route. The marking of these were equally broad-brush. Large, bold triangles denoted 'Dangerous Hills'; a smaller, lighter triangle was for 'Steep Hills'. No actual measurements were given, save for a few spot heights on some of the more obvious mountain and hill summits,

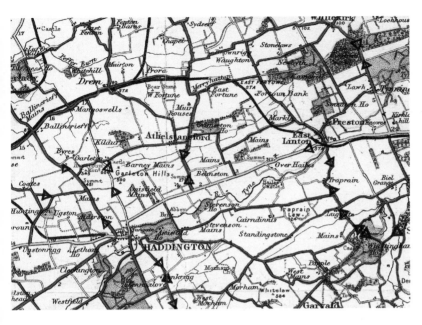

Left: An example of the Graded Road Map; the much-heralded colour shading looked sloppy, and the hill triangles woefully inexact

almost always some distance from the road itself. It was a brave attempt at a new map series, but it never really took off, and the onset of World War I finished it off for good.

It didn't help that Gall & Inglis's maps were in direct competition with Bartholomew and Ordnance Survey. Despite one of their biggest sellers being called the *Contour Road Book*, it was the complete lack of contour lines on any of their maps that probably did for them. Gall & Inglis's simplistic portrait of elevation compared particularly badly with Bartholomew's own half-inch series, which was lavish and precise in its use of colour to denote changing height. From 1897, Ordnance Survey had also started to issue their one-inch maps in full colour; they too offered far greater exactness with their use of contours. By comparison, Gall & Inglis's hill triangles looked crude and old-fashioned.

It was the easiest thing in the world for cartographers to tilt their wares at the new motoring market, for all it needed in the early years was a new title to the map or the addition of a cover illustration showing a pioneer motorist chugging through the countryside. The actual map

Overleaf: Contoured Road Map of Chatham & Maidstone (1921), Maidstone detail: the Graded Road Maps looked even more outdated once Ordnance Survey's flagship one-inch series had been updated with colour, shading and contours

itself needed no real updating, for the roads upon which the cars were forced to travel were the same rutted and dusty ones that had taken the bicycles and stagecoaches before them.

Just as the British had been late in their entry to the world of motor manufacturing, so they were when it came to building new roads to accommodate the cars. In other countries the love affair with the automobile was advancing full pelt, and new highways were being planned and built. In January 1902, *The Automotor & Horseless Vehicle Journal* reported that the Belgians were constructing a highway from Ostend to the national border, which could link up with a planned French highway to Paris, and that there was serious talk in the US about building a 100-foot wide route from New York to New Orleans. That didn't happen, but the New Yorkers got in early with another route: the Long Island Motor Parkway, built by the Vanderbilt family as a private road exclusively for motorists, and opened in October 1908. The Vanderbilts were early enthusiasts for motor racing, and the 45-mile Parkway was principally built as a track upon which young coves, after paying their $2 toll, could open up the throttle and go at whatever speed they liked. At the opening ceremony, the company Vice-President set the tone for a highway 'free from all grade crossings, dust and police surveillance':

> *Think of the time it will save the busy man. Speed limits are left behind, the Great White Way is before him, and with the throttle open he can go, go, go and keep going, 50, 60 or 90 miles an hour until Riverhead or Southampton is reached, in time for a scotch at the Meadow Club, a round of golf and a refreshing dip in the surf, and all before dinner is served, or the electric lights begin to twinkle.*

This was the voice of smooth modernity, and it was in stark contrast to the blustery outbursts back in the old country, where almost everyone outside of the wealthy motoring fraternity saw the car as either a disagreeable intrusion or a short-lived fad. Even the *Financial Times*, in a 1900 editorial, found plenty to be worried about:

We are sorry to see that there is indeed a demand for the abominations [cars]. All over the place one meets the hideous, noisome and noisy vehicles, dangerous alike to the wayfarers and to the passengers who think they are enjoying themselves on the rattling malodorous concerns. We mournfully admit the demand.

They could hardly do anything other than 'mournfully admit' the car's instant and growing popularity. The numbers spoke for themselves. Thanks to the 1903 Motor Car Act, enforcing registration of all vehicles, we can see the staggering rise in cars on British roads, from fewer than 8,500 in 1904 to more than 10 times that number just five years later. After a further five years, to the outbreak of World War I, there were nearly a quarter of a million cars and motorbikes on the road.

NEED FOR SPEED

There was one new road built solely for cars before World War I. It was 100 feet wide, 2.75 miles long and of no use to most motorists as it went round in a tight loop. This was the Brooklands motor racing circuit at Weybridge in Surrey, financed and opened in June 1907 by estate owner Sir Hugh Fortescue Locke-King. He'd been inspired by a trip to the Coppa Florio road race in northern Italy two years earlier, where he'd been shocked to see that there were no British competitors at all.

In 1907 the official speed limit was still only 20mph, a figure that remained intact until 1931. Although that had appeared sufficient for the first wave of cars, technology had developed so quickly that cars were now being produced that were routinely capable of more than three or four times the limit. Locke-King recognised the need for speed, and Brooklands was the result. Like the Long Island Motor Parkway and the AVUS track in Berlin, it meant that the first purpose-built roads for motorists were all designed as racetracks.

With a capacity for around a quarter of a million spectators, Brooklands became a mecca of motoring, in all its guises. As well as the speed and time trials, and numerous distance and endurance record attempts, the track was used for automotive testing. Only a year after opening, the course doubled up

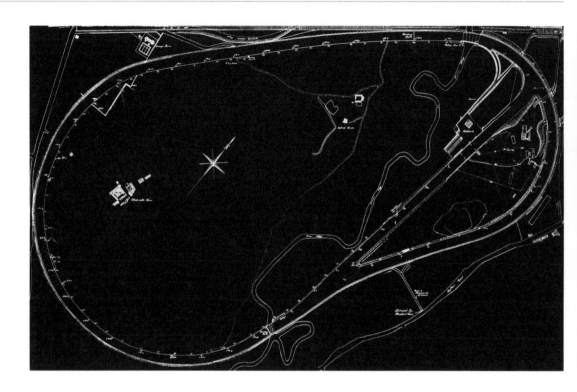

Above: A blueprint of the Brooklands circuit from 1907

for the first time as an aeroplane landing strip; in 1910 Britain's first flying school opened here. At first, women were banned from competing, but that was soon overturned and Brooklands became an unlikely front line of the nascent women's liberation movement. World War II saw the track's demise, after it had been requisitioned for aeronautic construction, and the vast concrete track, already crumbling in places, had to be breached.

There's a Brooklands Museum there now, chock-full of nostalgia for a glorious heyday, as well as a 'Driving Experience Centre' operated by Mercedes-Benz, a hotel, a shopping centre and a few housing estates, some of which have been built right over the original banked oval track. However, large parts can still be seen, mossed over and cracked, and all the more evocative of a vanished age for that.

'The Right Crowd and No Crowding' was one of the early slogans of the track, and here we see the beginnings of the cult of individualism that the motor trade

*Above: And they're off!
Race day excitement at
Brooklands in 1911*

has so successfully exploited ever since. In these early days, advertisements and editorials in many specialist publications emphasised individuality, status and taste, contrasting motoring with the mass collectivism of railways and their fixed routes. Even the choice of destination afforded by your means of transport became loaded: a train took the masses for their seaside holiday in some garish kiss-me-quick resort, while a car enabled the self-declared intelligentsia to pootle along the fishing harbours of the Cornish coast or check out a crumbling hilltop ruin. It's a distinction still much toyed with by car advertisers and advocates today, and one worth pondering if you visit the remains of the Brooklands motor track, particularly the great curving wall of cracked concrete along the side of Barnes Wallis Road in Byfleet. Once you've had an eyeful of this shrine to speed and individualism, turn round and gaze at the forest of hatchbacks in the gargantuan car park of a 24-hour supermarket, or the sullen queues of traffic at a petrol station. The romance of the road seems a very long way away.

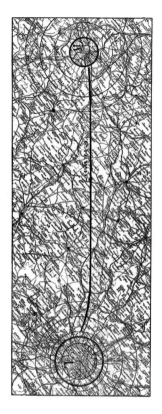

Above: A map illustrating
B H Thwaite's proposal
for a 'carway' from
London to Birmingham

Even amid the grumpiness of the early days, there were some high-level calls for the car to be taken seriously, and to be planned for with the building of fast new roads. In a House of Commons debate as early as May 1900, the future Conservative Prime Minister Arthur Balfour, an enthusiastic motorist himself, described his vision of the future:

> *I sometimes dream – perhaps it is only a dream – that in addition to railways and tramways, we may see great highways constructed for rapid motor traffic, and confined to motor traffic, which would have the immense advantage, if it could be practicable, of taking the workman from door to door, which no tramway and no railway could do. Such highways as I sometimes conceive in my mind would, of course, be in connection with the ordinary street system at one end, and the ordinary country road system at the other end.*

He conceded that his ideas 'may, to some minds, seem fanciful and imaginary', but he was far from alone. In the August 1902 edition of the journal *Nineteenth Century*, engineer B H Thwaite published an article entitled 'Why Not a Motorcar Way through England?' His proposal was for a new four-lane toll road from London to Carlisle, and ultimately thence to Glasgow and Edinburgh. The first section, a ruler-straight route between Edgware on the outskirts of London and Bickenhill, near Birmingham, was the only one seriously considered, but the proposal certainly caught the public's attention – Thwaite himself wrote a few months later that the idea had received 'from all parts of the country almost unanimous and enthusiastic approval'.

Particularly enthusiastic, of course, were the new breed of motoring evangelists, none more so than the Honourable John Scott Montagu MP, later the Second Baron Montagu of Beaulieu. He liked the theory of a motorcar way, though he far preferred the idea of one running from London to the ritzy playground of Brighton over one to grimy old Brum, 'as it seems that such a route would have been much more used than any running northwards from the metropolis…I doubt whether there are sufficient automobiles in Great Britain to justify such a scheme,' he wrote in *The Autocar* in August 1902. Montagu was perhaps the archetype of

Left: The Honourable John Scott Montagu MP, one of the most passionate of early motoring enthusiasts

the aristocratic auto-enthusiast, a regular driver on the European race circuit, founder and publisher of a number of motoring journals and close friend and supporter of Hugh Locke-King at Brooklands (see 'Need for Speed', p105). He commissioned the original statuette that became the Spirit of Ecstasy on the front of every Rolls-Royce; it was modelled on his mistress, Eleanor Thornton.

Thwaite's proposal versus that of Montagu crystallises the debate at the end of Britain's first decade of motoring. To many of the wealthy automobilists, motoring was all about speed and derring-do, a pursuit for chaps to fit in between shooting parties and gallivanting off on their other great love, pioneer aviation (motor cars and aeroplanes, born almost simultaneously, have fitted snugly together from the outset). Not for them any thought as to the likely economic, social or topographic revolutions that the car might bring; that was left to more sober politicians and planners. Montagu continued to press the case for a London to

Brighton motorway, publishing a pamphlet on it and even presenting it to parliament in 1906, where it was unceremoniously shunted aside.

The simple truth was that no new roads were yet forthcoming, as no one could work out who should pay for them, and how. As the number of cars climbed higher, including many bought by middle-class professionals such as doctors, it was ever more obvious that motoring was no flash in the pan, and that its development needed some strategic planning by government. Although the Local Government Act of 1888 had created the county councils and thus streamlined responsibility for highway maintenance, the arrival of the car had changed everything. In all, there were nearly 2,000 different councils – county, county borough, metropolitan borough, urban district and rural district – with responsibility for the roads on their patch. The Great North Road alone came under the aegis of 72 different authorities. Co-ordination was impossible.

However, the Edwardians were allergic to anything that smelled even slightly of nationalisation. Back in 1903, the committee that had initiated legislation for driving licences and a new speed limit shrank from the idea of statutory funding for the roads. Their only nod to central planning was the recommendation for a French-style system of road classification, into national and local routes, albeit still under the management of the county councils.

It was all change when the Liberals won the 1908 general election. In the near-revolutionary 1909 'People's Budget', Chancellor David Lloyd George increased licence duty on cars, and put a new tax of threepence per gallon on petrol; the funds thus raised went into a new Road Board, which could subsidise new road building or the improvement of designated national routes. The Road Improvements Act of 1909 put flesh on the bones, enshrining the idea of compulsory purchase of land for new roads. The measures were enough to alarm plenty, and not just the dwindling band of anti-modernists horrified by the very existence of the car. Some of the age's most voracious petrolheads were equally unconvinced. The RAC worried that it might mean motorists were excluded from 'ordinary' roads. Conservative MP George Bowles said that the idea showed 'a certain want of balance in the minds of those who can seriously make such a proposal'. Born into a very British chorus of mass fretting and pious nostalgia, the new Road Board spent its first few years funding the tarmacking of many major routes. Plans were mooted for the creation of a new arterial road, the Western Avenue, out of London, but World War I put the stoppers on that. By 1914 Britain had been turned inside out by 20 years of motoring, but not one inch of new public road to accommodate the revolution had yet been built.

Cartographers were not so slow off the mark. Though there was nothing new to show on their maps, there was a whole new market, and they lost no time in pitching for it. It was, after all, not a huge task to repackage a 'Cycling Map' as a 'Cycling and Motoring Map' or to add a vignette of a car to the front cover. The perception that motorists were classier customers than cyclists, however, resulted in other cosmetic changes. At the cheaper end of the market, G W Bacon had been an enthusiastic producer of cycling maps, often crammed with advertising both around the map's edge and even on the cover. Much of this advertising ephemera disappeared as they attempted to make their products look more upmarket, aiming to sell to motorists – even if the map itself remained the same.

There was some considerable new competition at the bottom end of the market, most notably from brash new *arrivistes* Geographia. Founded in 1908 by Alexander Gross (the father of Phyllis Pearsall, creator of the first London A–Z), Geographia maps were as cheap and shameless as Gross himself. At a time when most decent maps cost upwards of sixpence on paper and a shilling on cloth, his New Road Map district series, at 3 miles to 1 inch, initially retailed at just one penny on paper and threepence on cloth. You got what you paid for. The mapping was plain, dull and badly printed on coarse paper. You had to hand it to Gross, however, for the sheer brazenness of his marketing. It has long been commonplace for maps to depict on their cover stylised versions of their target audience, but with these maps Geographia took it to a new level. There on the juvenile monochrome cover drawing are a car driver, a cyclist and a walker all ascending a hill together, while only feet above them flies a very odd early aeroplane, seemingly drawn by someone who'd never actually seen one. It looks like a nightmare vision from *The*

Right: Road and town heights from Pratt's 1905 road atlas. Who would have thought that Birmingham was higher than Bradford, Sheffield or Manchester?

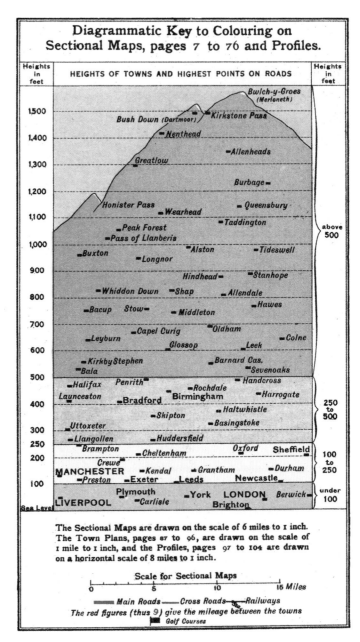

Diagrammatic Key to Colouring on Sectional Maps, pages 7 to 76 and Profiles.

Heights in feet	HEIGHTS OF TOWNS AND HIGHEST POINTS ON ROADS	Heights in feet
	Bwlch-y-Groes (Merioneth)	
1,500	Bush Down (Dartmoor) ▪ ▪Kirkstone Pass	
1,400	▪Nenthead	
	▪Allenheads	
1,300	Greatlow	
1,200	Burbage▪	
1,100	Honister Pass ▪Queensbury ▪Wearhead	above 500
	▪Peak Forest ▪Taddington	
1,000	▪Pass of Llanberis	
	▪Alston ▪Tideswell	
900	▪Buxton ▪Longnor	
	Hindhead▪ ▪Stanhope	
800	▪Whiddon Down ▪Shap ▪Allendale	
700	▪Bacup Stow▪ ▪Middleton ▪Hawes	
	▪Capel Curig ▪Oldham	
600	▪Leyburn ▪Colne	
	Glossop Leek	
	▪KirkbyStephen ▪Barnard Cas.	
500	▪Bala ▪Sevenoaks	
	▪Halifax Penrith▪ ▪H18ncross	
400	Launceston ▪Rochdale ▪Harrogate ▪Bradford Birmingham	250 to 500
	▪Skipton ▪Haltwhistle	
300	Uttoxeter ▪Basingstoke	
250	▪Llangollen ▪Huddersfield	
200	▪Brampton Oxford Sheffield Crewe ▪Cheltenham	100 to 250
100	MANCHESTER ▪Kendal ▪Grantham ▪Durham ▪Preston ▪Exeter Leeds Newcastle▪	
	Plymouth ▪York LONDON Berwick▪	under 100
Sea Level	LIVERPOOL ▪Carlisle Brighton	

The Sectional Maps are drawn on the scale of 6 miles to 1 inch. The Town Plans, pages 87 to 96, are drawn on the scale of 1 mile to 1 inch, and the Profiles, pages 97 to 104 are drawn on a horizontal scale of 8 miles to 1 inch.

Scale for Sectional Maps

0   5   10   15 *Miles*

▬▬▬ *Main Roads* ——— *Cross Roads* —▪— *Railways*
The red figures (thus 9*) give the mileage between the towns*
▪▪ *Golf Courses*

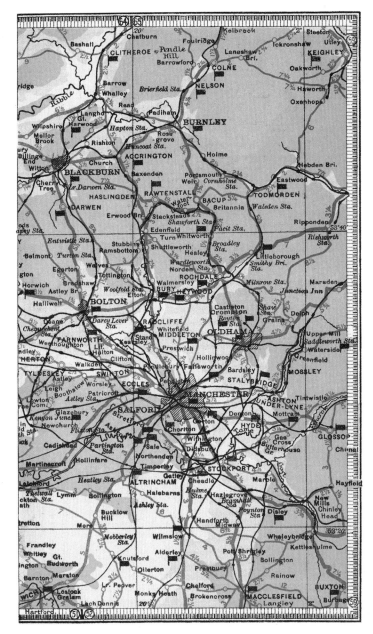

*Left: The roads become
the dominant feature in
the mapping from* Pratt's
Road Atlas of England
and Wales *(1905). The
black flags here represent
golf courses.*

*Above: An advert from
Pratt's Road Atlas
of England and
Wales (1905)*

Wizard of Oz. Whether any pioneer aviators actually used the maps is doubtful in the extreme.

Although plastering maps with adverts for railway hotels, spares shops and miracle rejuvenating tonics was firmly on the slide, there was a new breed of motoring map sponsors in the shape of oil companies. From the very beginning, such support was far more covert, and even classy – there was more chance of finding a gold-embossed crest on the leather cover than a brash advert. Such was the case with the very first road atlases, produced by Pratt's, a subsidiary of the Standard Oil Company, later Anglo-American Oil.

The first *Pratt's Road Atlas* appeared in 1905. Initially they were published on a regional basis, but came in a red leather folder that could hold a number of different maps as well as your driving licence. They were soon condensed into two atlases: one of England and Wales, the other of Scotland and Ireland. The maps, at a scale of approximately 8 miles to 1 inch, were by George Philip & Son Ltd, who had been producing popular maps, atlases and other reference works since the 1830s. The style of cartography is simplistic, if reasonably effective. The number of roads shown is relatively small, and all are in red, drawn thick for the main routes and thin for the 'cross-roads', a strangely dated term for minor routes that harks back to Ogilby. Height is demonstrated by simple use of colour shading on the ground: green for all land below 100 feet, yellow for 100–250 feet, buff for 250–500 feet and brown for everything over 500 feet. Distances are inscribed alongside the road between every settlement marked, but there are only a select few of each. Railways and stations are included, but at a fraction of the emphasis of the roads. Giving another nod to its intended clientele, the only other feature throughout is a flag symbol to mark golf courses.

This first road atlas already has many of the hallmarks of the genre that came to dominate 20th century road mapping. The emphasis on roads at the expense of any other feature of the landscape is nigh on absolute. Everything else is relegated, and the sheer size of the designated main routes makes each appear as wide as an airstrip – and this at a time when most of them were little more than dusty tracks. The use of such a bright red for the roads is telling too, for it is the colour of urgency, and the colour of blood: these, it boldly implies, are the pulsing arteries of the landscape, far more so than the thin black lines of the railways. With Bartholomew also choosing red – albeit a more muted shade – to denote main roads, and Ordnance Survey switching to the same hue after a brief flirtation with mustard yellow, this set in stone the colour we most readily associate with their depiction. The *Pratt's Road Atlas* is a statement of intention, of motoring supremacy, and it set the tone for the future. Soon, the confident red lines on the map would become reality.

EDINBURGH'S FINEST: JOHN BARTHOLOMEW AND SON LTD

Above: Bartholomew's majestic half-inch series in its signature blue cover

Until the end of World War I, Ordnance Survey maps had been almost incidental to the lives of most cycling and motoring enthusiasts. The commercial market for top-quality maps was almost entirely left to others, and none took up the challenge as brilliantly as Bartholomew.

The Edinburgh company had begun life in 1826, and soon became renowned for the precision and aesthetic quality of their engraved maps. It was a family firm, passed down from one John Bartholomew to the next, and it was during the tenure (1888–1920) of the third John, known as John George, that Bartholomew reached their peak. The late Victorian age was captivated by maps and exploration; the appetite for atlases, globes and beautiful maps was almost inexhaustible. Barts, as they were affectionately known, produced some of the finest.

Having pioneered the use of colour shading between contours to denote changing height, Bartholomew were in an ideal position to capture a significant slice of the cyclist and motoring markets. They licensed out some of their maps to many other commercial cartographers, but saved the finest for publication under their own name. Their flagship half-inch to the mile series, in its famous blue covers, was published from 1890 under the cover strapline 'For Tourists and Cyclists'; the word 'Motorists' replaced 'Tourists' after the war.

The Barts half-inch series has long been the favoured map of many travellers, whether on four wheels or two. It's not hard to see why. They

Above: Cartography is an occupation for those with phenomenal attention to detail, and Bartholomew had some of the finest

managed to pack in almost as much as the contemporary Ordnance Survey one-inch series, while covering more than five times the area. Ordnance Survey had their own half-inch series too, but compare the two and it's easy to see why Bartholomew sold over 10 of their maps to every one sold by Ordnance Survey. The Ordnance Survey half-inch series tried to emulate Barts by using colour shading to denote height, but it is done using a palette of deepening muddy browns, making the whole map – even in lowland areas – look faintly dirty. The yellow roads vanish into the brown murk, only the blue waterways really stand out, and the typography is cluttered and irregular. John George Bartholomew was exacting about his typography and colours (he refused to allow the brown one-and-a-half penny stamp on his premises, as he objected to its hue), and it shows, to dazzling effect.

As early as 1903, Bartholomew published a 'Motor Map' of the environs of London, and followed it up in 1907 with a *Contour Motoring Map* of the entire British Isles. This was hugely successful, and ran to seven reprints up to 1913, and a further three after the war. Aside from the lack of railways (and golf courses), it contains more information than Pratt's entire series of road atlases, but on one large, cloth-backed sheet. Distance charts from London, Edinburgh, Dublin, Glasgow and Belfast are given – the Irish ones, not surprisingly, only to other Irish destinations, but it is the same with Edinburgh and Glasgow, where only mileages to Scottish towns (plus Berwick and Carlisle on the border) are given. Bartholomew were proudly Scottish, and reserved some of their finest cartography for their home patch.

Around the perimeter of the map, exquisite city through-route maps of London, Edinburgh, Glasgow, Manchester and Dublin are placed in boxes. Roads are delineated quite clearly as main, secondary or other; even a handful of prohibited roads are marked. Road heights are given, mileages between towns and villages are clearly marked, and towns are categorised by the kind of dot used as to whether they have garages, and hotels or inns. The mapping is, of course, exemplary – and, ironically, all 'reproduced by permission from the Ordnance Survey', which seemed unable or unwilling to produce such a good map themselves. Well, not quite anyway.

Overleaf: Section of the Pembroke area from Bartholomew's Reduced Survey Tourists & Cyclists: the Bartholomew half-inch map combined aesthetic quality with practical utility in a way that has never been bettered

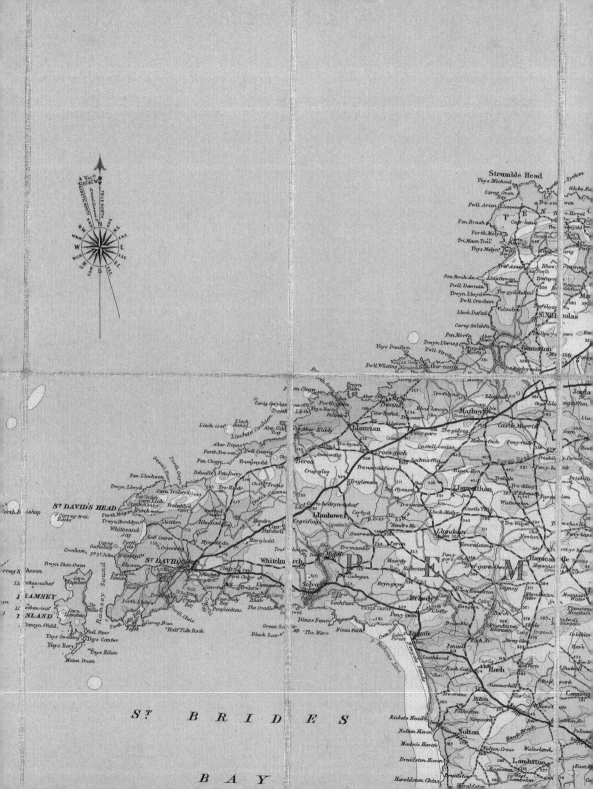

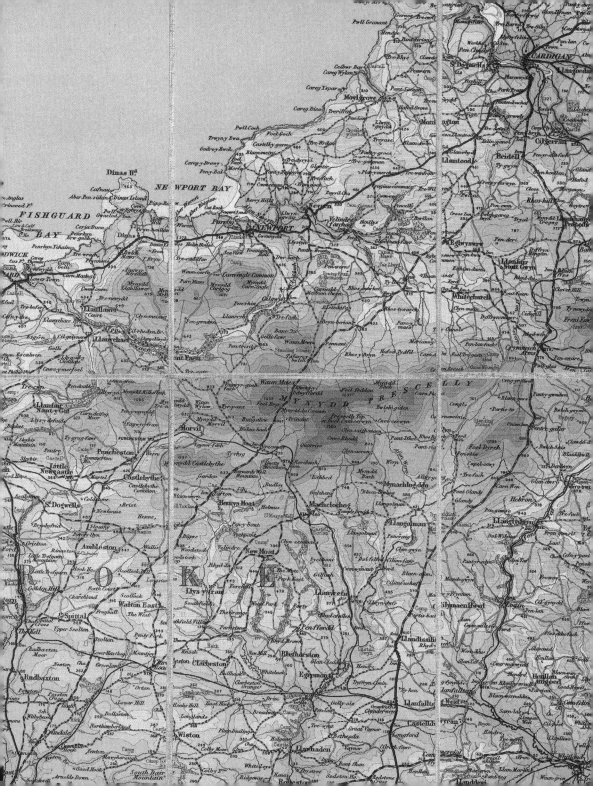

Chapter 4

THE OPEN ROAD

(1918–39)

At the end of World War I, Britain was devastated, even in victory. So many of a generation of young men had met a grisly end in the trenches, and the country's finances were in a parlous state. Road vehicles had been much used throughout the war, at home and abroad, and after the Armistice, planning began in earnest to shape the new landscape, with the car firmly at its heart.

It was a mode of transport that the fiercely individualistic British fell in love with almost immediately, and with the arrival in 1922 of the £165 Austin Seven, more people than ever could afford one. Even that was still a costly option, though – more than a miner's annual wage and nearly half that of an MP – and many people cut spending in other areas of their life to be able to afford one. *The Autocar* columnist Owen John quoted *Hamlet* to advise aspiring motorists: 'Costly thy habit as thy purse can buy, But not expressed in fancy, rich not gaudy, For the apparel oft proclaims the man.' A car was not just a means of simple transportation. It was liberation and status too.

The AA opened Britain's first roadside petrol pump in November 1919 at Aldermaston, on the Berkshire stretch of the Bath Road. Many others soon followed. Already there were mutterings about the price of fuel: a 1920 petition of protest collected 1,239,229 signatures. They had a point. Adjusted for today's measurements and prices, fuel was costing more than £2 per litre, the highest it has ever been.

World War I had ushered in many temporary measures that proved to be anything but. Most famously, pub opening hours were radically cut in order to dissuade munitions workers from drinking; the rules stayed on the statute books for the rest of the 20th century. An emergency import duty on vehicles and components of foreign origin was also brought in during the war. Briefly repealed in 1924, it was reintroduced a year later and remained in place until the UK joined the European Economic Community in 1973.

With the country's coffers so empty, the first post-war measures taken to accelerate the motoring age were largely administrative. The Ministry of Transport was launched in 1919; one of its first tasks was to attempt to streamline the country's aged, varicose vein network of tracks

Previous page: Pratt's High Test Plans (c.1930), popular between the wars, mapped the romance of the journey as much as the road

Left: Britain's first roadside petrol pump opened in 1919 at Aldermaston, near Newbury

and roads into something more befitting a modern power. Just before the outbreak of war, the Road Board had been contemplating a road numbering system based on counties, but following the example of the French, it was decided to adopt a national system of alphanumeric road classification. This would make signage, planning and navigation a great deal easier for all.

The better roads were to be classified as first class or second class, just as mapmakers such as Ordnance Survey and Bartholomew had been doing with the use of different colours for a decade or more. County councils were instructed to conduct a thorough audit of the roads on their patch; those that were busiest, or which connected places of some importance, were to be accorded T (trunk) status, those in the second tier L (link). These were soon changed to simple A and B.

Right: With their jazzy image, Michelin maps were quite different from the other road maps of the time

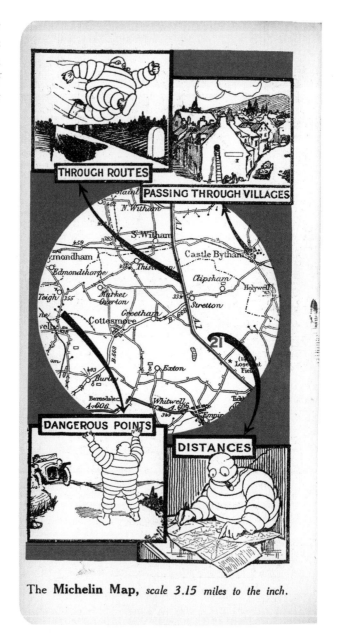

The **Michelin Map**, *scale 3.15 miles to the inch.*

BONJOUR M. MICHELIN

As is seen by the profusion of their words imported to describe aspects of motoring (automobile itself, garage, chauffeur, charabanc, corniche, cul-de-sac, a Grand Prix), the French were into the motoring age well before the British. André Michelin (1853–1931), founder and boss of the eponymous tyre company, wrote to the British government on numerous occasions to give advice on matters to do with the roads, including their classification. That we ultimately adopted a system based on the French one is no coincidence. Michelin even beat the Ministry of Transport in releasing the first map of the new scheme, with a nationwide plan published in 1922. On the front cover is Bibendum, the Michelin tyre man, happily smoking his cigar as he holds on to a sign saying 'What Road Numbering means!'

Note, from the Michelin Map, the numbers of the roads to be followed and, at the cross-roads, take those which, according to the sign-post, have the same numbers.

Above: Bibendum, the Michelin tyre man, helps explain the new MoT road numbering system to a befuddled Brit

As early as 1900, Michelin had started to publish guides and maps aimed specifically at motorists; in 1905 he came across the Channel and opened an office in London. In 1911, the company built a showpiece headquarters on the Fulham Road, and published their first guide to Britain. A series of 22 1:200,000 maps of the country soon followed (Michelin's road numbering map was overlain with their divisions in a nifty piece of cross-marketing). They were quite different from anything else being published at the time, and the last to use hachures to denote relief, which works surprisingly well, except in very mountainous areas. Main roads, as ever, are in red, although very many minor roads are omitted altogether.

Michelin's unique point was in detailing the state of the roads far more precisely than could possibly be achieved by the often rather vague categorisation of their rivals. As well as categories of general road quality, the Michelin maps also included annotation pointing out things like 'bad bump', 'deep gully', 'liable to floods' and the rather gnomic 'dangerous point'. Despite these apparent advantages, the series never did too well, and it was pensioned off in the mid-1930s.

With considerable encouragement from André Michelin, founder of the eponymous tyre company (see 'Bonjour M. Michelin', p125), the system developed by the Ministry of Transport was modelled on the French equivalent, where different numbered spokes radiated out from Paris and roads within each segment began with that number. In Britain there were two systems, one for England and Wales and one for Scotland. The former was based on London, with the spokes ascending in order in a clockwise direction.

The A1 went straight up to Edinburgh, the A2 to Dover, so that all main roads between the two were numbered A1x or A1xx. The A2s were between Dover and Portsmouth, the A3s a long tranche right to the far end of the West Country, the A4s a giant wedge that took in most of the Midlands and Wales, the A5s everything between the lines from London to Holyhead and Carlisle, and the A6s the remaining backbone of England, back round to the A1. The last three numbers – A7, A8 and A9 – were Scottish-only roads that were similarly centred on Edinburgh. The most important roads were accorded the shortest numbers.

There are places where the simplicity of the design didn't quite translate to the convolutions of real roads on the ground, especially around the border zones between the differently numbered segments. This inevitably became even more muddied as new roads were built, necessitating re-numbering and re-grading of older routes. That said, it's a system that has worked pretty well for nearly a century now, and no one has yet come up with anything better.

More than anyone, cartographers were thrilled with the new road numbering system, and raced to include the information on their maps, sometimes without fully checking their facts. In their eagerness, Bartholomew made an uncharacteristic slip-up by producing in 1922 a half-inch map of Northumberland that clearly marked the A7 running southwest from Berwick-on-Tweed. In fact, the A7 ran from Edinburgh to Carlisle, over 30 miles to the west; the route shown as such on the map has only ever been the A698. It would seem that the mistake came from a misreading of a 1921 internal memorandum within the Ministry of Transport, which, if true, suggests that Bartholomew had some well-placed friends.

The best set of maps to show the new system was the official Ministry of Transport Road Map series, issued via the Ordnance Survey in 1923. These have the stamp of officialdom all over them, and look as if they were never intended to be seen anywhere except on the wall above a transport planner's desk. The new A roads are overprinted in red, as is their number (likewise with B roads in green), but the number does not follow the road's course as most maps have chosen to show them ever since. Instead, it is plonked somewhere alongside – easy enough to match to its road when there are very few of them, but all getting a little congested in built-up areas.

The new system was an official diktat that did not always accord with the routes on the ground. This is best illustrated by the A1, the backbone of both the country and the new numbering system, which was decreed to head off its ruler-straight course north at Boroughbridge in Yorkshire, snaking its way instead up through Northallerton to Darlington and beyond. Drivers ignored this, and continued to use the old Roman Dere Street to Scotch Corner; it was a good road, and quicker. The A1 label was reapportioned to the more logical route within the decade.

THE CHANGING FACES OF THE ORDNANCE SURVEY

Throughout the Victorian and Edwardian upsurge in popular cartography, the one company failing to make much of it was the government's own Ordnance Survey. Ironically, other mapmakers plundered Ordnance Survey's work with impunity, often even marketing their wares as 'Reduced' or 'Improved' Ordnance maps. Before World War I, Ordnance Survey had attempted to address the situation and capture their due slice of the fast-growing market. Their first salvo was the 1911 Copyright Act, which established the concept of Crown Copyright on Ordnance Survey maps, a phrase that has appeared on them ever since. The first test case came in 1913, when Ordnance Survey took mapmakers H G Rowe & Co. to court and proved that their *Rowe's New Road Map for Cyclists & Motorists* was a direct photographic reduction of the Ordnance Survey map. Rowe were forced to destroy all copies of the map and the plates from which they were printed; Ordnance

Overleaf: Bartholomew's 1922 map of Northumberland – in their haste to be the first to map the new road numbering system, Bartholomew made an uncharacteristic mistake by mis-labelling the A698 as the rather more important A7

Forts
Cockburn Hill
Primrosehill
Whiteadder
Preston 311 298
Preston Ch.
326
Water
436
Preston
Cairnlaw
478
Ladywell 280
Ninewar
Plainfield
Duns Cott
Duns Law
Duns Law Mains
Rules Mains
Hen Poo
Wellfield Ho. 454
Chalkielaw 334
DUNS
Berrywell
Crumstane
Cairnbank
Peelrig
Cheeklaw
Nisbet Rhodes
300
Cairnhill
Mungo's Walls
Langton Burn
Nisbet Ho. 265
Kimmerghame Ho.
Pathead
Nisbet Hill
Mill Whitywalls
Caldra Ho. 326
Crunklaw
Bogend
Fogo Eastend
Fogo
Pilmuir
Fogorig
Charter Hall
Printonian
W. Printonian
Harcarse 253
Harcarse Hill
Ryslaw 239
Longbank
Swinton Ho.
Earnslaw
Swintonmill
Lochrig
Raecleugh
Mersington
Mersington Ho.
Highlands
Springwells Mains
Stainrig
Antonshill
Belchester
Grizelrig 175
W. Mains
Orange Lane
Bankhead
Moorsfield
Sunnyside
Todrig 166
Manse
237
Wester Whitrig
Eccles
Hatchednize

Lintlaw 361
Cruiksfield 251
E. Blanerne
Marden
Broom Ho.
Blanerne Westside
Edrom Ho.
Edrom Mains
Edrom Newton
288
Blanerne Ho.
Hammerhall
247
Chirnside Sta
Mill
289
Ninewells Mains
276
Inns
Chirnside
Newstead
Edrom
242
Edrom Sta.
Whitsome
Stuartslaw
249
Kellae Bastle
Allanbank
Whitsome
Kelloe Mains
Brieryhill
Kelloe Ho.
Bucklee 268
Manderston Ho.
Turtleton 260
Wedderburn Cas.
294
Mains
214
Whitelaw
Barns
Blackadder Mount
U. Fr. Ch.
Allanton
Whitehall
Broadhaugh
Blackadder Ho.
261
238
Blackadder
268
254
Mains 258
Blackadder bank
Heugh
Middlestots
235
228
Laws
Langrig
Whitsome
279
Frenchlaw
Leetside
Dykegatehead
262
Heriotbank
Hilton
Sinclairs Hill
The Laws 218
Mains
Greenknowe
Mount Pleasant 283
Bellshiel
Southlaws 190
250
204
Greenrig
Crowfoot bank
Morningbank 172
Swinton Quarter
U. Fr. Ch. 235
Swinton
Inn
Swintonhill
173
Walterstead
Upsettlington
142
Ladykirk Ho.
Swinton Bridgend
Lit. Swinton
168 200
235
178
Simprim Mains
Simprim
Ch.
178
Shiels
Sunnyside
Longrig
Bughtrig
Martfield
178
Ruthven
238 204 196
Butterlaw
West Mains
Milne Graden
Leitholm
Belville
Hawkslaw
246
Wyliecleugh
Skaithmuir
George Field
212
Sch.
168
Todhillrig
Lennelhill
Darnchester
Mains
172 225
Castlelaw
Hassel Law
170
Kincham Wood
Oxenrig 114
Coldstream Mains
Donaldson
Mellington
443
Harelaw
374
E. Harelaw
Wheatgores
363
Edington Hill
Maines Ho.
Chirnside
Cas.
Edington 233
Nether Mains
Edington Mains
Hutton Hall
Edington Mill
Hutton Castle
165
Hutton Cas.
Hutton
Carrybank
Broomdykes
206
Crossrig
Pistol Plantation
Jardinefield 182
Horndean
Inn
124
Fellowhills
Horndean
Ramrig
Ladykirk
Mains
Mountfair
Whitsome hill 224
224
240
Fort
W. E. Newton
Homefarm
120
Dropper Island
Raffingt
139
Twizel Castle
Ferry
Sta.
Twizel Mill
St. Cuthbert
177
140
Old Heaton
200
290

Mouldenhill • Greenfield
Maorpark • St Johns • Lamberton
421 • 649 • Witches • 313
Foulden Hag • Mordington • Knowe • Marshall • Marshall Meadows Bay
Mains • Meadows
Nunlands • Blinkbonny • New East Farm
258
Foulden • Mordington Ho. • Steps of Grace
Ho. • 274 • Mordington • 210 • Needles Eye
Newton • Edrington Ho. • Ch. • Halidon
Water • Edrington • Hill 537 • COUNTY OF THE BORO' & TOWN • Brotherstons Hole
Mains • P.U. Ch. • 1232 • Int.
High Cocklaw • OF BERWICK UPON TWEED • Sharper Head
dows • Chesterfield • St Leonards • Meadow Ho. • 156
Ladbad • N. Mains • Baldersburyhill • Nunnery • Golf • BERWICK • UPON TWEED
Meadowhouse • Ford • Low Cocklaw • High • Buckhall • Castlehills • 113 • Co.
Mains • Edrington • Letham • Sta.
Paxton • Cass. • Newmills • 47 • Castlehills • Meadow Haven
Spitalhaugh • Laudeughs • New • Yarrow • Lighthouse
Mains • 129 • Paxton • WaterHaugh • Slacks • Sandstell Point
field • Stir Mains • Old Toll Inn • 42 • Battery • Lifeboat Sta.
Factory • Gainslaw • Tweedmouth • Dock • Spital
bdean • 153 • Ho. • Pier
Paxton • West Ord • River Tweed • 120 • Signy • Seaview Works
114 • Ho. • Ho. • Hotel • side • L.C.
Tweedhill • East Ord • Cemetery
Fishwick • Union Br. • Inn • A.7.
k • Loan • Middle • Springhill
Mains • End • Ord • 289
Horncliffe Ho. • 223 • S. Ord • Colliery • Borewell
Horncliffe • Longridge • Scremerstono.C.
Inn • 178 • Towers • Billylaw • 600 • Richardsons • 235 • Sta.
Velvethall Sta. • 256 • Murton • Stead
Camp • Murton • Square • 235 • Unthank • Scremerston
Norham • Thornionpark • Roman • A.7. • Colliery
East Mains • Lime Works
West Mains • Royalty • 163 • Thornton • 125 • Adler Dean • Scremerston Cheswick
stle • 187 • Camp • Scremerstonhill • Black Rock
Salutation Inn • Shoreswood • 275 • Allerdean • 227 • Oxford • 145 • Cheswick • Ches S
135 • 260 • Shoreswood • Cheswick • Windmillhall • GOSW
Hall • 217 • Ancroft Greens • Ho.
Grieve Stead • Ancroft • Ladythorne Ho.
8 • 263 • Northmoor • Broomhouse
ndon • Ancroft Southmoor • Berrington • Olde
218 • Felkington • Berringtonlaw • Blackhill • 191 • New Haggerston • Th
245 • 356 • 369 • 195 • Berrington • The Lamb
Grindonridge • 236 • Berringtonlough • 233 • Turnstoops
200 • 232 • Bowsdenfoor • Camp • 139 • Lowly
213 • Duddo • Whistlebare • 252 • Bowsden • 209 • Lickar • Kentstone • 268
200 • Gatherick • 207 • Crookhouse • 175 • 214
Tindle Ho. • Hazely • New Dryburn • Hunting Hall • West
183 • Woodside • Castle • Lowick • Kylo
Bernhill • Woodend • Barmoor • Northfield • 269 • Lowick Law Stead

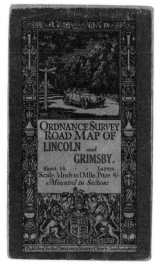

Above: Ordnance Survey Road Map of Lincoln and Grimsby *(1914): despite placing the motorist squarely on its cover, Ordnance Survey's own half-inch series never attained the popularity nor the sales of its Bartholomew rival*

Survey publicised the decision as widely as possible as a warning to other unscrupulous plagiarists.

The court case encouraged Ordnance Survey to establish a committee with the brief of working out why their toehold in the commercial market was so shaky. In truth, it was obvious. The most glaring reason was the drab, utilitarian packaging of their maps. Once the war was over, it was full steam ahead with a whole new image: gone was the ration-book look of the covers, to be replaced by illustrated scenes and seductive typography. Most were the work of Ordnance Survey's first dedicated artist–designer, Ellis Martin. He produced gorgeous images of areas from the Cairngorms to Cornwall, the Thames through London to the sharp peaks of Snowdonia. Cars made increasingly common appearances on the covers, but always in splendid isolation amid invigorating scenery, or with the car owners picnicking merrily by its side.

Martin's most important redesign was the generic one for Ordnance Survey's flagship one-inch series. On his cover of 1919 we see a young man, in tweed cap, Norfolk jacket and plus fours, sitting on a hillside, map outspread, overlooking a lush valley. Leaning against a nearby bush is his trusty bicycle. He is assured, casual, independent and an indissoluble part of the scenery he surveys. By the early 1930s the hill-sitter was looking way too old-fashioned for the free-thinking, pipe-smoking chaps who were now the mainstay of Ordnance Survey's market, so Martin redrew the exact same scene for the new age. Another young man, a hiker, replaced the Edwardian cyclist: gone too was the headgear and the scratchy outfit, to be replaced by a leisurely rake in rolled-up shirt sleeves and a tank top, casual trousers and with a bulging knapsack on his manly back. Subtly, but with a typical eye for detail, Martin had even made the trees in the valley below grow a few feet in the intervening years, and had given the surrounding vegetation an extra bounce.

These covers followed the standard cartographic code of picturing their target audience, much as the photographs on today's Explorer maps tend to portray punters cycling, sailing, kayaking or hiking (ironically, you'll never see a car on an Ordnance Survey map cover now). Martin's 1930s covers for the one-inch Tourist, Popular and District maps took this rule to its inevitable conclusion, shoehorning every possible target map-buyer into the frame. The picture is dominated by a young chap in the foreground, puffing away

Left: Ordnance Survey Contoured Road Map of Chatham & Maidstone (1921): *the cyclist still reigned supreme on the cover of Ordnance Survey's standard one-inch series in the classic design by Ellis Martin*

ORDNANCE SURVEY
"ONE-INCH" MAP

Dorking & Leith Hill
(Mounted on Cloth)
Price - - - Three Shillings

Above: Some Ordnance Survey one-inch maps (this example c.1925) covered all bases of potential markets: walkers, cyclists, motorists and daytrippers in their charabanc

on his pipe as he leans against a stone wall to consult his beloved Ordnance Survey map. On the road ahead of him a Morris car travels one way, a group of cyclists the other. In the distance, outside an inn at a country crossroads, a touring bus sits waiting. Here is the golden countryside, the map declares, and this is your passport to it, however you choose to arrive. Ironically, in the 1930s massive areas of the finest countryside remained out of bounds, for landowners were loath to see the Great Unwashed from the cities stomping across their grouse moors. Violence erupted periodically, most famously at the Mass Trespass on Kinder Scout in the Peak District, in April 1932. There is no hint of any of that kind of nastiness in Ellis Martin's dream-like portraits of a quintessential England.

Perhaps even more interesting on the early Ordnance Survey maps are the sets of red dotted lines, indicating roads planned but yet to be built. Beyond London, there weren't many: just a short bypass for Ormskirk in Lancashire and the 6.5-mile Portway, linking Bristol city centre with Avonmouth. This was an ambitious plan, carving a road through the Avon gorge and under the Clifton Suspension Bridge. Work had begun immediately after the war, but in 1924 a 200-yard section of the uncompleted road slid down into the river, and delayed the project further. When it finally opened in 1926, it was the most expensive road in Britain, having cost a princely £800,000.

Inevitably, it was around the capital that most of the new road building was concentrated, for congestion there had long been a hot topic. As far back as 1903, a Royal Commission on London Traffic had been established, which, in its report two years later, favoured the solution of an American-style grid of wide arterial roads to be imposed upon the chaos of the London streetscape, for cars and trams alike, and with tunnels beneath for new underground railways. This would demand massive demolition of overcrowded housing stock, which would be compensated for by the creation of new suburbs and garden cities along and between these new arterial routes.

These pre-war plans for new arterial roads were dusted down and re-examined, but the Haussmanesque vision of sweeping away large parts of the city for a massive grid of thoroughfares was undone by the lack of funds. Furthermore, the world was a very different place to the one of not quite 20 years earlier. The Commission had come from an age where horse-drawn carriages and trams were far more plentiful than cars, but by the close of the war, the car had won. Roads for cars, along with an expansion of the Underground system, were the driving forces of the new thinking.

Arterial roads were the buzzword, with a sprinkling of giddy references to a new Roman age of building great highways. Motoring evangelists have always invoked the image of Britain as a body, and the roads as its arteries, pumping lifeblood to every extremity. Such a metaphor also lends itself to portentous imagery of those arteries clogging up with too much traffic, the need for life-saving surgery, and so on.

The dotted lines on the Ministry of Transport map showed that the arteries of London were in for massive expansion. Bypasses around Sutton, Croydon, Kingston, Shooters Hill and Bexleyheath, Edmonton and Enfield, Hendon and Watford were all soon built – roads that were 'bare, open, shadeless and shameless, as shiny as steel and as hard as the rigours of commerce', said *The Times*. In terms of raw mileage, the most ambitious projects were for a new arterial route from the East End to Southend-on-Sea (the A127), and a continuation of the A2 from Dartford to just outside Rochester, bypassing Gravesend. That this was largely on the route of tiny lanes and paths that had once been the great legionary highway of Watling Street only gave further credence to the idea that we were entering a golden age of road building worthy of the Romans. Compared with the dogleg turns and crooked perambulation of the roads that had evolved throughout history, these new roads did indeed look quasi-Roman on the map – smooth and straight, ignoring settlements as they allowed the motorcar to whoosh imperiously by.

On the Ministry of Transport's 1923 map too are various dotted sections to knit the proposed North and South Circular roads into a vaguely coherent whole. From the 1903 Royal Commission right through the rest of the century, planners toyed with the dream of building a great series of concentric circles around the capital, linked by in-and-out arterials. This giant spider's web of tarmac reached some sort of fruition

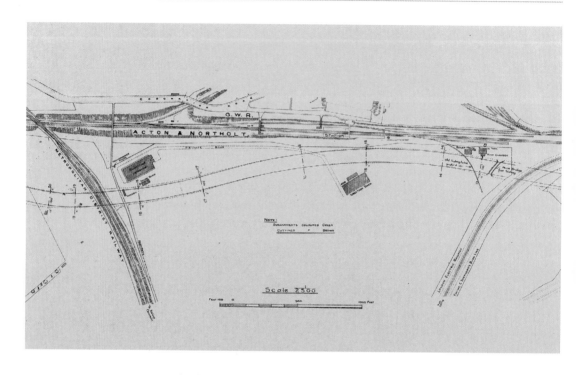

Above: Detail of a Middlesex County Council plan (c.1924) for the new Western Avenue arterial road between Hanger Lane and Willesden Lane

with the opening of the M25 in 1986, but that, and the North and South Circular roads, hardly constituted the series of massive planned ringways. Compared with other countries and the multi-lane highways through and around their big cities, the British way was always more piecemeal and compromised. With hindsight, looking at what we could have lost and how we might have condemned millions to motorway-side living, we should perhaps be glad of that.

There was lofty ambition, of course, and nowhere was it seen to better effect than in a couple of new 1920s arterial routes in the west of London.

Before the war, the western and southern approaches to the capital were identified as the ones in most urgent need of improvement; by the early 1920s the need was acute. In the west there were two particular pinch points along the exceedingly narrow confines of Brentford High Street on the A4 Bath road, and just a couple of miles north at Ealing Broadway on the A40 to Oxford.

The nomenclature was as airily ambitious as the roads themselves, and made these little corners of ramshackle Victorian London sound as if they had dropped out of a Hollywood 'talkie'. First, Brentford was bypassed by what was christened the Great West Road, while north of Ealing the grand sweep of Western Avenue was constructed through the semi-rural patchwork of Perivale and Northolt.

Above: The Hoover factory on the brand new Western Avenue, 1932

These were not just new roads; they were gleaming highways into the future, flanked by seductive art deco factories the like of which no Britons had ever seen before. Many of these were new European headquarters for American companies, and all so achingly modern: Firestone tyres, Pyrene chrome, Macleans toothpaste, Gillette razors, Burgoyne wireless sets, Currys electricals, Hudson-Essex cars and Henley's garage ('the world's biggest petrol station') along the 'Golden Mile' of Brentford's Great West Road. The crowning glory of Western Avenue, as it is still, was the magnificent pseudo-Egyptian palace of the Hoover headquarters.

Above: New tube lines and new roads combined to lure Londoners out into the suburban wonders of Metroland

The factories were something of a Hollywood stage set too: all showy facades and elaborate trimmings, though the real work was being done in nothing more fancy than great sheds at the back. And around these new roads, away from the glare of pearly white Americana, grew thousands of semi-detached houses, peeling off into an endless suburban yonder. It is often assumed that it was the expansion of the Underground in the interwar years that gave rise to the growth of Metroland, and so it did to a large extent. Here in the west of London, the Central line was being plotted out to Hanger Lane, Perivale and beyond, while Piccadilly line extensions – a northern branch to Park Royal on Western Avenue in 1931, a southern branch to Osterley and Hounslow by the Great West Road in 1933 – put some black lines on the map alongside the new red ones. But they were not the only impetus for growth; the roads were just as crucial, and many a new Metroland semi had its little garage to prove it.

It was the same all over London, and beyond. This rush of roads produced new suburbs almost overnight. Billboards along the arterial routes and bypasses advertised vacant building plots, and there was no shortage of takers. To many, it was a dream come true to leave cramped inner-city dwellings and head into a new three-bedroomed semi in the suburbs, with its fitted kitchen and indoor bathroom. Roads and property development went together with an unstoppable momentum that obliterated farmland and swallowed villages with barely a pause for thought.

The maps tell the story better than a thousand words. Look at the one-inch Ordnance Survey maps from the beginning of the 20th century, next to their counterparts of 30 or 40 years later. Marvel at Perivale, Wembley or Hendon; Mitcham, Morden and Malden; Penge and Cheam; Ruislip, Eltham and Chigwell. Or Surbiton, suburbiton, the queen of the pack. As the new roads arrived, these small, self-contained towns and villages ballooned into monsters, stretching out on all sides until they nestled up against their similarly expansive neighbours. You can spot the between-the-wars estates just from their look on the one-inch map. No longer the right-angled grids of Victorian terraced streets, sharp and hemmed in between railways and factories. Instead, the gentle curves and concentric rings of avenues, drives, gardens, groves and closes. Somewhere in the middle will be a boulevard or a parade, with its trim selection of shops, a 'Tudorbethan' pub, and either a railway station straight out of a Hornby model train set or a Tube station built as an improbable modernist dare. A golf club – quite probably a choice of golf clubs – will never be far away.

A full third of our national housing stock was built in this 20-year period between the wars. With a wary eye on what had recently happened in Russia, this massive expansion of the suburban middle classes, said Lloyd George after the war, was 'visible proof of the irrelevance of revolution'. Although the 1920s and 30s were a period of greatly raised expectations and comfort for many, it was also a time of chronic economic uncertainty and massive unemployment. Alleviating this by investing in huge infrastructure projects was a central plank of government economic policy; much of this was seen in the road-building programme.

One of the loveliest of the first tranche of arterial routes was the London to Southend road, which began in the capital as the Eastern Avenue (now the A12), before becoming the A127. Opened in March 1925, it was a serpentine 38-mile canter across virgin countryside that

Below: Detail of the new Southend arterial road brushing past an infant Basildon, shown on the 1926 Daily Mail Motor Road Map of South-East England by Edward Stanford

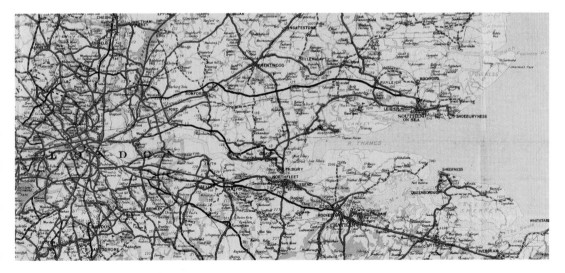

deliberately avoided existing settlements. Original plans had been for it to go no further than Romford, but the authorities in both Southend and Billericay were desperate to give work to many recently demobbed war veterans, who were taken on as navvies as the road was pushed further east. It was a similar tale on the new East Lancashire Road, an arterial route connecting Manchester and Liverpool that had first been mooted in 1912, but wasn't completed until 1934. Most of the work was undertaken by Lancashire County Council, one of the most pioneering of early road-building authorities, but the first 12 miles from Liverpool were built by unemployed men from the city's labour exchanges.

The most breathtaking of new roads – as both ends in themselves and remedies for unemployment – were the cluster built to link up the coal-mining valleys of south Wales. The economic downturn had hit the region with devastating force, and the misery was only compounded by the area's singular geography. During the rush for coal in the middle of the 19th century, hitherto isolated rural valleys had been squeezed full of pits, railways, roads and miles of vertiginous terraced housing, all fighting for space. Few of the valleys connected up; there was only one way in and out. In the 1920s and 30s, ambitious schemes to build roads out of the top of the valleys and up over the mountains beyond them were hatched, and, with a workforce of unemployed local miners, they were soon constructed. These high passes, grinding up the steep slopes in low-gear gradients and numerous hairpin loops, are some of the most distinctive on the map of Britain, looking like twisted red worms splayed out over the green Welsh hills.

The effect was enormous: the Valleys were no longer a dead end. When the June 2001 issue of *National Geographic* magazine featured Wales, the photo they used as the centrepiece of the article was not of St David's Cathedral, Snowdon or the Millennium Stadium, but the ice-cream van at Bwlch-y-Clawdd on the A4061, the most famous of the miners' mountain passes. And there is something of Wales-in-a-nutshell about the view: the tight terraces of the Rhondda far down below, the switchback sweep of the road against the uncompromising hills, the roaming sheep scavenging for titbits. There is a sense of continuity too, for the lady now dispensing the cornets and lollies is the granddaughter

Left: One of the enterprising Welsh-Italian families of the Valleys

Overleaf: Some of the most distinctive roads on the map of Britain: the intestinal tracts of tarmac built in the 1920s and 30s by unemployed South Wales miners brought not just work, but an end to the isolation of dead-end valleys (detail of Ordnance Survey Great Britain New Popular one-inch Map Cardiff, *1947. The best examples can be seen on the left of the map)*

of the Welsh-Italian ice-cream maker who, when the road first opened in 1928, used to wheel his wares up the mountain on an ice-laden cart from his cafe down in Treorchy. Since the day it opened, this has always been one of the great Valleys days out, especially for courting couples – though at 1,500 feet, it's just as well that you can get a cup of hot tea as well as a '99'.

THE BRIGHT YOUNG THINGS

Unemployed miners building roads over windswept mountains was a far cry from the image of motoring in wealthier parts of the country. The pre-war auto enthusiasts were almost entirely drawn from the moneyed classes, and their love of cars continued apace in the years that followed. Far from being just a route through to somewhere else, the new arterial roads became destinations in their own right, as roadhouses, golf courses and country clubs sprang up alongside them, especially around the big cities.

Like the factories of the Great West Road, the roadhouses – a name and concept straight out of America – were often sleekly modernist and aspirational, although, this being Britain, many others harked back to a mythical golden age with a riot of mock Tudor gabling, gothic twirls and even thatched roofs. Usually sited at major intersections, they were designed to be both admired and desired, fun palaces to lure in the Bright Young Things of the Roaring Twenties.

London was ringed with them. There was the Berkeley Arms on the Bath Road in Hounslow, built in 1932 as a bastardised version of a French château and promising 'the delicate sophistication of a Mayfair restaurant complete with jazz band'. Or the Thatched Barn on the Barnet bypass at Borehamwood, home of tennis courts, a swimming pool, gymnasium and shooting gallery, and second home to the minor starlets of the nearby Elstree film studios. The Clock, between the Great North Road and the Welwyn bypass, advertised Saturday night dances at six shillings for couples, three shillings and sixpence for singles, refreshments included and 'Dress Optional'. The Spider's Web, on the Watford bypass, became a celebrated centre of British jazz, though there were always whispers that more extracurricular activity was the main focus of the place.

The cool crowd loved a risqué reputation, and nowhere cultivated it more assiduously than the most famous roadhouse of them all, the Ace of Spades on the Kingston bypass. Serving food 24 hours a day, it included a ballroom, polo ground, riding school, golf course and open-air swimming pool. Arriving by car was not the only option either, for it even had its own airstrip. When the dance halls of the West End closed at midnight, customers would hotfoot it down to the Ace of Spades and continue dancing through the night. Noël Coward even sang its praises in his ditty 'Give Me the Kingston Bypass'.

In 1932 and 1933, British Pathé shot a number of films that only augmented the dark allure of the Ace of Spades. In one entitled *Roadhouse Nights (Filmed on the Kingston Bypass)*, and subtitled 'Hot nights – and cool waters', footage was of acrobatic divers and beauties parading in their scanties at the pool. The semi-dressed theme continued, as we went indoors to watch lithe young things in thin strips of chiffon performing daring dance routines. Brylcreemed chaps in tuxedos and skinny girls with kiss curls applaud through the fug of cigarettes and hormones. A feeble comedy double act tell us perhaps all we need to know about the audience, when one asks the other, 'So then, who was Atlas?'

'A giant supporting the world on his shoulders', replies the stooge.

'And who supported Atlas?'

'I expect he was on the dole', comes the instant retort. There is a huge, hearty laugh from the crowd.

As road building accelerated around and between all the big cities, mutterings about the despoiling of the countryside began, and soon swelled into a roar. For many of the establishment intelligentsia, it was largely an aesthetic argument that teetered on the edge of outright snobbery. Poet and essayist Stephen Spender described the new road-borne settlements as '*laissez-faire* run mad, a huge inflation of Tudor villas on arterial roads, wireless sets, tin cars, golf clubs – the paradise of the bourgeoisie'; planner and polemicist Thomas Sharp sniffed that 'every little owner of every little bungalow in every roadside ribbon thinks he is living in Merrie England because he has those roses round the door and…sweet williams and Michaelmas daisies in his front garden'.

It was a common theme. The hoi polloi could not be trusted to do it right, and therefore should not be trusted to do it at all. For some commentators, there was the distinct whiff of regret that such people had even got their hands on a steering wheel, let alone a place in the ever-expanding suburbs. In his 1935 book, *The Heart of England, Guardian* journalist (and later editor of *The Observer*) Ivor Brown wrote of the hell of driving back to London from Suffolk on a summer Sunday evening. Hell, as ever, was other people, particularly the 'myriads of East Enders

packed seven or eight in an antiquated car which has been bought for a few pounds and seems almost to be held together by string and straps… jogging home from a day at Clacton or Southend…Thirty years ago these people never left the town, except perhaps for one week in the year. Saturday night was spent in the gin-palace and Sunday morning was spent in sleeping it off.' Now, though, he fulminated, thanks to 'the new democratic week-end', they spent their spare time 'covering decent sand with orange peel and cigarette cartons'.

The 'roadside ribbon' was the phrase of the moment; the developments that strung themselves out along the new arterial routes like gaudy necklaces. In the interwar years, 862,500 new houses were built in hitherto rural districts, the vast majority of them owner-occupied. As we've seen, many of these were in Greater London and the Home Counties, where the number of cars was also far higher than elsewhere. Towards the end of the 1920s there was one car for every 22.6 people in Surrey, compared with one per 87.2 in Glamorgan, and one per 128.5 in County Durham. And that wasn't the full picture, for city dwellers were buying up picturesque country properties in their droves, and using their cars and the trains to commute back into town.

It was happening way beyond the overheated southeast too, in and around every major provincial city. In Glasgow, the city with the highest population density in Britain, and packed into some of the worst conditions, there was no sense of regret at the new arterial roads to the west (towards Dumbarton) and east (the new A8), for these gave the city a much-needed chance to breathe out. Massive new municipal estates were built along each: Knightswood to the west and Carntyne in the east, joining an earlier post-war development at Mosspark on the city's south side. In stark contrast to many interwar developments in other cities, these are all still some of the lovelier, and leafier, parts of Glasgow.

Outside London, the greatest example of interwar arterial roads reshaping our urban landscape came in the West Midlands, particularly the building of the New Road – as it has been known ever since – linking Wolverhampton and Birmingham. To outsiders, the West Midlands conurbation can seem like one endless sprawl, but that is to misunderstand the very different identities of Birmingham and the cluster of towns that make up the Black Country to its north and west. While Brum has always been a cosmopolitan melting pot, known as 'the city of a thousand trades', many of the Black Country towns grew up around one dominant small industry: locks in Willenhall, leather in Walsall, glass in Stourbridge, chains in Cradley Heath, bolts and nuts in Wednesbury and Darlaston, springs in West Bromwich. Even today, the Black Country is an area that looks like a city, but often feels like a village.

Back in the 1920s, this sense of the singular isolation of Black Country towns can be clearly sensed from the Ordnance Survey and Bartholomew maps of the area. Roads, railways and tramways duck and dive with no apparent coherence, while the towns and villages appear straggled across the pocked landscape like debris. And then, on the 1927 Ordnance Survey one-inch map, there is a smooth new red line carving its way through the mess: 'In course of construction' it says. The new A4123 tiptoed around the dark clumps of Coseley, Tipton, Dudley and Oldbury, before coming to rest on the Hagley Road, Birmingham's main thoroughfare to the west. Drive it today and it is an almost unbroken boulevard of interwar suburbia, plugging the gaps on the map, but unrooted and almost unreal.

The only major interwar arterial road that didn't attract ribbon development was what became known as the East Lancashire Road (after its intended, but never attained, destination), the A580 between Liverpool and Manchester. Aside from a few large housing estates at the Liverpool end, there was very little development of any kind by its side until long after it had finally been turned into a dual carriageway in the 1960s. In many ways, this only enhances the feeling that the East Lancs, opened in 1934, was the nearest we have to a prototype motorway, in as much as it seems to glide across both the map and the landscape without touching either very much. Furthermore, it was engineering of motorway-scale ambition: it was intended to be three carriageways – two outer ones for slow local traffic, the centre one for faster through traffic – which made it a generous 120 feet wide throughout its 30-mile length.

RUS IN URBIS

Not all of the new housing was in suburban semis strung out along busy arterial routes. The Garden City movement, which had taken root in Letchworth before World War I, was held up as a model for good planning, and the 1920s and 30s saw many such developments come to fruition. The idea harked back to an idealised version of medieval settlements gathered around the church and the market place, and took hold in some of the planned workers' estates built in industrialised areas towards the end of the Victorian age; the best examples are Bournville in Birmingham, Saltaire in Bradford and Port Sunlight on the Wirral.

Those were workers' estates appended to particular factories; with Letchworth, Ebenezer Howard wanted to build an entire, mixed town along similar principles. Much influenced by the rustic yearnings of William Morris, John Ruskin and the Arts and Crafts movement, Howard founded Letchworth in 1903 as the embodiment of *rus in urbis*, the countryside in the city, or 'a new town that pretended to be an old village', as Jonathan Meades had it. George Orwell was even more blunt, writing that Letchworth was the natural home of 'every fruit juice drinker, nudist, sandal wearer, sex-maniac, Quaker, nature cure quack, pacifist and feminist in England'.

After World War I, Ebenezer Howard inaugurated another new town 15 miles south of Letchworth towards London. Welwyn Garden City was born of beautiful maps and planners' models, carefully crafted and annotated in rustic typefaces. Residential avenues all curved gracefully; the only straight roads were the grand boulevards at the town's heart, most notably the mile-long Parkway scything through the town in a way that wouldn't have looked out of place in Mussolini's Albania, albeit with added poplar trees. Unlike teetotal Letchworth, where evening options comprised non-alcoholic tipples in the Skittles Inn or something wholesome from the Food Reform Restaurant in the Simple Life Hotel, Welwyn was allowed pubs, though mainly scattered around its leafy edges. Inevitably, these were named with the same rustic determination that infused the whole project: the Waggoners, the Bull, the Beehive, the Pear Tree, the Cherry Tree, the Woodman.

The garden city concept was also implanted deep into the urban jungle, somewhat counter to Ebenezer Howard's vision. Perhaps the most famous

Overleaf: The prototype of the motorway: Lancashire County Council's 1934 plan of the East Lancashire arterial road

LIVERPOOL-EAST LANCASHIRE ROAD.

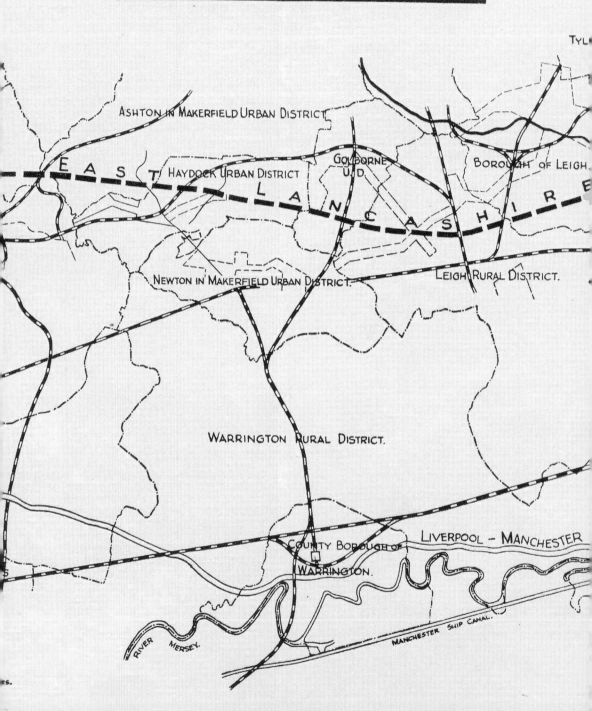

ASHTON IN MAKERFIELD URBAN DISTRICT

GOLBORNE U.D.

BOROUGH OF LEIGH.

HAYDOCK URBAN DISTRICT

E A S T   L A N C A S H I R E

NEWTON IN MAKERFIELD URBAN DISTRICT.

LEIGH RURAL DISTRICT.

WARRINGTON RURAL DISTRICT.

LIVERPOOL — MANCHESTER

COUNTY BOROUGH OF WARRINGTON.

RIVER MERSEY.

MANCHESTER SHIP CANAL.

TYL

UNEMPLOYMENT RELIEF WORKS.

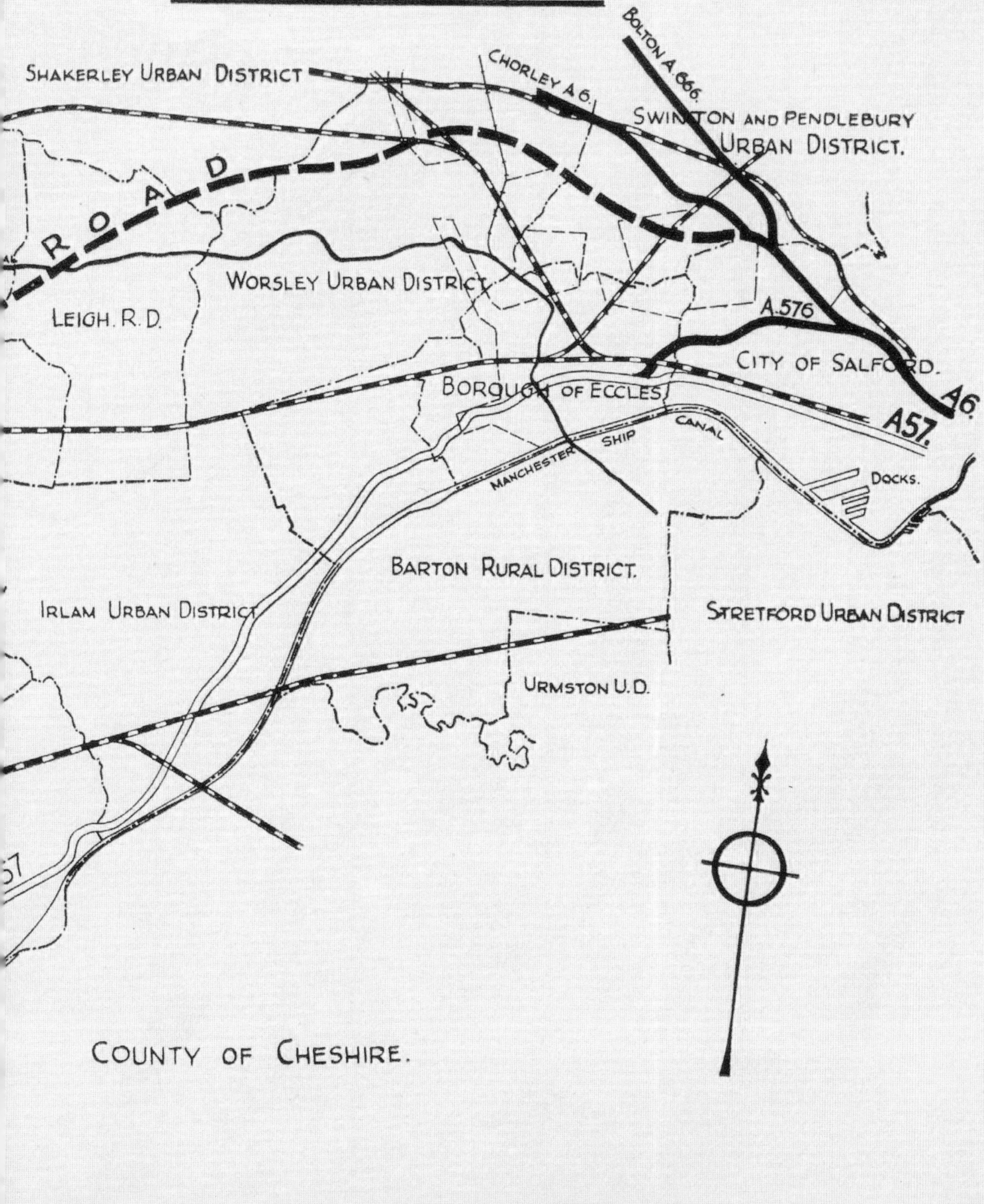

SHAKERLEY URBAN DISTRICT

BOLTON A 666.

CHORLEY A.6.

SWINTON and PENDLEBURY URBAN DISTRICT.

R O A D

A.576

LEIGH. R.D.

WORSLEY URBAN DISTRICT

CITY OF SALFORD.

A.6.

A.57.

BOROUGH OF ECCLES

MANCHESTER SHIP CANAL

DOCKS.

BARTON RURAL DISTRICT.

IRLAM URBAN DISTRICT

STRETFORD URBAN DISTRICT

URMSTON U.D.

57

COUNTY OF CHESHIRE.

LOCKLEYS PARK

WELWYN STATION
BUILDING SITE

Beehive Works

BUILDING SITE

DIGSWELL WATER

WOOD

WOODED PARK

DIGSWELL PARK

TEWINWATER PARK (Wooded)

WOODED PARK

TO TEWIN

ROLLING LAND

OPEN FLAT LAND

For 40,00
Factory Area
Shopping Area
Town Area: 16
Ultimate Populat

FARM HOUSE

ROLLING LAND

Attimore HALT

WOOD

OPEN FLAT LAND

WOOD

To Hertford via Cole Green

TOWN AREA (Houses)
Part to be first developed

AGRICULTURAL AREA

SHOPPING AREA
————— Existin
—•—•—•— Proposed

FACTORY AREA
Alternatively Residential

WOODLANDS

TIMBER RECENTLY CUT

TO S.ALBANS

ROLLING LAND

HATFIELD

OPEN FLAT LAND

FARM

ONE MILE FROM HATFIELD STATION

AREA OF POSSIBLE EXTENSION OF

BRICK WORKS

BUSH HALL

OPEN FLAT LAND

TO HERTFORD

example is Hampstead Garden Suburb in north London, a 243-acre residential estate, cut through by the A1 and with the new A406 North Circular road as its upper limit. Most of its original aims – tree-lined roads, low housing density, an emphasis on quiet – have been upheld, and are common to many other comparable garden suburbs. The first aim, that it should 'cater for all classes of people and income groups', has been rather less successful. Hampstead Garden Suburb's most famous street is The Bishop's Avenue, known as 'Britain's Blingiest Road' (*The Times*, 2005). Of the 66 houses in the Avenue, at the time of writing 10 are owned by the Saudi royal family and two by media magnate Richard Desmond. Other residents include the Sultan of Brunei, Asil Nadir, steel tycoon Lakshmi Mittal and Nursultan Nazarbayev, the oligarch president of Kazakhstan.

The vast estate of Wythenshawe, in southern Manchester, was the first garden suburb planned around the car. Two parkways, for free-flowing traffic, formed the backbone of the estate; these were firmly segregated from residential roads. This was no theoretical encouragement towards car ownership, for the nearest station was a mile or more away and there were, in the early years, no shops or amenities on the estate itself. Nonetheless, it was a popular place to live, and by the end of the 1930s had a population of nearly 40,000.

Opposite: The first sketch plan of Welwyn Garden City, by Frederic Osborn, 1919

New roads meant new maps, and plenty of them. Petrol companies, motoring organisations and commercial cartographers were all pumping out atlases and maps aimed at the motorist, with the roads emphasised above everything else. Red had settled down as the colour of choice for the main routes in nearly all cases. Ordnance Survey one-inch and even Bartholomew half-inch maps, while hugely admired by cyclists, were thought to be far too detailed for general motoring needs; the main market was in those between 3 and 6 miles to 1 inch. There were similarities, of course, but they were not of equal quality. Consistently awful were the motor maps produced by G W Bacon at 5 miles to 1 inch. In the pre-war years it had just about been possible to get away with printing new maps from very old plates, but with all the new roads, that time was over. Except for Bacon's. Still using plates from the mid-19th century, they attempted to make an asset of it by overprinting 'new roads

Right: The AA teamed up with Bartholomew to produce a popular interwar touring map aimed at motorists

and bypasses now open' in dark blue. It doesn't work, especially as some of them are so crudely placed as to be useless.

Most of the new arterials succeeded in opening up previously isolated regions, or in providing a catalyst for development to take vast numbers of working class people out of the slums of the inner cities. They were largely forces for good, but the vocal opprobrium against them swelled by the day. Inevitably, nearly all the focus on their detrimental effect came from London and the Home Counties, where the commentators and politicians were based. Their experience of the new developments was restricted to sighing at them in undisguised horror as they rolled past in their Daimlers, but it was enough to create both the tone of the debate and the resultant legislation.

The topic was raised frequently in parliament. In a Lords debate of April 1935, the Marquess of Lothian bemoaned 'the rapid conversion of country roads into streets', which was 'fast destroying the landscape as a whole'. His charge was not on aesthetic grounds, however. The 1934 Road Traffic Act had reintroduced speed limits after their abolition three years earlier, and it was this to which he – and many others – objected.

This was a regular rallying cry of the motoring lobby. These shiny new roads demanded speed, and here they were being forced to crawl along them at 30mph, the new limit in built-up areas. Furthermore, there were dark mutterings and simplistic assumptions – as there have been ever since – that as it was the taxes on motoring that largely paid for the new roads, the motorist should be allowed to do as he pleased on them. If people chose to live on these main routes, that was their lookout. Moving onto the Western Avenue, for instance, was hardly like moving onto an ordinary street, however much people liked to pretend that it might be. As *Autocar* put it in January 1937, 'every time it is the motorist who pays out vast sums to find a way of avoiding all danger to children and pedestrians, and every time these pedestrians settle down like a swarm of bees around the amenities which he, the motorist, has provided – and then complain of the danger!'

However much some motorists wanted to make light of it, the danger was horribly real. In 1934, 7,343 people were killed on the roads, at a time when there were only 2.5 million cars in the entire country; now we have over 15 times as many cars, and about a quarter of the fatalities. When the 1934 Act had become law, new Transport Minister Leslie Hore-Belisha almost became one of the statistics himself. To demonstrate the efficacy of his 'foot passenger crossings' – a set of white lines painted on the road and a signpost marked with a C (for 'crossing') – he staged a press photocall on Camden High Street, when a sports car shot past without stopping and nearly flattened him. It was enough to persuade him to beef up the crossings, with studs placed across the road and flashing orange globes on black-and-white striped poles at either side. The press swiftly christened them 'Belisha beacons', and the name stuck.

There were some very revealing contributions to the debate. Speaking in the Commons against the reimposition of any speed limit, Conservative MP Lieutenant-Colonel John Moore-Brabazon sought to distinguish between dangerous 'little cars' and his own 'great big car', which was of course perfectly safe. He proposed a minimum rather than a maximum speed limit, and, of the deaths on the road, said, 'It is no use getting alarmed over these figures. Over 6,000 people commit suicide every year, but nobody makes a fuss about that. It is true that 7,000 people are killed in motor accidents, but it is not always going on like that. People are getting used to the new conditions...No doubt many of the old Members of the House will recollect the number of chickens we killed in the old days. We used to come back with the radiator stuffed with feathers. It was the same with dogs. Dogs get out of the way of motor cars nowadays and you never kill one. There is education even in the lower animals. These things will right themselves.' Moore-Brabazon later became the Minister of Transport.

These chilling assumptions were fuelled by envious eyes being cast across the Channel, towards Germany and Italy in particular. While Britain was getting its lacy undergarments in a twist at a few new arterial roads and their accompanying development, Hitler and Mussolini were going full speed ahead by building Europe's first motorways. These had restricted access, graded junctions that allowed through traffic to continue without stopping, and no speed limit. To many motoring

evangelists, Germany and Italy were something of a holy grail. A 224-strong Road Delegation, made up of politicians, civil servants, engineers and representatives of the AA and RAC, visited Germany in September 1937 and were welcomed wholeheartedly by their Nazi hosts. All were impressed by the new *autobahnen*; a few were evidently as excited by the ideology that underpinned them.

In 1935 the Restriction on Ribbon Development Act was passed; in the same year London County Council launched the first green belt scheme to preserve some rural pockets threatened by the spreading suburbs. Visions were regularly invoked of rustic arcadia cowering beneath an onslaught of tarmac, cars, fumes, signage, litter, garages, tea shops, campsites and common city dwellers. Ironically, the same dream-like notions of rustic idylls were being used to attract more people into

Above: Leslie Hore-Belisha, the Minister of Transport, with Gordon Selfridge at the launch of a Safety Week Exhibition at Selfridges in 1935

the countryside, both as visitors and inhabitants. Even more ironically, the reality of life in rural Britain barely got a look in.

As people in the 1930s became increasingly nervous of what lay ahead, the attraction of four-square, old-fashioned life was dangled before them as never before. Stationers' stalls were thick with guide books and cheap novels celebrating Olde England; motoring magazines waxed lyrical about Sunday spins through quaint lands of legend and unbroken history. Usually written in the most turgid and flowery prose, they offered an essentially romantic and deeply conservative view of the country, which threatened to kill the very thing it purported to cherish – but it worked like magic.

Walking and bicycling boomed as never before, but it was the car that allowed ever greater numbers of people to tour the churches, castles, coves, moors, hills, villages and stately homes of the land, perhaps make a few days of it and stay in a farm bed and breakfast, a campsite or one of the new youth hostels. In 1934 the AA issued 700,000 itineraries (an average of 1.4 per member), with strip maps and route sheets. They also offered a selection of 'Tourlet' half-day

Right: The 1937 British Road Delegation in a convoy of vehicles on a German autobahn. A British motorway was still 21 years away

motoring excursions, 'Day Drive' booklets and longer popular routes, taking in picturesque scenery en route to destinations such as Brighton, Oban, Monmouth and the Wye Valley, Scarborough, Torquay, and the Lake District.

Whether imbibing the purple prose of H V Morton or Arthur Mee, or gallivanting around the country following an Ordnance Survey Tourist Map in its sylvan cover, the view of the countryside was invariably an urban one, as a place of unchanged sanctuary. In truth, the countryside was in the throes of a revolution every bit as major as the one ripping through urban Britain. Massive gentry estates were parcelled up and sold off after World War I, often to their own tenant farmers. Within 10 years of the war's end, a quarter of the British countryside had changed hands; the greatest transition since the Dissolution of the Monasteries. Unfortunately, this coincided with agricultural prices dropping sharply and the collapse of many traditional rural industries.

To those living in the countryside, motoring provided a lifeline. Ownership of cars meant far less rural isolation, but, even better, there were economic opportunities galore in catering for the hordes of

Below: AA itineraries provided their members with the chance to see parts of Britain for the very first time

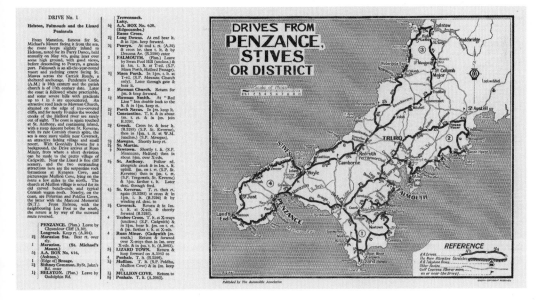

157

Right: A thatched petrol station, such as this one at Blashford in Hampshire in 1930, combined Olde England with new technology, but can't ever have seemed like a very good idea

motorists thundering out of the cities, in charabancs and coaches as well as private cars. Farmhouse bed and breakfasts, campsites, souvenir shops and tea rooms proliferated. As did petrol stations, for the sale of land for garages was a much-needed boost for many farmers struggling with their new mortgages. By 1929, only 10 years after the very first one had opened, there were 54,000 petrol stations in Britain, most individually owned.

Metropolitan commentators were horrified by the 'urbanisation' of the countryside, citing in particular the many small garages and the rash of wayside advertising for the new cafes and bed and breakfasts. Never mind that renting out roadside pitches was another much-needed source of income for farmers; this wasn't the Olde England that the books and guides had promised, and they wasted no time in demanding their removal. As for the petrol stations, things took on a distinctly surreal turn in attempts to appease the naysayers. In 1930 *Autocar* suggested 'English architecture for English soil' in the design of new garages, and was especially keen on seeing them built in Tudor and Queen Anne styles. The Council for the Protection of Rural England produced a booklet on the matter, recommending building materials for garages that included timber-framed walls and thatch for roofing. *Architect* journal labelled their suggestions 'incomprehensible and dangerous'.

With the same irony, the maps, books and advertisements most often promulgating the myth of unspoiled Merrie England, Romantic Scotland or Rugged Wales were often the ones paid for by oil companies. Most famously, Shell produced dozens of posters by leading artists of the day that depicted stylised versions of beauty spots, beaches, castles and unspoilt villages. Rarely was a car seen in any of them. In 1934 they launched their evergreen Shell Guide series, under the editorship of that most arcadian of poets, John Betjeman.

The maps that most embody this spirit came from Pratt's, a branch of Anglo-American Oil. They'd created the first road atlas of Britain back in 1905, and in the 1930s came out with a series called Pratt's High Test Plans. These were road maps at their most romantic. Some featured a specific route, such as the Great North Road or the Bath Road, while others were regional plans that included all of the main roads. Little illustrations and annotations peppered the map – a castle here, a half-timbered inn there, a hunting scene between them – while bits of verse and folksy sayings decorated the edges. In the typography and symbolism for the towns, and the elaborate cartouches, town crests and compasses, there was more than a nod to the great road strip maps of old, Ogilby and Cary in particular. This was heady nostalgia in map form, as likely to be framed on the wall as popped in the glove compartment.

Overleaf: Pratt's High Test Plan of the Bath Road: *poetry and soaring spires adorned the gorgeously romantic Pratt's plans of some of the great roads, instead of the rather more prosaic truth of traffic jams and accidents. And was 'World's Biscuit Capital' really the best thing they could find to say about Reading?*

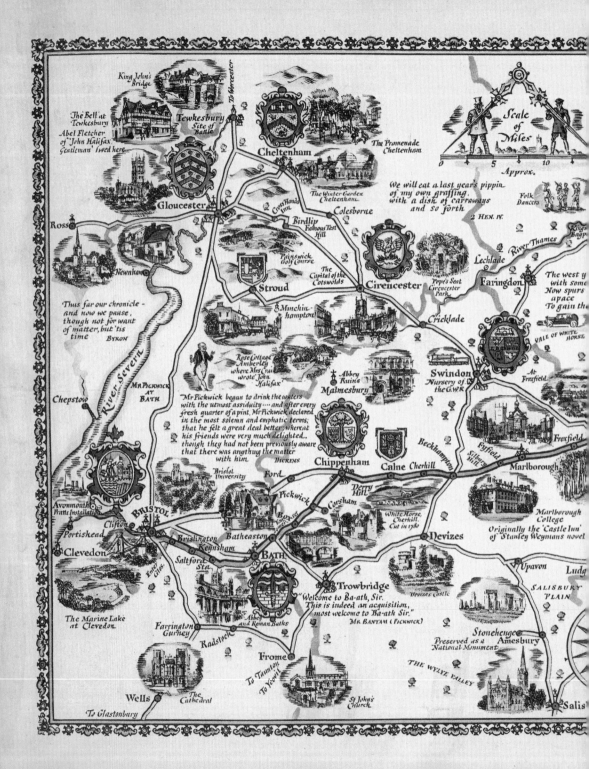

King John's Bridge

The Bell at Tewkesbury Abel Fletcher of 'John Halifax Gentleman' lived here

Tewkesbury
Site of Battle

To Worcester

The Promenade Cheltenham

Cheltenham

Scale of Miles

0   5   10
Approx.

Gloucester

The Winter Garden Cheltenham

Cross Hands Inn

Colesborne

Birdlip Famous Test Hill

We will eat a last year's pippin of my own graffing, with a dish of carraways and so forth
2 HEN. IV.

Folk Dancers

Ross

Newnham

Painswick Golf Course

River Thames

Lechlade

King's Bagp

The Capital of the Cotswolds

Stroud

Pope's Seat Cirencester Park

Faringdon

The west y with some Now spurs apace To gain the

Cirencester

Thus far our chronicle - and now we pause, though not for want of matter, but 'tis time   BYRON

Minchin-hampton

Cricklade

VALE OF WHITE HORSE

River Severn

Rose Cottage Amberley where Mrs Crai wrote John Halifax

Abbey Ruins Malmesbury

Swindon Nursery of the G.W.R.

At Froxfield

MR PICKWICK AT BATH

Chepstow

Mr Pickwick began to drink the waters with the utmost assiduity.....and after every fresh quarter of a pint, Mr Pickwick declared in the most solemn and emphatic terms, that he felt a great deal better, whereat his friends were very much delighted, though they had not been previously aware that there was anything the matter with him.   DICKENS

Chippenham

Calne Cherhill

Beckhampton

Fyfield

Silbury Hill

Froxfield

Marlborough

Bristol University

Ford

Pickwick

Corsham

Derry Hill

White Horse, Cherhill, Cut in 1780

Marlborough College

Originally the 'Castle Inn' of Stanley Weyman's novel

Avonmouth Watts Installation

BRISTOL

Clifton

Box

Devizes

Portishead

Brislington

Keynsham

Batheaston

Upavon

Ludg

SALISBURY PLAIN

Clevedon

Saltford Sta.

BATH

Devizes Castle

The Marine Lake at Clevedon

Abbey and Roman Baths

Trowbridge

"Welcome to Ba-ath, Sir. This is indeed an acquisition, most welcome to Ba-ath Sir."
MR BANTAM (PICKWICK)

Stonehenge
Preserved as a National Monument

Amesbury

Farrington Gurney

Radstock

Frome

THE WYLYE VALLEY

Wells

The Cathedral

To Taunton
To Yeovil

St John's Church

Salis

To Glastonbury

Right: The Highways Plan, 1937 – roads were in desperate need of improvement, and the AA presented the MoT with a proposal in 1937. War soon put a halt to proceedings

REPRINTED FROM

THE TIMES

Thursday November 25 1937

A HIGHWAYS PLAN

COORDINATION OF DEVELOPMENT

A.A. AND A NATIONAL PROGRAMME

A provisional scheme for the development of the main highways of Great Britain in order of their importance as traffic arteries, which has been prepared by the Automobile Association, was outlined yesterday by the secretary, Sir responsible to the Minister of Transport, with duties and functions analogous to those carried out by Telford a century ago.

All the roads are numbered on the accompanying map. The first six, in order, are:—

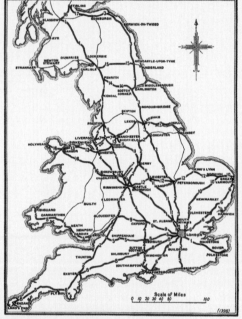

Stenson Cooke. The plan provides for the coordinated treatment of 18 highways of major importance—in two instances roads are coupled—and it is proposed that each of these should be in the charge of a road engineer, appointed by and directly

Dover—Glasgow
Exeter—Doncaster
Brighton—Edinburgh
‡Southampton—Birmingham
‡Liverpool—Preston
London—Bristol (across the Severn)—Fishguard
Portsmouth—London—Yarmouth

1939 ON THE GREAT NORTH ROAD

For an intense flavour of the roads of this era, it's worth looking on the internet for a colour film of the Great North Road, shot in August 1939. So familiar yet foreign, the tone is set at the beginning as a street cleaner obediently stops his hand-pushed cart at a red traffic light. Buses, cars and people bustle by. Soon we're out of London, through Stevenage and Biggleswade, Buckden, Stilton and Stamford, along a road that seems to alternate between being blissfully deserted and full of terrible drivers tailgating each other and overtaking wildly.

The paraphernalia that we know so well is already in place: the inns and cafes, the signs, the telegraph poles (in their early oversized incarnation), the traffic lights, the advertisements and the pedestrian crossings (with Belisha beacons, but no zebra crossings as yet), all unfurling along the soft grey tarmac stretching into the distance. It looks so timeless, and yet... a banner strung across the street calls for ARP volunteers, and overhead an airship hovers. The skies are blue, but we know all too well that dark clouds are gathering once again.

Maps such as Pratt's were a far cry from the ones being produced by the Ministry of Transport. The new arterial roads had been deemed a success, and they wanted more, particularly in the southeast. In December 1937, two detailed maps were published of Inner and Outer London to show the roads being planned. These included many new arterials, bypasses and extensions and a ringway around the capital on a route very similar to the M25 of decades later. Plans for the city itself included some lengthy flyovers (quaintly called 'viaducts' in the key): two over Wimbledon, one along the Chelsea Embankment and some whoppers around Deptford and the Elephant and Castle. Tunnels were projected too: under the Thames at Woolwich, through Islington and under the entire width of Hyde Park. Roads were to be driven through many residential areas, especially poorer ones, necessitating wholesale demolition. Within just a couple of years, the Luftwaffe were doing the job for them.

Chapter 5

BRAVE NEW WORLD
(1939–73)

Just a quarter of a century on from World War I, the country was once
again battered by international conflict. This time, there were not just
emotional and economic scars, but brutal physical ones too, for British
towns and cities had been systematically levelled by airborne bombs on
a scale far beyond the limited Zeppelin raids of 1915–18.

From 'Black Saturday' – 7 September 1940 – London was attacked
every night for two months. After a brief respite, the Luftwaffe campaign
against the capital intensified, reaching a grotesque crescendo under the
full moon of 10 May 1941, when 100,000 bombs came down in one
night, leaving nearly 1,500 dead. Throughout the eight-month campaign
28,500 civilians lost their lives in the London Blitz.

Ports and industrial cities everywhere were similarly targeted
through the dark days of 1940 and 1941. Massive swathes of Liverpool,
Southampton, Portsmouth, Plymouth, Manchester, Belfast, Cardiff,
Swansea, Bristol and Glasgow were destroyed. As the great Midland cities
that built cars also built weaponry and aeronautic components, they
were systematically targeted; Coventry's burned-out cathedral became
one of the most iconic images of the war. Many Luftwaffe raids on the
north of England returned home using the Humber as a navigational
guide, jettisoning any remaining bombs on Hull. Some 95 per cent
of the city's buildings were destroyed or damaged; half of its 300,000
population were made homeless.

The shock to the national psyche, of wartime victory amidst such
utter devastation, was profound, and led to some highly un-British
thinking. Sloughing off our usual hesitant caution, change was embraced
in everything, from the landslide afforded Clement Attlee in 1945 to the
wholesale reshaping of our landscape for the modern age. And the car
was at the heart of it.

*Previous page: No stone
unturned: plans for
the M23's arrival in
Streatham, south London.
It was never built*

OFF THE MAP

As with many other sciences, it is in times of war that great leaps are made
in cartography. Ordnance Survey was established to counter the threat from

Left: The Battle of Britain: a Heinkel He 111 bomber flying over the Isle of Dogs in the East End of London, at the start of the Luftwaffe's evening raids on 7 September 1940

Napoleon, and in the 20th century it was the two World Wars that advanced aerial photography as a mainstay of mapmaking. From its tentative beginnings in the first war, and its early adoption by Ordnance Survey between the wars as an aid to surveying archaeological sites and the changing shape of our towns, it became a crucial part of reconnaissance of enemy territory throughout World War II. Inevitably, this was often a highly dangerous mission, never more so than for the solo pilots who surveyed and mapped the Normandy coast in secrecy to prepare for the D-Day landings. In order to escape radar detection, they sometimes had to fly below 100 feet. Not all returned.

The enemy had us mapped too, of course. Luftwaffe pilots, often flying by moonlight, had laminated maps printed with the main targets in luminous

Above: Under wartime restrictions, even location names on AA telephone boxes were painted out

yellow. Also tinted were places to avoid bombing, mainly camps holding German prisoners of war. These were produced from British maps bought commercially, aerial reconnaissance and on-the-ground espionage. Similarly, throughout the Cold War the USSR produced highly detailed maps of Britain at many different scales. The shapes are very familiar, but the Cyrillic alphabet makes them objects of great curiosity.

Ironically, during the Cold War the Soviets had more detail on their maps of Britain than we did ourselves. Since the 1920s, sensitive sites of military or strategic importance had been kept off official maps, including the Ordnance Survey plans available to the general public. The number of omissions grew steadily, reaching its peak in the 1960s, when 5,000 such 'key points' (as defined by MI5) were missing from our maps. One that always used to baffle me as a youngster was the Fylingdales early warning station on the North Yorkshire moors; images of its famous golf-ball domes were readily available on postcards and in guide books, but on the local Ordnance Survey map there was nothing. Some of the gaps on the map – especially the bigger research bases – looked even more suspicious than any accurate portrayal of them would have done. It was only in 2006, a full 15 years after the collapse of the USSR, that the British government finally rescinded this policy, and not for any reasons of openness, but because of 'the availability of this information from open sources' – that is, Google Maps and the like.

Map sales were restricted throughout the war years. The Control of Maps Order 1940 banned selling them at any scale larger than one-inch to anyone without a permit, and outlawed the sale of any map to 'aliens'. Smaller-scale road atlases had to remove all their city street plans to stay within the regulations. It was the same thinking that underpinned the removal of direction signs and village name plates, in a bid to confuse the enemy should rogue parachutists land in the countryside, or in the event of a full-scale invasion. These measures did not much inconvenience British drivers, for petrol was the first commodity to be rationed as soon as the war broke out; impresario Ivor Novello was imprisoned for four weeks for using petrol ration coupons stolen for him by a fan. For most people, the family car, their pre-war pride and joy, rusted quietly away throughout the war, and took some serious kick-starting once it was all over. Petrol was taken off rations at the end of the war, but soon restored at an even smaller quantity; the ration remained until May 1950. Even in such trying circumstances, the British public returned to driving with enthusiasm. A Gallup poll of 1949 showed that one in seven people went for a Sunday drive, the same number that went to church.

It wasn't just the blank canvas of bombed cities that provoked Britain's radical redesign. Under wartime emergency measures, many new parts of the countryside had been tarmacked over, for military airfields and their substantial accompanying infrastructure; 38 were constructed in the area between Oxford and Swindon alone. Towards the very end of the war, another one, on the fertile plains at Heathrow, was snuck in under emergency measures, though there was never any plan to use it for military purposes. It was an almost inevitable outcome that the great new highways of west London were to point towards the nation's major airport. Furthermore, as part of the 'Dig for Victory' campaign, massive areas of town parks, common land and heath had been turned over to agricultural usage. Change had already erupted all around, and there was to be no turning back – at least, not for now. For the next quarter of a century, Britain's obsession was with the future, not the past.

Even in the depths of wartime, planners had been turning their thoughts to the new roads that would be needed when it ended. But the 1945 Labour government had more pressing calls on their depleted coffers: housing, health, food, energy and education. The future direction of road building was clearly signposted, however, in the 1949 Special Roads Act, which legalised the construction of routes restricted to particular users. For the first time, a road could be built upon which pedestrians and cyclists, for example, were not allowed. Motorways were here – or at least would be, when we could afford them.

Even in bomb-ravaged cities such as Plymouth and Southampton, the building of major new roads was a glacially slow process. In Coventry, the city that had become such a potent symbol of the horrors of war, there was much talk of redevelopment – but then there had been long before the first bomb had dropped. The opening of the city's southern bypass in 1940 had whetted local appetites. Pre-war plans for the city centre, showing wide roads and pedestrianised squares, were dusted off,

Below: An integral part of Coventry's post-war redevelopment plan was this 1945 proposal for the creation of an inner ring road

updated and enthusiastically pursued. As the war ended, an exhibition was held at the city's Drill Hall, the centrepiece of which was a large architect's model of the planned new city centre. It was clear that what the Luftwaffe hadn't achieved, the city fathers would. The bombing had destroyed only about one-third of Coventry's medieval buildings; most of the rest fell to the bulldozer and the wrecking ball.

Out of the ruins grew the new city centre, its straight new thoroughfares bearing no resemblance to the palimpsest of streets

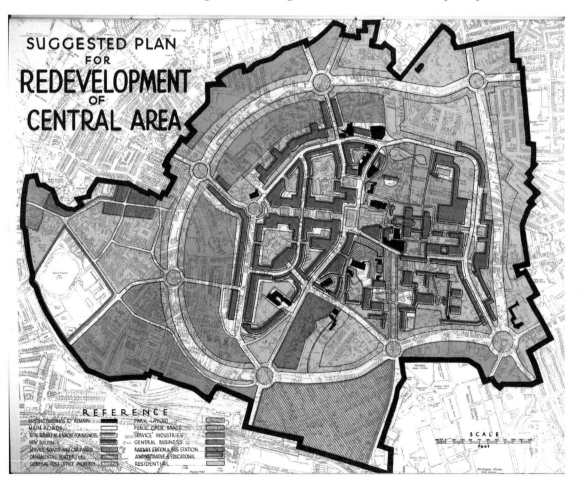

beneath. Council documents and plans talked of a fully capitalised New Coventry, a Jerusalem on the plains of the English Midlands. The dreams were big. Britain's first carless shopping precinct, in a cruciform shape angled towards the ruined cathedral's spire, drew admirers from afar and provided the prototype for others across Europe. Basil Spence won the competition for a new cathedral with a startlingly modern design, knocking out the numerous offerings that had largely wanted to replicate what had been lost. In the spirit of reconciliation, Coventry inaugurated the concept of twinning with foreign cities, the first being Stalingrad (now Volgograd) in 1944. (Inevitably, its sister cities have mainly been drawn from a pool of those similarly blitzed by war, so that a list of Coventry's twin towns – all 27 of them, more than anywhere else in Britain – reads like a roll call of the once-damned.)

Below: Junctions galore on the Coventry Inner Ring Road, perhaps the most choking of all 'concrete collars'

All of the city centre development was to be pinned in by a new ring road, which appeared on the very first post-war plans as a ground-level circle intersected by seven roundabouts. Separate cycle paths were planned on either side, with landscaped grass verges to finish it off. Construction began in the late 1950s; two days before Christmas 1959 the first section, to the south of the city centre, was opened when the Lord Mayor cut the ribbon. A commemorative film shows him going for a spin along the new road in the municipal Daimler, while two cyclists swoosh by on their dedicated track alongside. The street maps of the time show a first roundabout and the loop of ring road curving gently away towards the railway station.

Plans soon changed, and completely. The idea of a roundabout-laden, ground-level ring road, resembling all too much the slow, congested arterials of the 1920s and 30s, was swiftly jettisoned. The city planners looked to America for inspiration instead, and found the grade-separated dual carriageway, which could swirl cars in an endless loop of flyovers and underpasses around the city centre, with no need to stop. The building recommenced to the new plan, and in 1962 a short stretch of elevated dual carriageway, Ringways Rudge and Queen's, was complete. By 1964 about half was done, though it took a further full decade before another ribbon-cutting ceremony, by another Lord Mayor, finally opened the entire circuit. The last bit in the link was the airborne upgrade for the original ring road of 15 years earlier.

There were no cycle paths, no pedestrians and no grassy verges this time. This was undiluted tarmac city, so futuristic that the plans included roof-top car parks on the high-level junctions (abandoned on cost grounds) and an experimental under-tarmac heating system to beat frosty mornings (installed on one slip road, but it never worked very well, cost too much to maintain and was also abandoned). There was no shortage of junctions: nine in all, on a circuit measuring less than two miles, meaning that slip roads from the last turn-off almost overlapped with those for the next. Driving the Coventry ring road is not for the faint-hearted. (It might not be for anyone much longer, for although the tarmac tourniquet has been an unqualified success in moving the city's traffic around with great efficiency, the mood of the moment has firmly changed. Plans for the city's future now all include the 'taming' of the ring road – which might translate as anything from pedestrian crossings and a few flowery verges to outright demolition.) In both the initial construction of its concrete collar, and the latterday urge to flatten and floralise it, Coventry is replicating exactly the story of its equally car-crazy, car-building big brother, Birmingham.

From the initial low-key post-war plans for the Coventry ring road, to their radical overhaul in 1960 as a highway-in-the-sky, something obviously changed in the national mindset. That something was the long-awaited arrival of the motorway age, and with it the green light for roads designed with only cars, and their speed, in mind. 'What was Britain's first motorway?' used to be a good pub quiz question, as you could reliably expect half the room to answer 'the M1'. Not any more: such was the excitement over its half-centenary in 2008, and such is the growth in internet-fuelled geekery, most quiz punters now know that the answer is the Preston bypass.

Above: The official opening of the Preston bypass, Britain's first motorway, on 5 December 1958. Note the wide central reservation that was soon to become a third lane on each side

Lancashire had long been in the vanguard of road building. Before the war the county council had been the first to erect its own road signs, had built one of the country's first bypasses at Ormskirk, and had created the most motorway-like road of its age, the East Lancashire arterial. They had also drawn up pre-war plans for a north–south motorway through the county, even protecting the relevant land from any other development. After the war, pugnacious County Surveyor James Drake bullied the Ministry of Transport into agreement for an eight-mile motorway-standard road around Preston, the most notorious bottleneck on the long A6 route to Scotland.

Against Drake's recommendations for two carriageways of three lanes each, the ministry insisted that the new road should be only two lanes in each direction. Drake knew that widening the route would be inevitable, and so built it with an extra-wide central reservation. The third lanes were much needed, and added with the minimum of fuss only seven years later.

Work started in June 1956, and was endlessly interrupted by ferocious weather. Fortunately, the day of the opening ceremony – Friday 5 December 1958 – was uncharacteristically dry, allowing the Prime

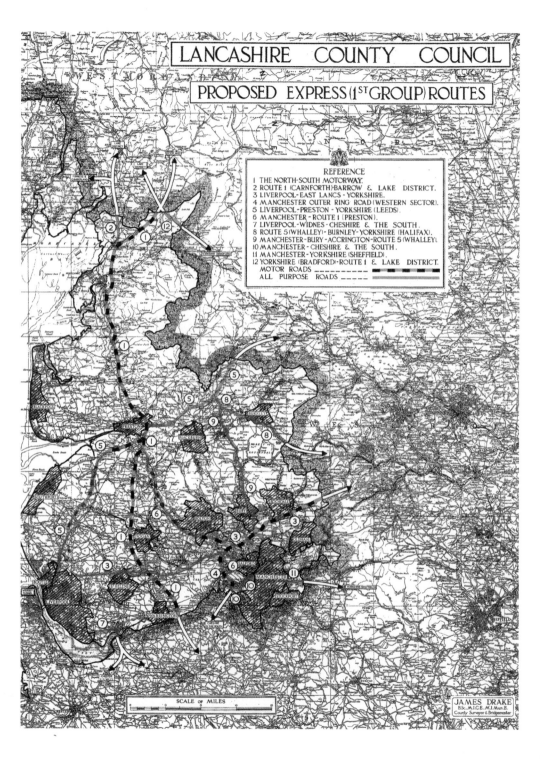

LANCASHIRE COUNTY COUNCIL

PROPOSED EXPRESS (1ST GROUP) ROUTES

REFERENCE
1 THE NORTH-SOUTH MOTORWAY.
2 ROUTE 1 (CARNFORTH)-BARROW & LAKE DISTRICT.
3 LIVERPOOL-EAST LANCS-YORKSHIRE.
4 MANCHESTER OUTER RING ROAD (WESTERN SECTOR).
5 LIVERPOOL-PRESTON-YORKSHIRE (LEEDS).
6 MANCHESTER-ROUTE 1 (PRESTON).
7 LIVERPOOL-WIDNES-CHESHIRE & THE SOUTH.
8 ROUTE 5 (WHALLEY)-BURNLEY-YORKSHIRE (HALIFAX).
9 MANCHESTER-BURY-ACCRINGTON-ROUTE 5 (WHALLEY).
10 MANCHESTER-CHESHIRE & THE SOUTH.
11 MANCHESTER-YORKSHIRE (SHEFFIELD).
12 YORKSHIRE (BRADFORD)-ROUTE 1 & LAKE DISTRICT.
MOTOR ROADS
ALL PURPOSE ROADS

SCALE OF MILES

JAMES DRAKE
B.Sc., M.I.C.E., M.I.Mun.E.
County Surveyor & Bridgemaster

Minister, Harold Macmillan, to wax lyrical in his speech by quoting a poem by Robbie Burns:

> *I'm now arrived – thanks to the gods!*
> *Thro' pathways rough and muddy,*
> *A certain sign that makin' roads*
> *Is no' this people's study.*

'What Lancashire has today, other parts of the country will have tomorrow,' he told the assembled dignitaries, before launching the cavalcade off on 'the country's first motor way' – in his cut glass tones it was two distinct words rather than one. There was much talk of Britain entering the modern age with its eight-mile motorway, some 26 years after Germany had inaugurated its first *autobahn*, and a full 33 after Italy's inaugural *autostrada*. Rather underlining the point, the mechanism that had been erected to cut the ribbon and unveil the granite memorial failed, and the job had to be done manually. Even more regrettably, and rather more publicly, just six weeks later the entire motorway had to be shut for carriageway repairs after a sharp frost and rapid thaw had gouged holes out of the tarmac. The press had a field day.

Nonetheless, we were off! No 'pedal cyclists, mopeds, invalid carriages, animals, agricultural vehicles, learner drivers', as the new signs had it, and, most thrillingly of all, no speed limit either – that didn't arrive until 1965. Not that you could get up much of a head of steam on such a short road: Lancashire constabulary monitored the first month of the motorway and noted the 'remarkable feature being the moderate speeds that vehicles are travelling. Our radar checks have only, on one occasion, found a driver going faster than 75mph, whilst most people drive at 40–50mph.'

Bigger, better racetracks were just around the corner, however. On the day the Preston bypass opened, a Whitehall press release stated that 'the total length of motorway covered by the present roads programme' was 'about 380 miles'. This included two more Lancashire county council projects: another section of the putative M6, around Lancaster, and the Stretford–Eccles bypass, now part of the M60, which included the magnificent Barton Bridge over the Manchester Ship Canal.

Nothing could compare though with the excitement that was steadily building in the south Midlands, as a 70-mile trench of mud gouged its way across the landscape. The M1, together with its M10 and M45 extensions at either end, was fast a-coming. At three o'clock on Monday 24 March 1958, Harold Watkinson, Harold Macmillan's Minister of Transport, started construction work by pressing a button to send a signal flashing along the entire 55-mile Luton to Rugby route of the M1 itself. Just over 19 months later – nine fewer than it had taken to build the Preston bypass – his successor Ernest Marples was there to open the finished motorway.

Used as we are these days to protracted inquiries, delays and protests for nearly all great infrastructure projects, the story of the building of the M1 makes for staggering reading. Twenty-five thousand maps like complicated coloured jigsaws detail every parcel of land on or by the motorway's route. More than 300 landowners needed to be convinced to sell up; anyone expressing doubt was personally visited by Sir Owen Williams, the chief engineer of the project. Most were heartily in favour of the motorway, as was the whole country, for this leap into modernity chimed precisely with the mood of the time.

THE WATFORD GAP

The only landowners to refuse outright Sir Owen Williams' exhortations to sell up for the M1 were the Thorntons at Brock Hall, just north of Weedon Bec in Northamptonshire. The family had owned the Jacobean pile since 1625, and had in previous centuries tried to block the construction of both the Grand Union Canal and the main London to Birmingham railway across their land. As on those two occasions, their attempt failed. As Tom Rolt put it in his 1960 commemorative book *The London–Birmingham Motorway*, 'in each case they were unsuccessful because their parkland lies athwart a natural trade route'.

For this is the Watford Gap, one of the most legendary – if mysterious – locations in Britain. It is a name known to all, not least because of the M1 service station named after it (Britain's first), but it has long been confused in

Left: A fleet of AA vans gets ready for action on the opening day of the M1 in November 1959

many people's minds with the town of Watford, 68 miles further southeast. Watford Gap became the defining point of the north–south divide, and your lot in life was due to which side you came from.

Although this busy corner of Northamptonshire appears so physically unremarkable, it is in some ways the crux of the nation. It is the narrowest and lowest point in the limestone wolds that slice diagonally across England, the border between the wealthier south and east and the hardier north and west. To the eternal frustration of transport planners, it is also geologically unstable. The Romans built Watling Street through the gap, but when Thomas Telford came this way with his highway to Holyhead, he was forced off their route here by quicksands – which is why the A5 makes a sudden westward lurch into Kilsby village. The same problem afflicted the canal engineers, who had to alter the line of the Crick Tunnel, and Robert Stephenson with his railway tunnel at Kilsby.

Blessed with technological advances, the motorway engineers managed to take the M1 almost exactly over the route of the Roman road as it crests the

Overleaf: London Yorkshire Motorway Crick to Doncaster By-Pass Draft Scheme Plan *(1960): land ownership maps, for every parcel of land over which the M1 was destined to pass, reveal what a logistical knot the project was, and how remarkable was the speed with which it was achieved*

C1

767

766

773

771

770

768

772

769

WATLING STREET

L. & N. W. R. (RUGBY LINE)

ROMAN ROAD

CANAL

Crick

Scale - Six Inches to One Mile or 880 Feet to One Inch

100 FEET 500   0   1000   2000   3000   4000   5000 YD.

FURLONG

C3

C4

763

764

762

758

757

759

761

756

760

summit of the Watford Gap. Just below is the village of Weedon Bec, where the canal, rail and road – the north–south A5 crossing the east–west A45 – all converge. This small, dusty village should have grown, you feel, into a major city; perhaps even a national capital.

For a few miles north of Weedon Bec, the A5, M1, Grand Union Canal and West Coast mainline railway all run in tight parallel. I've journeyed on each of them; the most fun was on a narrowboat at a steady 4mph, as the trains and cars hurtled by on either side. Every time I pass, I marvel at the imprint of successive centuries as they shoot through the same narrow gap, and wonder what this century will add to the mix. It won't be the HS2 rail link, if it ever gets built – although initially ploughing a familiar furrow between London and Birmingham, the plan is to route it the other side of Daventry.

But back to the Thorntons of Brock Hall. After begrudgingly having to accept the canal and the railway, the motorway finally did for them, and they sold up in 1969 after more than three and a half centuries there. The house was carved up into upmarket apartments – one is on the market as I write, and in its lavish prospectus, much is made of the fact that it is 'conveniently placed for access to the M1'.

Right: The AA launched its new retriever unit vehicles for the motorway age; they were in great demand

The construction of the M1 was helped by the fact that amazingly few houses needed to be demolished outright; the only casualties were the five houses and three bungalows that once made up Clyde Road, between Dunstable and Luton, and now lie buried under one of the slip roads of junction 11. Quite how much people were prepared to put up with in the name of progress is evident in the films and aerial photographs of these western Luton suburbs. The route of the motorway carves through a vast chalk cutting, with houses and gardens tottering on the brink above.

Once building began, it roared along at a pace we now associate with modern-day China. On average, a full mile of new road was completed every eight days, and one of the 183 new bridges every three. The work was tough: men with picks and shovels digging deep into difficult clays and chalks against a backdrop of yet more record-breaking rain and floods. In the middle of the first August, firemen had to pump half a million gallons of water from a cutting near Northampton; it was 10 feet deep in places.

Excitement was building, especially in those communities near the road. The *Luton News* regularly published massive aerial photographs of the motorway's progress through the town's outskirts, while the *Northampton Chronicle & Echo* published a special 'Motorway Survey' in April 1959. 'Seven months remain until the historic moment when the Motorway is scheduled for completion,' it chirruped, 'when 100mph motoring will become a safe reality in Britain at last.'

Bang on time, and within its £16 million budget, the M1 opened that November; the *Chronicle & Echo* was there. 'MOTORWAY "OFF" TO WAVES AND CHEERS' hollered its main headline, followed by page upon page of ecstatic coverage. In one story, the paper reported that a couple of days before the opening, Mr Geoffrey Sloan of the Swan Revived Inn, Newport Pagnell, had taken his 1902 Benz for a spin on the M1. He said that he did it in 'a fast time', despite having to stop to mend a blown exhaust valve, but refused to say how he gained access to the road, as he didn't want 'to get anyone into trouble'. Among the pages of breathless excitement, only one word of caution was sounded, by builder Stan West of Woburn Sands. 'I have never been on anything like it,' he told the paper, 'but I should think it could get monotonous.'

The national press was just as agog with excitement, and all sent correspondents to see what speeds they could clock up on the new road. The winner was the *News Chronicle* reporter, who claimed to have reached 157mph in his Aston Martin. Speed was the main object for many, even if they didn't have quite such a glamorous vehicle. Car ownership had more than doubled between 1949 and 1957, and was now at around the 8 million mark. Finally, after years of bottlenecks and tailbacks through bomb-cratered streets, there was the chance to really put your foot down, and people jumped at it. All along the M1 in those first few weeks, big ends blew, tyres burst, engines overheated, fan belts snapped and petrol tanks swiftly emptied as a battered armada of Fords and Morrises were pushed to, and often well beyond, their limit.

Everyone has an M1 anecdote or two. Some are bespoke: mine include regular memories of tagging onto the queue of hitch-hikers at Brent Cross while at university in London; of having my dad's Audi for a fortnight while he was abroad, and tanking it from Leeds to London in well under two hours one winter's night, bellowing along to the Eurythmics as the orange lights streaked by in a blur; of a tyre blowing on my mum's overpacked Mini as we headed to visit aunties in Yorkshire, and none of us noticing until a lorry flashed us onto the hard shoulder. Like most of us, I've had nine lives on that motorway.

Death inevitably looms large in the collective memory of the M1: not just the road accidents (the worst, in March 1972, near Luton, involved 200 vehicles and killed nine), but the Kegworth air crash of 1989, when a struggling plane failed to make the runway of East Midlands Airport and landed on the side of the motorway, killing 47 passengers but miraculously no one on the ground. For years, the bald patch by the side of the road was an ominous reminder that always left your palms sweaty on the steering wheel. And who could forget the M1's strangest hour, when in 1997 tens of thousands of people crowded onto overhead bridges and even down onto the silent carriageway itself to stare at the flower-strewn hearse taking Princess Diana back to Althorp?

It is almost impossible now to conjure up the excitement of those first years of motorway life, but it was everywhere and seemed to infect everyone. L T C (Tom) Rolt, the heritage transport enthusiast best known for his campaigns to preserve canals and steam railways, wrote a highly enthusiastic little book about the M1, which he described as 'a broad double ribbon of asphalt reeled out across the shires'. Nikolaus Pevsner, the architectural historian known for his love of old churches and stately homes, put an entry about the M1 ('the twentieth century version of Watling Street' with bridges that 'impress by a cyclopean rudeness') into his 1961 county guide to Northamptonshire, part of his esteemed Buildings of England series. He even afforded it the rare privilege of a photograph. Thirteen years later, discussing the intrusion of the M6 in the introduction to his new Staffordshire volume, Pevsner felt obliged to apologise for his earlier over-enthusiasm.

In these pioneering days, people didn't quite know how to react to the motorways – and neither did cartographers. With most mapmakers sticking to the convention of showing main roads in red, the question of how to give extra emphasis to the motorways was dealt with in an assortment of ways. In April 1960, in direct response to the opening of the M1, Ordnance Survey introduced on its one-inch maps a beefed-up red road, with thicker black lines encasing it, to denote all motorways and dual carriageways. In 1964, on their 1:625,000 (1 inch to 10 miles) Route Planning Maps, they adopted the blue colour of its signage system to delineate the motorways on the map, and this soon became the standard colour for most commercial cartographers. However, Ordnance Survey didn't use the blue on their flagship one-inch series until they replaced it with the new metric series in 1974.

Above: Even Nikolaus Pevsner fell briefly under the spell of the motorway age, giving the M1 a write-up and the honour of a photograph in his 1961 guide to Northamptonshire

SIGNS OF THE TIMES

Rarely do we get something so right first time as we did with the new signage system born with the motorways. Until 1958, waymarking of roads and destinations had been achieved by a jumble of signs produced by local authorities, motoring and cycling organisations and private concerns. Realising

that this was a safety issue as much as an aesthetic one, the government commissioned Jock Kinneir, who'd designed the new signs for Gatwick Airport, to come up with a system for the motorways. It was installed on the very first, the Preston bypass, and to great acclaim.

Kinneir, and his former student Margaret Calvert, were then charged by the 1963 Worboys Committee with updating the signs on the entire road network. They took the rules of their motorway signage and applied them throughout. The main features were a mixture of upper and lower case lettering in a clear sans serif font, installed on direction signs that resembled a simple map oriented towards the driver. Pictograms were similarly plain, but effective. Calvert even smuggled in a few nods to the age: gone was the Enid Blyton-esque boy in shorts and a cap to warn of a nearby school, to be replaced by a thoroughly modern little miss pulling along her smaller brother.

The original colour schemes stuck. From the outset, the motorways have been signed in white lettering on a blue background, like the sky of a summer's day. Primary destinations on main roads are shown as white on green, with yellow used for the road numbers, and all other minor places and routes are shown as black on white. As motoring has become more complicated, the signs have had to be adapted for many uses that Kinneir and Calvert could never have anticipated, but it is testament to the power of their design that the system has coped admirably, has been copied all over the world, and, after more than half a century in use, still looks fit for purpose today.

Another problem facing mapmakers was the question of currency, for people needed maps with the very latest information on them. It was all too easy to get it wrong. The first section of the M1 was a very well publicised – and highly anticipated – route; all cartographers knew that they must incorporate it, but during construction it was decided to take the new motorway a further two miles north of its intersection with the M45, in order to decant north-going traffic at a better place in the existing A road network. This small extension terminated at the A428, just west of Crick village (now junction 18). Ordnance Survey were caught napping on the 1960 update of their half-inch map No. 37, *Leicester*. The northward extension, opened at the same time as the M1 and M45, appears only as a dotted line, while the M45 is shown as a seamless continuation of the M1, and intersecting almost immediately with the A5, where there has never been a junction. Anyone trying to go up to Leicester with this map would end up miles out of their way. Worse, after the M45 has ended near Dunchurch, and the A45 taken over on its route to the Coventry bypass, the A road is erroneously marked as the M1 many miles out of its way.

Not surprisingly, maps that promised to be bang up-to-date became the ones that people used. Venerable companies such as Ordnance Survey and Bartholomew, who produced such a variety of maps that they could only possibly update them every few years, became the preserve of those who wanted to use the car to explore the country lanes, and perhaps go walking or cycling. To the new generation of motorway addicts, the road

Overleaf: Ordnance Survey were caught on the hop in trying to map the new M1 in 1960. They had failed to anticipate its actual end at Crick, mapped a junction with the A5 that didn't exist, and had mislabeled the M/A45 as the M1 all the way past Coventry

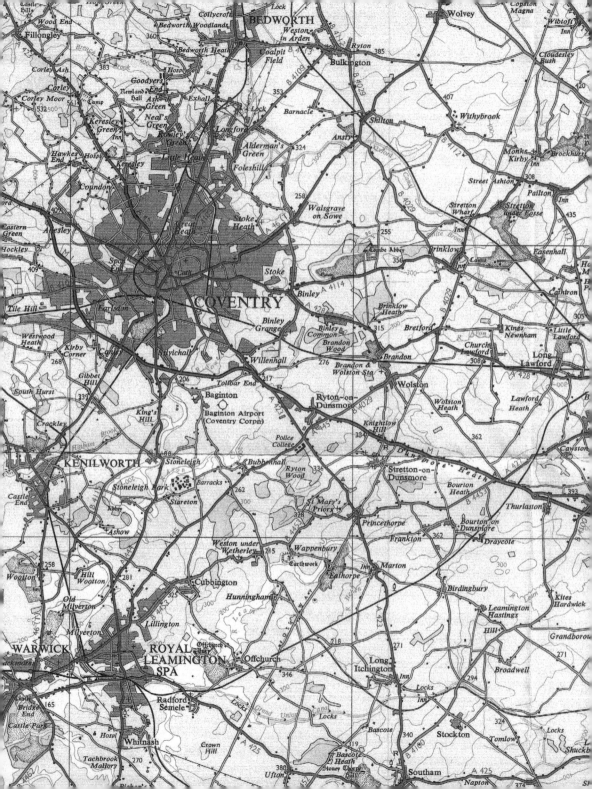

atlases, AA or RAC handbooks and branded petrol station maps were far more useful. Their main appeal was that they were regularly updated – annually, in most cases. This year's date on the front cover became more of a selling point than the quality of the cartography.

Many of these maps were cheap and cheerful, sold at a nominal price or given away free as part of a promotion or membership package. New motorways and dual carriageways were given huge prominence over everything else. Railways shrank in proportion or disappeared entirely from the maps, as did smaller roads, more isolated settlements, and any information about places of historical significance.

THE ANNUAL MEMBERS' HANDBOOK

Membership of the AA or RAC brought numerous benefits, none more used than the annual members' handbook, invariably found in a car's glove compartment. The AA introduced theirs in 1908; at first little more than a list, by town, of garages and mechanics across the country. The following year a directory of hotels was added and, from 1912, these were rated according to a pioneering star system. This idea came from the system used to classify brandy, for the AA Secretary, Stenson Cooke, had in a previous existence been a wine and spirits salesman. He defined a three-star hotel as 'a really decent, average middle-class hotel'.

Lists of hotels and garages continued to be the handbook's backbone, along with its 'service map' of the whole country at the motorists' standard scale of ten miles to the inch. In the post-war but pre-motorway years, the thickest lines on the map were of 'roads regularly covered by AA patrols'; mainly A-roads but a few B-roads too, though a note rather enigmatically promised that 'AA patrols will also be found on many other roads at times of peak traffic'. A special category in the Scottish Highlands denoted roads that would be patrolled only 'during the Touring Season'.

The handbook's cartography was simple, mostly clear and aimed squarely at drivers: little mention of physical geography or places of interest, but meticulous coding of towns and villages to show which had AA-recommended hotels, AA garages or both, where the motoring organisation's phone boxes and offices could be found, and where petrol was available at night. There's not a railway in sight, though car ferries and airports are shown, with a special 'cross channel airport' category for those on the south coast where you could load your car on to a plane. This was a service that began at Lympne Airport in Kent in 1948, and remained a mainstay of glamorous continental motoring through the 1950s and 60s.

The AA launched its new square logo and sleek contemporary look in 1967, and the handbook was duly revamped for the motorway age too. Between the 1960s and the 1980s, it was an annual thrill to open the latest handbook to see what new blue lines had been inked across the page, for there were always plenty, and they came so thick and fast that it seemed like the novelty would never end. For many, their choice of destination became shaped by the fast roads – if a new blue line pointed towards it, then let's give it a try. Even more excitingly, the updated map would contain a whole new set of dotted lines of intention, of bypasses, ring roads and motorways that, it was to be hoped, might be inked in fully by next year.

In the handbooks, there were growing sections of motorway strip maps, marked with every service station and every junction and its interconnecting A-roads or other motorways. They did not bother with actual geography; the lines were ruler-straight and made no mention of hills, bends, direction or places – however important – en route. While obviously following the cartographic tradition of Ogilby and Cary, these were more the automotive equivalent of Harry Beck's London Underground map, with all extraneous information cut away, leaving just perpetual forward motion and intersections. You could travel all over the country with them, and barely know where you were.

Although with added colours and more modern typefaces, the general mapping of the country barely changed from the early days. It remained at ten miles to the inch, and continued to differentiate the towns and villages with an entry in the accompanying gazetteer – i.e. with at least a hotel, a garage or both – from those without. It also continued to show all motoring organisation phone boxes, and, in more remote areas, general GPO boxes too. For 80 years, the members' handbook remained the one-stop shop for a motoring holiday, secure that the might of the motoring organisations was there if anything went wrong.

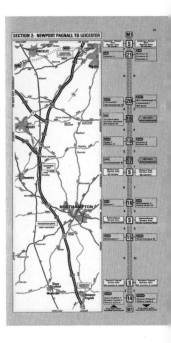

Above: The motorway brought us back to the strip map, seen here in the 1976 AA Handbook

The covers changed significantly too. Pre-war and 1950s maps had tended towards bucolic imagery of old-fashioned villages and lovely scenery. The dawn of the motorway age coincided with a radical new design aesthetic (on the new road signs as much as anywhere else; see 'Signs of the Times', p183), and covers shifted acutely to reflect this. The Gulf petrol *Route Planning Map* of the late 1960s is a fine example, with its sharp brushstroke drawing of what looks like any urban ring road in the land, an angular forest of slip roads, signs, lamp-posts and the distant sight of two new tower blocks overlooking the scene. A couple of pedestrians, walled in by railings alongside the dual carriageway, are perhaps about to descend into the subway under the roundabout, which appears as nothing more enticing than a big dark hole. To a cynical 21st-century eye, the scene looks like a guaranteed recipe for urban decay and squalor. To a 1960s motorist, it looked like the cutting edge of modernity.

Just as the early years of the car had coincided in so many ways with the growth in elementary air travel, so the space age (and jet age) of the 1960s helped ease the way for the massive new road-building programme. The prevailing mood was no longer about tentative post-war optimism and the end of rationing; all eyes were on the future, and that came equally in the race for the moon and the race to a streamlined motorway network. So much of the road imagery and architecture of this age took its cue from all things aeronautic, most famously the Pennine Tower at Forton services on the M6, where little boys of all ages could eat their chips and dream of being a pilot or an astronaut.

Throughout the 1960s, dotted red and blue lines spread like a contagion across the map. Shortly after the opening of the M1, the government announced their intention of having 1,000 miles of motorway open by the end of the decade. Nothing was allowed to stand in the way, and no one much wanted to, for people loved the new motorways and were eager for more. The necessary routes were fairly obvious – the H shape of roads, with the crossbar through the West Midlands, had been a mainstay of all speculative motorway maps since the turn of the 20th century, and could be said to hark back to the roads of the Romans. Completing this shape, together with an east–west link through Wessex and into south

Wales, and another somewhere across the Pennines, were the building blocks of any plan, and they were all on the drawing board.

So much the odder then that the second significant motorway to open, beyond various bypasses later to be slotted in to the network, was the highly rural M50, threading through Worcestershire and Herefordshire to Ross-on-Wye in Gloucestershire. It opened in 1960, and for two years languished in quiet isolation before the new M5 arrived at its eastern end and linked it northwards to the outskirts of Birmingham – not that even that turned it into a major highway. Planned originally as a fast route through from the coalfields of south Wales to the industrial heartland of the West Midlands, it was soon superseded by the M4/M5 over the Severn Bridge, and has never been busy. Personally, it is one of my favourite motorways; its most startling feature is the right-angled junction 3 onto a quiet B road, the whitest-knuckle ride of any motorway junction in Britain.

After the first part of the M5 was built, work continued on extending both the M6 and the M1 as the major 'legs' of the H shape. By 1965 the M6 extended from Lancaster all the way down to Stafford, and the M1 had nearly reached Nottingham. Meanwhile, Britain's most piecemeal motorway, the M4 – it opened in 19 different segments between 1961 and 1994 – was tiptoeing west. In 1966 there were three sections in place: from London to Maidenhead, from northeast of Bristol across the new Severn Bridge to Newport, and the five-mile bypass at Port Talbot, initially christened the A48(M).

These last two sections perfectly encapsulate the 1960s attitude to motorway building, both for better and for worse. Firmly in the latter category is Port Talbot. Even calling the A48(M) a bypass is a misnomer, for it does not circumnavigate the town, but instead thunders right through and above it, towering over terraced streets and forming dark, dank no man's lands beneath its concrete stilts. On the eastern side of town, Groes, the picturesque estate village to Margam Abbey, was erased completely from the map and now lies entombed under junction 39. The motorway – one of the very first to be announced in 1954 alongside the M50 and the bypasses of Preston and Lancaster – has been an undiluted curse for the town, which has regularly topped national pollution tables ever since.

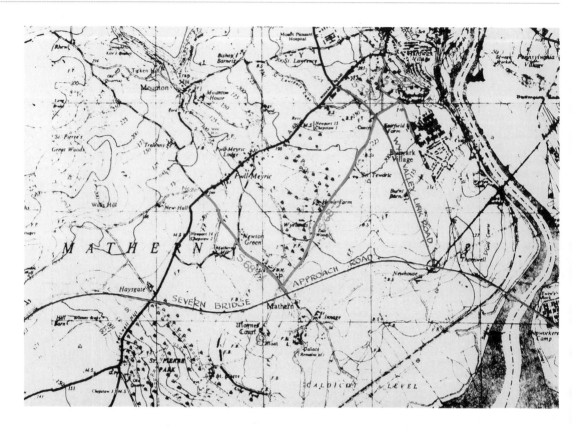

Above: Department of Transport plan c.1960. One of the earliest parts of the M4 was also one of its most challenging: planning and building the Severn Bridge connecting England and Wales

The Bristol to Newport stretch included two far more optimistic symbols of the new age. The Severn Bridge, a graceful arc of steel and concrete over one of the most extreme tides in the world, was opened by Queen Elizabeth II on the morning of 8 September 1966. She then motored seven miles to open the Almondsbury interchange north of Bristol, where the embryonic M4 was destined to meet the future M5 (still five years away). As Britain's first major motorway intersection, Almondsbury was conceived with all the extravagance and excitement that the age could muster: a 100-acre junction in the shape of a Maltese cross, with roads on four levels intersecting at its heart. After inspecting it shortly before the opening, transport minister Barbara Castle wrote in her diary that these blasts of highway Americana 'are the cathedrals of the modern world';

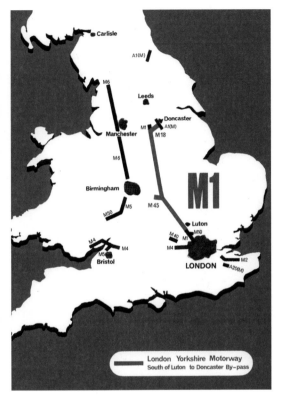

London Yorkshire Motorway
South of Luton to Doncaster By-pass

MOTORWAYS COMPLETED
MOTORWAYS PROJECTED
THE MIDLAND LINKS AND
ASTON EXPRESSWAY

Scale of Miles
0 10 20   40   60   80   100

Map of Midland Links and Aston Expressway in relation to
the rest of the country

the cross shape was perhaps not entirely incidental. But there were signs that the enthusiasm was already beginning to wane, and the next crop of big interchanges, such as Worsley near Manchester and Birmingham's Spaghetti Junction, were far more cramped, conflicted affairs.

Above: Motorways complete in 1967 (left) and 1972 (right)

It's worth taking a moment to compare the 1960s spread of new roads with the rapid shrinking of the rail network at the same time, for the two went hand in hand. If you look at a decent map from the early 1960s, it is a snapshot of a unique moment in time when the two briefly co-existed, and is enough to make a transport buff faintly giddy.

In March 1963 the Beeching Report into Britain's railways was published, recommending the closure of 5,000 miles of track, and 2,363 stations. Trains were the past; the car was the future. Beeching, a

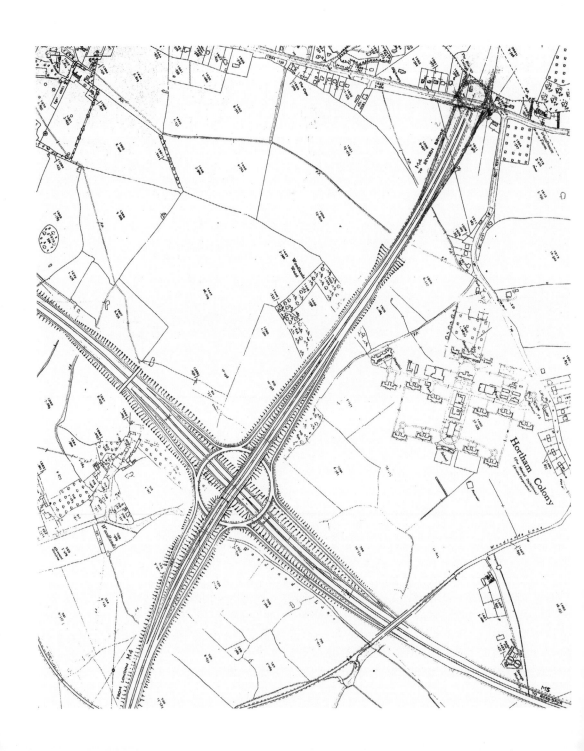

director at ICI, had been commissioned by the Conservative transport minister Ernest Marples. Marples was also the founder and owner of a civil engineering company, Marples Ridgway, which had won some of the motorway-building contracts. When a conflict of interest was pointed out, Marples reluctantly promised to sell his 80 per cent share. After being blocked from selling it to his business partner, he sold it to his wife instead. He became Sir, and then Lord Marples, before fleeing his Belgravia apartment one night in 1975 for Monaco, to avoid charges of tax fraud. He never returned to Britain.

Opposite: The Ministry of Transport's tentative plan for the M4/M5 Almondsbury interchange, near Bristol

However loaded was the evidence against the railways and for the roads, in fairness Marples and his like were pushing at an open door. The public wanted the freedom and convenience of the car, and they wanted fast roads on which to use them. A few voices were being raised to question whether the rush to concrete over swathes of the country was the right plan, but they were easily drowned out by the palpable excitement of almost everyone else. Driving had become the national hobby – at least for the male half of the country. By the late 1960s, still only about 15 per cent of women held a driving licence.

THE GOOD, THE BAD AND THE UGLY

Asked to nominate their favourite motorway, most people plump for one of two impressive stretches opened a year apart at the very beginning of the 1970s. The first was the Westmorland section of the M6 from Lancaster to Penrith, where the carriageways divide and swoop through the green fells (and as an added bonus, it's also home to everyone's favourite service station at Tebay).

The second is even more dramatic, if melancholy: Britain's highest motorway, which peaks at 1,221 feet. The need for a reliable trans-Pennine route was urgent; the A62 between Manchester and Leeds was at breaking point, and would often be blocked for weeks in the winter. To get the M62 over just seven miles of upland moor took seven years of grinding hard work, the hardest ever endured by any motorway constructors. Twelve million cubic yards of peat had to be removed; some of the excavating vehicles were swallowed whole by it. Millions of tons of rock were blasted out, broken down and compacted to create retaining walls

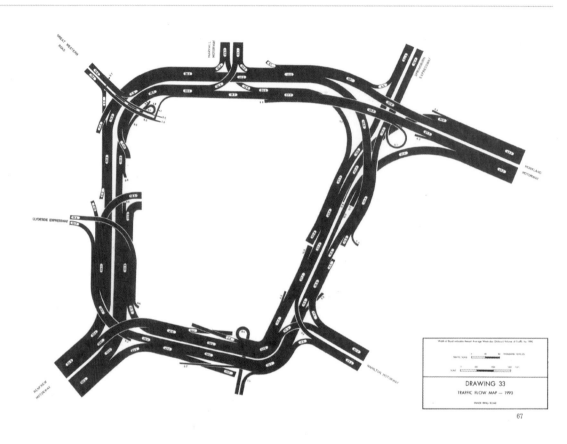

DRAWING 33
TRAFFIC FLOW MAP — 1990

67

Above: Glasgow's brutal 1960s plan to encircle the city centre with a tourniquet of tarmac

and the dam at Scammonden along which the motorway runs. And all at over 1,000 feet in the bleak Pennines, in weather of dense – and often freezing – fog, biting gales, snow and some of the highest rainfall in the country. Such was the scale of the job that, every Sunday, day trippers from surrounding towns would pack a thermos and drive over for a look. And still we come now, to sit in one of the designated picnic sites overlooking the motorway or to photograph perhaps the most iconic sight on the network: the 18th-century Stott Hall Farm, which sits between the two separated carriageways. My late uncle Jim, a proud West Riding man, took me to see it when I was 12 and told me of the gritty farmer who'd forced the motorway around him by refusing to sell up. It was, sadly, untrue – the carriageways diverge here for purely pragmatic reasons of geology.

The folk that overlook the M8 through Glasgow don't generally do it out of choice. It's hard to know which section of our motorway network is the most brutal, but this must be a strong contender. As detailed in Chapter 4, Scotland's largest city has long been a pioneer of grand, sweeping schemes. Add the knock-it-down, start-again spirit of the 1960s, and anything was possible.

It's often said that Glasgow, with its tight central grid of streets veering up and down the contours of Blythswood Hill, is the closest we have to an American city, and it was to the US that the city fathers travelled for inspiration. Not for them the effete British obsession with roundabouts and polite arterials; the plan that they drew up was for freeways, slip roads, ramps and underpasses speeding traffic unchecked around a multi-laned Inner Ring Road. Only half got built, in a tight bend around the north and west of the city centre, including the 10-lane Kingston Bridge over the Clyde. There are many tantalising signs of the never-built east and southern sections: the gargantuan junction at Townhead with its knot of slip roads pointing south into sudden backstreet anonymity, the strange curved dualling of Laurieston Road in the Gorbals, which was destined to be the ring road's southeastern corner, an assortment of 'bridges to nowhere' and, most famous of all, the truncated pair of carriageways sticking out into the sky and known as 'the ski jump'.

This mammoth scheme was never just about the roads; it was also a concerted effort at slum clearance, and moving people out into the tower blocks of brand new estates on the city's edge, such as Easterhouse and Castlemilk. But the same idea was inflicted on older areas of the city, such as the Gorbals, Sighthill, Pollokshaws and Govan; these too became a forest of tower blocks. It was all about getting rid of the hated, cramped tenements that were the mainstay of the city's housing stock. Of course, those now are highly prized and in great demand; you can see why if you visit the lovely Tenement House Museum in Buccleuch Street. It's the final house in the street now, for the rest were swept away to make way for the M8 thrumming past the window.

A look at a late 1960s road atlas gives a clear picture of the new world emerging, but also the unwelcome touches of the old world in the shape of the notorious bottlenecks and pinch points in the system. They're as plain as day: numerous roads converging on the centres of York, Chester,

Carlisle, Reading, Bath, Cardiff, Cambridge, Edinburgh, Bedford, Sheffield, Birmingham, Lincoln, Newcastle, Perth and so many more. To ease them, the map shows an increasing number not just of motorways, but of bypasses and ring roads too. The inner ring road, pioneered so boldly in Coventry, was a staple of 1960s planning, never mind what it did to a town's history or geography. In Dewsbury, the 13th-century Moot Hall was demolished for a ring road, while just down the road in Huddersfield, a tight dual carriageway around the town's Victorian heart was the only way to ensure, as the council put it, that 'the car becomes the servant and not the master'.

The promised 1,000 miles of motorway was duly delivered by the beginning of 1971. A new target was set, of another 1,000 miles by 1980, but attitudes were already turning. Surprisingly perhaps, it was not the sections of motorway through virgin countryside that caused most doubts, but those that squeezed their way into towns and cities. As long as those towns were as marginalised and downtrodden as the likes of Port Talbot, Glasgow and Eccles, then no one much got to hear about it. But as soon as the road builders took on the highly vocal residents of rapidly gentrifying west London, it was a call to arms heard by the whole country.

The saga of the Westway, now relegated for political reasons back to the status of mere A-road after 30 years as a motorway, is part of a much larger story of the great plan for a series of four concentric ringways around London. This had been a planners' dream since the 1903 Royal Commission on London Traffic, though it first attracted serious attention in the post-Blitz ruins of the 1940s. Town planner Sir Patrick Abercrombie produced two wartime reports on the rebuilding of London; he presents his ideas in a fascinating 1946 Ministry of Information film, *The Proud City: A Plan for London*, which can be seen online. The film's opening words ('London – the greatest city the world has ever known') sets its rather pompous and patrician tone, alongside exhortations that we must, as a nation, be bold in our new thinking. In the film, Abercrombie talks of 'London as a machine', hampered by a chaotic lack of planning and 'an out-of-date street system'.

Opposite: Few UK cities went as wholeheartedly for urban motorways as did Glasgow, as shown in this aerial view of the M8, slicing through the city centre

Overleaf: August 1969: an aerial view of the Western Avenue Extension under construction in west London, at its junction with the proposed West Cross Route. White City stadium can be seen top left

Abercrombie's plans were partially realised, although lack of finances rather than lack of political will meant that the development was piecemeal, and concentrated mainly on slum clearance and rebuilding residential neighbourhoods shattered by bombing. His costly new ring roads were quietly shelved; in a pattern that has become all too familiar, comprehensive rebuilding became the far cheaper option of rebranding instead. Abercrombie had wanted brand new roads to form the South and North Circular routes, but while the names survived, they were attached instead mostly to existing roads. As Sutton and Cheam MP Richard Sharples put it in a 1955 House of Commons debate: 'The South Circular Road exists solely by courtesy of the excellent sign-posting arrangements which have been made by one of the motoring organisations. But for that, I do not think that the South Circular Road could be said to exist at all.'

The plans for four concentric ring roads were once again dusted off when the new Greater London Council (GLC) came into being in 1965. It was keen to establish its credentials with streamlined and radical ideas; the ringway plan fitted that perfectly, though it may well have proved to be an idea too far. The modernist thirst that had erupted in response to the war was still humming in areas of planning and transport, but its days were numbered, and the hubristic plans for massive new roads through and around London helped seal its fate.

Although the M25 is a legacy of the plan – it's a hybrid of the outer ringways 3 and 4 – the only parts of the scheme in inner London that made it to fruition were the East Cross Route from Hackney to the Blackwall Tunnel, formerly the A102(M), and the West Cross Route in Shepherds Bush, formerly the M41. Connecting to the latter was the A40(M), the Westway, and although not strictly part of one of the ringways, it was designed as a link from ringway 1 to the Marylebone Road, and very much along the same lines. Britain's longest continuous chunk of concrete was to be a much-needed link, picking up where the Western Avenue had so abruptly come to a halt 40 years before at White City. Traffic coming in from the west was disgorged onto the already-congested roads of Shepherds Bush. Rat-running and accidents were commonplace.

In the 1960s North Kensington and Paddington were rundown areas with transient, often immigrant, populations. The area was still smarting from the Notting Hill riots of the late 1950s; local radical black newsletter *The Hustler* wrote in 1968 that 'North Kensington is a running sore on the rich fleshy arse of South Kensington'. Add to that the growing number of middle classes moving in, attracted by the cheap Victorian housing, and there was a potent mix brewing.

Site clearance began in 1964; hundreds of houses were demolished. Building the 2.5-mile elevated road took four years, and made life miserable for residents. Streets were severed, others left just yards from the side of the new motorway as it thundered past bedroom windows; compensation for such inconvenience was not yet a statutory requirement. When the road was opened by Michael Heseltine in the summer of 1970, protestors heckled his speech, disrupted his official cavalcade as it took its tour of inspection of the new road, and hung a massive banner along the length of the Victorian terraces of Acklam Road, hard against the Westway's concrete shoulder. It read 'GET US OUT OF THIS HELL – REHOUSE US NOW'. Heseltine commented that 'you cannot help but have sympathy for these people', thus helping ensure that such a scheme was unlikely ever again to be thrust through a British city. Although it took a few more years to be officially confirmed, London's ringway scheme was dead.

A BRIDGE TOO FAR

If Sir Patrick Abercrombie's ideas for London were radical, his proposals for the uniquely hilly – and uniquely beautiful – topography of Edinburgh were nothing short of revolutionary. In contrast with London, the Scottish capital had suffered very little wartime bomb damage, although there was a considerable slum problem in the city. It is clear that Abercrombie's thinking came from a philosophical belief in streamlining modernism, rather than a practical one.

In 1949, he published the *Civic Survey and Plan for the City & Royal Burgh of Edinburgh*, which advocated several jaw-dropping measures. He wanted the wholesale replacement of Princes Street by uniform buildings, with an upper

*Opposite: Abercrombie's
1949 proposal for a
radical remodeling of
Edinburgh's monumental
city centre, which formed
the basis of even more
controversial plans well
into the late 1960s*

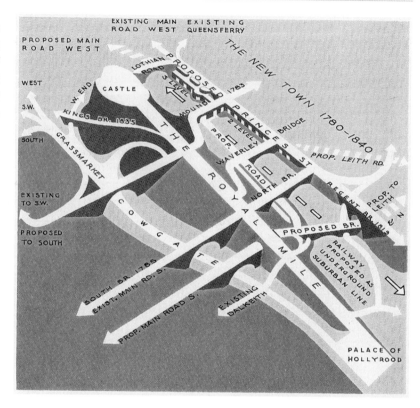

level along them to produce a second street of shops and a subterranean
new road beneath it, open at the side to overlook the gardens beneath the
castle, to form part of a fast inner ring. Other sections of the proposed ring
included a new fast road tunneled underneath Calton Hill, before resurfacing
at a large intersection, where one new road would roar through Princes Street
Gardens beneath the Walter Scott memorial, and another be barreled under
a new bridge beneath the Royal Mile. The car was unequivocally king, for the
proposals included downgrading Waverley station for local services only and
burying it underground, and the relocation of long-distance rail services to a
terminus away from the city centre.

Although the plan was never realised in full, elements of it did get built,
and it formed the basis of more extreme proposals in the 1960s for even larger

dual carriageways and looping motorway intersections in the city centre, the University quarter to the south, and the Tollcross district of the West End. This was to be a fully-dualled inner ring road, tightly encircling both the Old and New Towns of the city centre and causing maximum damage where the twin rock plugs of Calton Hill and Arthur's Seat forced it towards the city's heart.

Had it been built, a section of the Royal Mile would have been demolished for the new bridge, as proposed by Abercrombie – but, by now, the proposed road underneath had been upgraded to an urban motorway. One of the most celebrated medieval thoroughfares in the country would have been irreversibly destroyed. Some demolition of old housing stock took place to facilitate the 1960s plans, but they thankfully stalled, save for a few strange gaps in the city's skyline and the preparatory roundabout and dualling of Leith Walk.

There is another significant remnant of this Utopian vision still visible today, in the various 1960s buildings along the north side of Princes Street. Abercrombie's 1949 proposal for a two-tier street in the modernist style was enthusiastically taken up by the Princes Street Panel in its 1967 plan, and some of it was built. The first floor walkway, envisaged as a whole new high-rise street of shops, can still be seen along the front of Edinburgh's venerable New Club at 84–87 Princes Street, the Boots store at 101–103 and the recently vacated British Home Stores at number 64. In total, seven new buildings sprung up in this style, but the idea was dropped in the 1970s, leaving not a continuous, high-level street but a disjointed collection of brutalist blocks with over-generous balconies. More than perhaps any other city in Britain, the story of what might have happened to Edinburgh produces the greatest shiver down the spine.

The bubble of space-age can-do optimism, which had been steadily inflating since VE Day a full quarter of a century before, was threatening to pop. But first, the main H grid of motorways needed to have its last piece slotted in: the section of the M6 in Birmingham that would link up the entire system. Way before it was opened, the Gravelly Hill Interchange was already known by all as Spaghetti Junction, a name that had been coined by the Birmingham *Evening Mail* back in 1965. It didn't help assuage the public's growing ambivalence towards the motorways. A government memo harrumphed that 'the term "spaghetti" should be

*Above and opposite:
Birmingham's Gravelly
Hill interchange – far
more widely known as
Spaghetti Junction – on
a planning map and in
concrete reality*

strictly discouraged. It was the use of this nickname that helped to give rise to many fears about the junction before it was opened, which have since proved groundless.'

Despite its scale and fame, Spaghetti Junction is not the apex of the motorway system – that accolade probably belongs to the great triangle of flyovers two junctions further up the M6, where it meets the M5. It's really only a local junction, for traffic into the city, up to Erdington and Sutton Coldfield, or along the A38. All the same, it is possibly the most iconic symbol of both the motorways and – much to the chagrin of the city's tourism bureau – of Brum itself. An aerial view of the tangle of roads has been the city's best-selling postcard for decades. As an ex-pat Midlander, it still thrills me every time to rise high over the chaos and drop down onto the A38(M) into the city, clocking glimpses of the Jacobean Aston Hall and the neighbouring Villa football ground, and, in the distance, the glittering towers of the city centre. It's a fitting entrance to Motor City.

Spaghetti Junction was opened on 24 May 1972. The basic frame of the British motorway system was finally in place; you could now drive unhindered – except by jams or accidents – from Carlisle to London, or Bristol to Leeds. The opening ceremony was conducted by Peter Walker, the first occupant of the new post of Secretary of State for the Environment. Sticking slightly desperately to his brief, he informed the assembled dignitaries and media that the Gravelly Hill Interchange was 'an illustration of how motorways can improve environments'. The good people of west London, or Glasgow, or even Birmingham might have had something to say about that. And if no one was really listening to them, there were louder voices in the Middle East that would soon make themselves heard loud and clear.

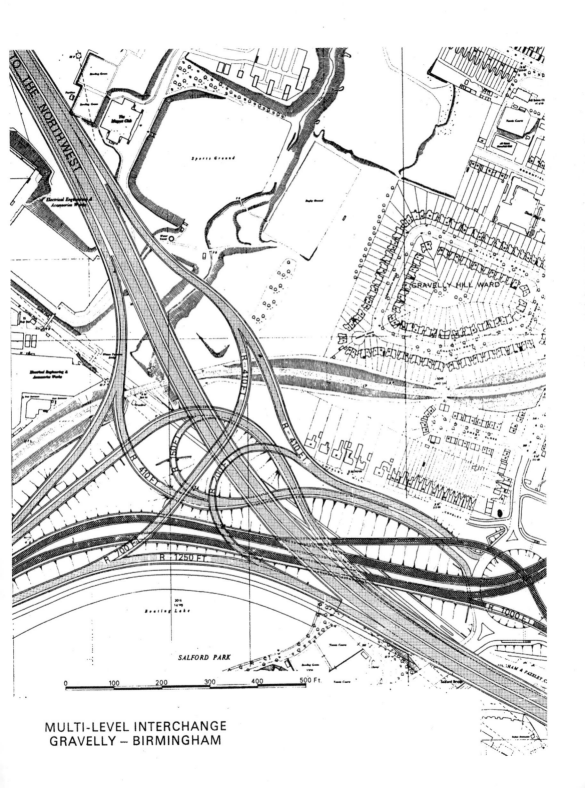

MULTI-LEVEL INTERCHANGE
GRAVELLY – BIRMINGHAM

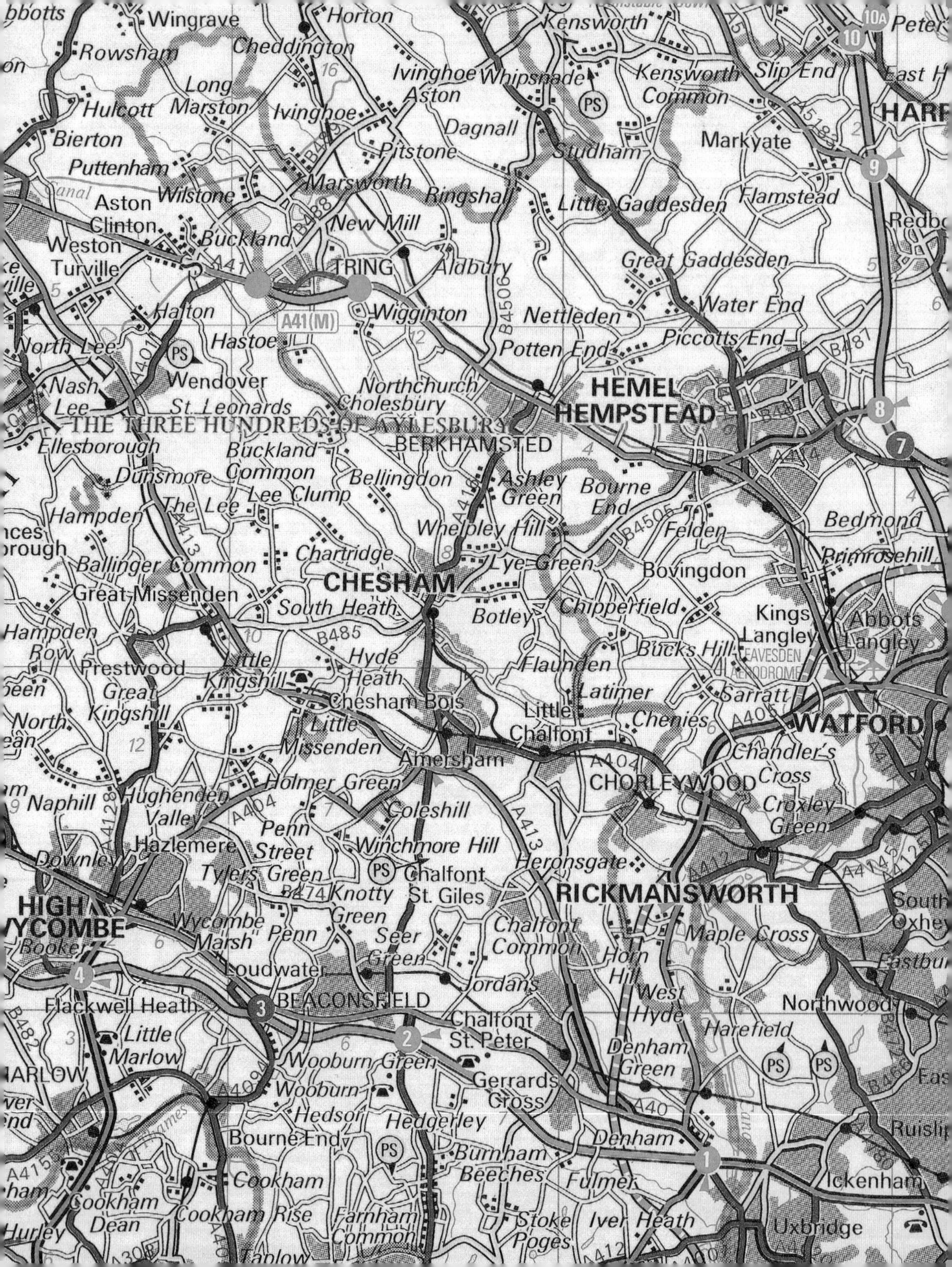

Wingrave
Horton
Kensworth
Rowsham
Cheddington
Ivinghoe Aston
Whipsnade
Kensworth Common
Slip End
Long Marston
Hulcott
Ivinghoe
Dagnall
Markyate
Bierton
Pitstone
Studham
Puttenham
Marsworth
Ringshall
Little Gaddesden
Flamstead
Canal
Aston Clinton
Wilstone
New Mill
Buckland
Weston Turville
TRING
Aldbury
Great Gaddesden
A41
Halton
A41(M)
Wigginton
Nettleden
Water End
Hastoe
Potten End
Piccotts End
North Lee
Wendover
Northchurch
Nash Lee
St. Leonards
Cholesbury
HEMEL HEMPSTEAD
THE THREE HUNDREDS OF AYLESBURY
BERKHAMSTED
Ellesborough
Buckland Common
Dunsmore
Bellingdon
Ashley Green
Bourne End
The Lee
Lee Clump
Hampden
Whelpley Hill
Felden
Bedmond
Chartridge
Lye Green
Primrosehill
Ballinger Common
Bovingdon
CHESHAM
Great Missenden
South Heath
Botley
Chipperfield
Kings Langley
Abbots Langley
Hampden Row
B485
Hyde Heath
Bucks Hill
LEAVESDEN AERODROME
Prestwood
Little Kingshill
Flaunden
Great Kingshill
Chesham Bois
Latimer
Sarratt
North Dean
Little Missenden
Little Chalfont
Chenies
WATFORD
Amersham
A404
Chandler's Cross
Naphill
Hughenden Valley
Holmer Green
CHORLEYWOOD
Croxley Green
A404
Coleshill
Penn Street
Hazlemere
Winchmore Hill
A413
Downley
Heronsgate
Tylers Green
Chalfont St. Giles
HIGH WYCOMBE
Knotty Green
RICKMANSWORTH
South Oxhey
Booker
Wycombe Marsh
Penn
Seer Green
Chalfont Common
Maple Cross
Loudwater
Jordans
Horn Hill
Eastbury
Flackwell Heath
BEACONSFIELD
West Hyde
Northwood
Chalfont St. Peter
Little Marlow
Harefield
MARLOW
Wooburn Green
Denham Green
Gerrards Cross
Wooburn
A40
Hedsor
Hedgerley
Ruislip
Bourne End
Denham
Burnham Beeches
Cookham
Fulmer
Ickenham
Cookham Dean
Cookham Rise
Farnham Common
Stoke Poges
Iver Heath
Uxbridge
Hurley
Taplow

Chapter 6

AUTO ADDICTS

(1973–92)

Above: Exquisite illustrations from the 1966 AA Illustrated Road Book of England & Wales

Previous page: The AA Motorists Atlas from 1985 sees the M25 gradually taking shape around London

On 16 October 1973, in response to Western intervention in the Yom Kippur war, the Organisation of the Petroleum Exporting Countries (OPEC) raised the price of a barrel of crude oil by 70 per cent, from $3 to $5.11. Their decision also to cut production, and the jitters produced by the crisis in the West, meant that, by the turn of 1974, market forces had taken the price of crude oil to $12, four times the price of a year earlier.

The effects were instant, and dramatic. Fuel shortages returned for the first time since the late 1940s; there was even talk of a return to ration books. Prices rocketed on and off the forecourt. The UK's GDP went from a growth of 5.1 per cent in 1972 to a 1.1 per cent contraction in 1974. Strikes, power cuts, three-day weeks and two general elections in eight months demonstrated all too clearly that a new, far less confident era was beginning.

Even the road maps reflected the new mood. Since the late 1950s the friendly petrol station and its up-to-date maps, often given away or sold at cost price, had been a major part of people's lives, and they were often very loyal to their chosen brand. The crisis tainted this for ever, dredging up as it did the rather less appealing realisation that oil companies had all been indulging in price fixing and post-colonial strong-arm tactics, and that what was happening was the inevitable comeuppance. In a 1974 BBC interview the personable Saudi Minister for Oil, Sheikh Yamani, was asked if this 'was a change in the world balance of power, between the developing nations like you, the producers, and us, the developed, industrialised nations?' Yamani gave an enigmatic smile and quietly answered, 'Yes. It will be.'

In order to cut costs, petrol stations were rapidly turned over to self-service operations, and trappings such as the free maps disappeared. To fill the gap, commercial cartographers started to produce more road maps and atlases, though these of course were far from free. In the 1950s and 60s, such road atlases as there had been played to their market, which was mainly the motoring middle classes off for a jaunt around stately homes and tea shops. To that end, many of the products on offer were gazetteers as much as maps, full of historical notes and beautiful illustrations. To my eye, the loveliest of all were the AA's Illustrated Road

Books of *England & Wales* and *Scotland*, where the gorgeous Bartholomew mapping constituted only about one-tenth of each book's considerable bulk. Most of the rest was a spectacularly detailed gazetteer of cities, towns and villages, and their points of historical interest. As well as the churches and manor houses, there was a healthy interest in all sorts of oddments, from follies to bridges, gibbets to odd signposts. Every other page of the gazetteer was given over to half a dozen pen-and-ink illustrations of some of the highlights mentioned opposite. They are books that many of us still use today.

ALWAYS A WELCOME – THE SERVICE STATION

Above: Bringing a blast of Americana to Lancashire, the Grill & Griddle restaurant on the bridge over the M6 at Charnock Richard service station, mid-1960s

As the oil crisis and ensuing recession bit, the big sibling of the petrol station – the motorway service area – also had to trim its offerings to suit the new reality. When the first services had opened on the M1, back at the tail end of the 1950s, they were bright bubbles of 24-hour, neo-American glamour, the hang-out of choice for the cool crowd. Many 1960s rock stars wax lyrical in their autobiographies about post-gig 2am stops at Newport Pagnell; it's said that when Jimi Hendrix arrived in Britain, he thought that the Blue Boar (the name of the operators of Watford Gap services) was some funky London club, as he'd heard about it so often.

The services were happy to build the aura of glamorous mystique. In the 1960s, customers were often welcomed at the door by young women who looked more like air hostesses. Some offered silver service cuisine – at Leicester Forest East, on the M1, this was in the Terence Conran-designed Captain's Table restaurant, with waitresses dressed as sailors and an in-house pianist. Like many service station eateries, the Captain's Table was located on the connecting bridge overlooking the motorway, which seemed like a marvellous idea at the time, but which soon proved to be the last view most frazzled motorists wanted to gaze at. For the first few years of the Farthing Corner services on the M2 in Kent, the bridge restaurant was largely al fresco.

Come the 1970s, the companies started to give up on trying to make service stations destinations in which to linger, and moved towards the more familiar idea of minimum loitering and maximum throughput. Even then, they held an air of excitement and anonymity, a place in limbo where anything might happen. And probably did; the pre-CCTV service station was the obvious place for illicit trysts, criminal assignations, gatherings of ravers and the swapping of subdued children between divorced parents. It was all a great deal more thrilling than the food, which – to absolutely no one's surprise – was condemned by restaurant critic Egon Ronay as 'pig swill'.

The map of motorway service stations brought a sweet, fleeting fame to obscure villages all over Britain. Who would ever have heard of Charnock Richard, Gordano, Leigh Delamere, Woolley Edge, Toddington or Pease Pottage without them? Even that poetic (and polite – it's nice to thank your hosts, after all) trend is disappearing. Like the old names of football grounds being elbowed aside in favour of various flavours of MegaCorp Arena, current thinking is that instead of naming the services after their nearest village, however insignificant, they need more recognisable, even aspirational, handles. And so it's been farewell Scratchwood, Farthing Corner, Forton, Rothersthorpe and Harthill, and hello instead London Gateway, Medway, Lancaster, Northampton and the Heart of Scotland.

People in the 1970s, rather brutalised and cynical by comparison with their motoring forebears, just wanted to get from A to B as quickly – and, more importantly, as cheaply – as possible, and the new breed of road atlas reflected that. Gone were the flowery descriptions of Tudor gabling and literary connections, to be replaced by far more pragmatic needs. The AA's *Motorists Atlas*, first published in 1977, cut to the quick with its first 20 pages, as detailed in the Contents:

Emergency Situations	4–5
Mechanical Failures	6–7
Emergency Problem	8–9
Preparation for Emergencies	10–11
Skidding	12–13
Skid Pans	14–15
Emergency Quiz	16–17
Emergency Toolkit	18

Everyone can prepare themselves to cope with emergencies. Each time you go out in a car, whether as the driver or not, you should observe and study the road in order to anticipate what will develop. Accurate anticipation often prevents emergencies. Keep asking yourself what you would do if the situation ahead of you changed suddenly and dramatically.

You should take every opportunity to practise and improve your car control. This should not be done on a public road but on a specialised training area, skid-pan, or a disused airfield.

Several specialist courses are available in advanced and high speed driving and these are extremely useful as a start towards preparing yourself to deal with emergencies. A most valuable feature of these courses is that they reveal any weaknesses or bad habits in your driving, enabling you to overcome them. After that, continue to practise the relevant techniques.

ANTICIPATION AND CONTROL

Most emergency situations can be prevented by good observation and intelligent anticipation. Careful reading of the road scene and gentle car handling should ensure that you enter each situation at the right speed and in perfect control.

BRAKING

The general rules about braking, whether in an emergency situation or not are:

1. Brake in plenty of time.
2. Brake firmly only when travelling in a straight line.
3. Vary the brake pressure according to the condition of the road surface.

When preparing to handle a possible future-emergency situation, an important aspect of car control is to practise braking from speed. You should know just how hard you can brake in your car without locking the wheels and losing steering control.

Practise, off the public roads, driving at a series of different speeds, then slowing the car down in a straight line by adjusting the braking pressures. When you have mastered control at one speed try a slightly higher one.

Once you can control the braking of your car from speed, start gently swerving to one side while braking and keeping steering control at all times. This will increase your confidence in your own driving ability and will help you to react positively to emergencies.

Reading the road well ahead enables you to spot hold-ups such as lorries turning in good time, so you can avoid braking harshly.

Sharp observation is needed when driving in busy streets to spot the pedestrians stepping into the road, as well as other hazards.

When following a large vehicle, particularly on a narrow road, keep a safe distance and when possible look along its nearside.

The parked van actually conceals some road works, as the observant driver will have noted from the warning sign ahead.

Observing the road beyond the lorry would have given you advance warning of the parked car.

Seeing the broken-down lorry in plenty of time helps you make an early lane change, minimising disruption to traffic flow.

UNDER-STEER

A small degree of understeering characteristics are designed into most modern cars. This gives them stability in a straight line at speed, under crosswind conditions and also when cornering.

The front of the car tends to run wider than the curve of the bend and this must be countered by greater movement of the steering in the direction of the bend.

OVER-STEER

The behaviour of an over-steering car on a bend is the opposite of one with understeer. The car tends to turn in towards the bend, because the centrifugal force moves the rear of the car outwards. This requires a steering correction in order to maintain control. An oversteering car will not have the inherent stability of an understeering one in gusty crosswinds, and will need constant steering correction. Correction will also be required on roads with pronounced changes in road cambers.

As the speed at which a bend is taken is increased, so the steering characteristics of a car will change. One which normally has a degree of understeer will, at high speed on a corner, develop neutral steer and then change to over-steer. This transition should, ideally, be progressive and predictable. If it takes place too rapidly it can be unexpected and dangerous.

CAR CARE

However proficient the driver in coping with an emergency, it is essential that the car behaves and responds reliably and as expected. This is only achieved if it is maintained in good condition.

Great stress will be thrown on the brakes, tyres, steering and hydraulic dampers in dealing with an emergency, and these should always be kept in first class condition. The driving exercises above will indicate whether any of them is deficient.

Brakes If these are not working at full efficiency, it will take you longer to stop. Have the brakes and brake fluid levels checked regularly and do not wait to replace friction linings until they are worn down.

Tyres The steering response can be critically affected by the wrong, or incorrectly inflated, tyre. Tyre pressures should be checked regularly, and tyres inspected for signs of over- or under-inflation.

Hydraulic dampers Weak dampers can cause the car to pitch badly with an increased tendency to roll. This can seriously affect braking and steering, particularly in an emergency situation.

Windscreen A clean windscreen free from smears will aid observation and visibility, particularly if an emergency should arise. Good windscreen wipers and an effective screen wash are also important.

Headlights Properly adjusted headlights will maximise your own vision when driving at night, and also minimise dazzle to others.

Seat belts Make sure your seat belts work properly, and, if you have children, install approved safety restraints to the back seat. Front seat passengers must now wear seat belts, by law.

Parcel shelf Keep the rear parcel shelf free from loose objects which could fly forward during a collision, into the necks of the driver or passengers. Even light objects can be dangerous if propelled with enough force.

Roll-over bar If driving an open car have a roll-over bar fitted. If a car without one turns over, the occupants have no protection.

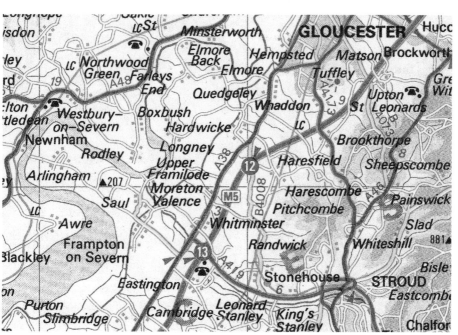

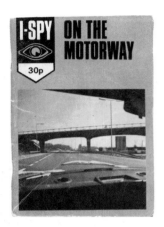

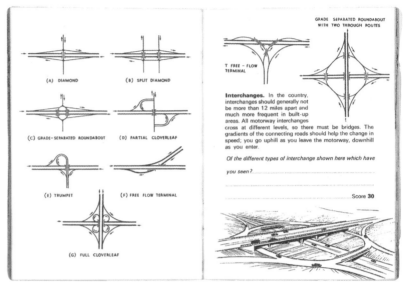

Above and right: Before headrest DVD players and iPads, what children did for fun on car journeys: the I-Spy on the Motorway book (1977), first published in the 1960s

No pretty ink drawings here, just a catalogue of grainy photographs showing a series of grim, and very staged, examples of Ford Capris overtaking badly, having their windscreens suddenly shattered and performing skids worthy of *Starsky & Hutch*. This was followed by the mapping, which was similarly functional: no relief shading nor spot heights on the road (major mountain summits, way off the road, were the only points of elevation given), and very little historical or tourist information either. 'AA viewpoints', with their blue semicircle hatching symbol, are mentioned in the index, but they are very few and far between. There are apparently none at all in the Scottish Highlands, the Lake District, nor the whole of Wales; instead, you'll find them by the M5 at Gloucester, on the outskirts of Portsmouth and in the middle of Portishead on the Bristol Channel. There's a similarly random selection of picnic sites marked, but that's it. Not a cathedral or abbey, no mention of the site of the Battle of Hastings, nor, for that matter, Alton Towers or Longleat, both doing a roaring trade by then.

All in all, the mapping has a real 1970s flavour to it, that of a slightly rootless, technotronic age. With no sense of height anywhere, save for a few arrows on particularly steep gradients, it implies that driving around Britain was a breeze on the smooth blue motorways, green trunk roads and red A roads. It was the grown-up version of my 1974 *I-Spy on the Motorway* book, which encouraged us to know the difference between split diamond, trumpet and full cloverleaf junctions and to 'think of your car as a magic carpet'. The reality was very different.

WELSH WAYS

From the 'flower power' of Carnaby Street to the social revolutions being enacted in parliament, the late 1960s and early 1970s saw rapid political change in all areas of life, and in all corners of the land. In Wales, a new nationalist spirit emerged, a fact that was soon especially evident on the roads.

A significant part of the fervent new politics was around the Welsh language, which, despite being the mother tongue of most of the population in huge areas of Wales, still had no legal status. The new road signs that had appeared throughout the 1960s in the wake of the Worboys report were stubbornly monolingual; even towns that had names in both languages, and where Welsh remained the *lingua franca* of everyday life (such as Carmarthen/Caerfyrddin, Holyhead/Caergybi and Cardigan/Aberteifi) were identified only by their English appellation.

For activists of the Welsh Language Society, road signs were an obvious, high-profile target, and the sight of daubed or uprooted signs became commonplace on road verges from Barry to Bangor. The campaign was ultimately successful, and since 1972 it has been policy to have both languages on road signs, with the Welsh first in areas where the language is strongest, and English first elsewhere. In the same spirit, names of other towns that had been anglicised, usually by the Victorians, reverted to their historic Welsh orthography: Dolgellau for Dolgelley, Llanybydder for Llanybyther, Aberdyfi for Aberdovey.

1972 also saw the birth of an unlikely icon of Welsh nationhood: the A470 trunk road. From Roman times, nearly all main arteries in Wales – road and then rail – have run east to west; the *Western Mail* newspaper ran a campaign to reclassify some existing A-roads running north to south as a single entity and

Above: The sight of a daubed-out road sign has been a common one in Wales since the late 1960s, as seen here on the A5 at Cerrigydrudion

an exercise in nation-building. And thus was born the A470, 'The Welsh M1', as a Radio 4 series optimistically titled it.

As befits a road hammered out of many others as they wind their way through Wales' sparse upland interior, the A470 makes a song-and-dance of its 186 miles between Cardiff and Llandudno, and is blessed with some very Welsh quirks. The great highway shrinks to a crowded urban street through Blaenau Ffestiniog, Builth Wells and Llanrwst. It hovers in spectacular indecision at the most bewildering junction in Wales, the clock tower in Rhayader, Powys, where it crosses the A44. And, nearby, the road's creation led to its midpoint becoming a designated primary destination on the national road sign network, up there with the big boys. For scores of miles on either side, all signs lead to Llangurig. By the time you reach it, you could be forgiven for expecting some great metropolis, rather than a tiny Montgomeryshire village sleeping quietly in the hills. Only Scotch Corner, that legendary intersection on the A1 that's signposted for miles, comes close in the blink-and-you'd-miss-it stakes.

Throughout the decade, large parts of the country were one big contraflow system as new motorways, bypasses and ring roads – all conceived in the heady days of the 1960s – ground their way through towns and across the landscape. Actress Meera Syal, growing up in the old mining village of Essington near Wolverhampton, captures the mood beautifully in her novel-memoir, *Anita and Me* (1996), as a new motorway interchange (the M6/M54) is built practically on top of them. The disruption, the dust and the diggers 'as shiny and solid as tanks' shatter their tight-knit little microcosm for ever.

The prevailing belief behind most new road building of the day, as espoused in Colin Buchanan's defining study *Traffic in Towns* (1963), was that cars should be separated from everything else, and nothing should impede their way. It was in marked contrast to schemes in other countries, which often incorporated pedestrians, bicycles, light rail and trams into the new road systems.

Buchanan's prescription was faithfully enacted throughout Britain, particularly in the inner ring roads that were causing some of the greatest upheaval. Conceived as the most efficient way of getting traffic through a town, which was possibly true, they were promoted to the towns themselves as being great municipal improvements, which undoubtedly wasn't true. Residents, newly formed civic societies, local newspapers and – eventually – even some politicians and local authorities started to get cold feet. The sight of a dual carriageway ripping its way through the guts of their towns didn't make them – or the town – feel like they were sharing in the space age. It just made the place a little more bleak and disjointed.

As a result, and with money getting ever tighter, many were never finished. Look at any succession of Ordnance Survey maps over the last 50 years and you'll see the telltale signs: roads gingerly creeping, stage by stage, around the centre of numerous towns and cities, the time lapse between editions showing progress slowing down and then finally grinding to an ill-tempered halt. In many cases, the areas of town that were due to be tarmacked over, but which never happened, ended up with the worst of both worlds: a ruinous space carved out by compulsory purchase orders and wholesale demolition, which then mouldered away as wasteland.

It's a phenomenon especially obvious in towns that are rarely on the heritage trail: Croydon, Hinckley, Loughborough, Luton, Dunfermline, Stafford, Oldbury, Hanley (Stoke-on-Trent), Darlington, Leicester, Halifax, Carlisle, Yeovil, Rotherham, Burnley and Watford, to name just some. It's one I know well, as I grew up through the 1970s and 80s in another town that belongs on that list, Kidderminster in north Worcestershire. Three sections of the town's inner ring road had been powered through in swift succession in the late 1960s; the first obliterated by far the most handsome and historic part of the town centre. Although a few people warned that it would prove a mistake, local politicians and newspapers were almost unanimous in pushing it, claiming that the scheme would 'open up a new vista' of the medieval parish church. Indeed it did, although said vista was across five lanes of a busy dual carriageway.

I remember the fourth section of the ring road opening in August 1973, as the local paper was full of hype that the 320-metre sculpted concrete retaining wall was the longest of its kind in Europe. I had no idea what it meant, but it was enough to make me feel vaguely proud (I was only six). The momentum of the whole project then seemed to drain

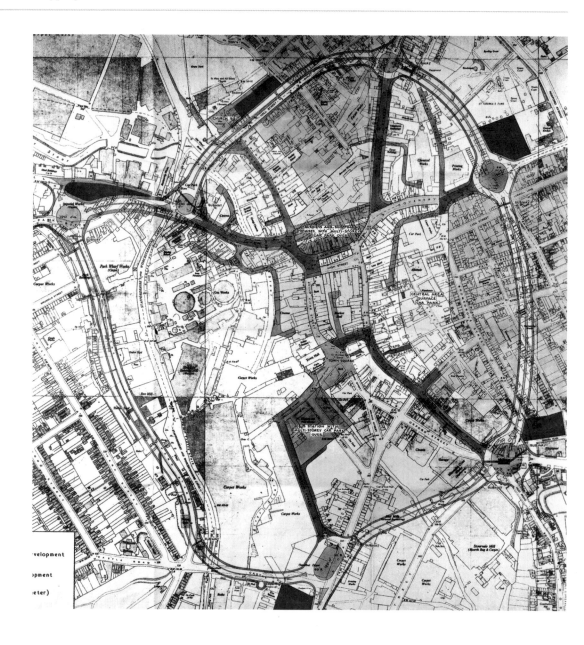

Left: Construction of Kidderminster ring road's massive sculptured concrete wall in the early 1970s. The textured surface, designed by sculptor William Mitchell, aimed to improve the natural weathering of the concrete over time

Opposite: Initial proposed plans for Kidderminster's inner ring road. In the event, the southern section took a different, longer route, and the western side was never built. Note too, the planned obliteration of large parts of the town centre for car parks

away. Plans were outlined for the last two sections; the fifth being finally completed in 1984, many years after the demolition work for it had taken place. In 1978 it was announced that the sixth and final section would not begin for 10 years. Civic dithering escalated, making many people's lives a misery as they faced years of uncertainty. Eventually, in 1996 it was announced that the final segment was not going to be built after all. Now, of course, the redevelopment talk is all about taming the 'concrete collar' ('concrete horseshoe' would be more appropriate), of making the ring road an 'urban boulevard', which mainly translates as putting in a few surface-level pedestrian crossings and a lot of trees. The same follow-the-herd, me-too thinking that caused all the problems is now being touted as their solution.

Kidderminster's sorry story is the tale of so many of our towns. So headstrong and certain were the planners, and so pliant the politicians and press, that the legacy of ring roads and dual carriageways that ran out

Opposite: Looking at the 1945 City of Norwich plan, it's easy to guess which part of the inner ring road never made it off the drawing board: the awkward southernmost section of sharp angles and a prohibitively expensive tunnel

of steam can be found even in some of our county towns and cathedral cities. Canterbury, Worcester, Hereford, Gloucester, Nottingham and Derby all suffered similarly. Salisbury didn't manage to finish its ring road either; one part that never got built was a multi-storey car park, although its considerable access road – which had necessitated the demolition of a number of houses – was ready and waiting. This legendary 'road to nowhere' was finally demolished in 1984 after becoming a national joke (though not as much as Nuneaton's miniature, roundabout-heavy ring road, regularly derided on Terry Wogan's Radio 2 breakfast show).

Norwich, the medieval second city of England, has possibly the oddest road network. It has two incomplete ring roads, an inner and an outer, and the missing chunk in both is the southeastern quadrant. If you're travelling around the outer ring road in this part, the alternatives are either to head in and use the single carriageway section of the inner ring that has been cobbled together out of existing city streets, or to head out a couple of miles and use the A47 bypass. Across the other side of the city centre, the original 1960s/70s inner ring road demolished a medieval church and threw a flyover above one of the city's oldest streets, from which it has never really recovered.

Even cities that are on every tourist's itinerary were roughed up a little before protests pushed the tide back out. Plans to construct an inner ring road across the meadows of Christ Church college in Oxford were bitterly fought over before they were ditched, although the south-western segment of the road, not far from the Thames, went ahead and immediately killed that whole tranche of the city. A similarly truncated scheme was half-built in Cambridge too. The eastern section, well away from the colleges, was put in place, and spawned a new shopping precinct, the Grafton Centre – a strange, in-town version of an out-of-town retail park, kept safely away from the tourist honeypot of the city centre. Nothing else came of the plans, leaving Cambridge physically divided, as in so many other areas of life, between town and gown.

Even Edinburgh, widely held to be the most aesthetically thrilling of all British cities, wasn't immune to the pressures of the age (see 'A Bridge Too Far, p203). The 1949 plans for an inner ring road that would have inflicted untold damage on the city centre resurfaced again and again

Right: Magdalen Street, one of the oldest thoroughfares in Norwich, was ripped in two by the city's inner ring road

right through into the 1970s, before it was finally killed by a changing public mood.

Looking at so many of the early plans for both motorways and urban dual carriageways, plans that were often later watered down or cancelled, there is one striking constant, and that is that the most controversial bits almost always seem to have been constructed first. Were planners aware that they were pushing their luck, and needed to get the worst over at the outset? Thus it was with the M4 through Port Talbot, the M8 through Glasgow, the M25 through Egham and Chorleywood and the M3 through Camberley and Farnborough.

As was so lamentably the case in my home town of Kidderminster, this trend was even more marked with the urban ring roads and expressways. The Derby inner ring road is a good case in point. It's also a graphic timeline of the changing priorities of the last half-century. The first major section, opened in 1969, flattened the city's only surviving Georgian square and demolished St Alkmund's church. The only reminder now comes in the fact that this impenetrable urban motorway, between four and eight lanes wide, is named the St Alkmund's Way.

The next, equally brutal stretch opened in 1972, and then the plan stalled, leaving a large swathe to the southwest of the city centre unbuilt. In 2000 the council announced their intention to complete the ring, and the final two sections were opened in 2010 and 2011. They are wholly different from the other side of the ring road: ground-level roads, sometimes only single carriageway, awash with crossings, calming measures, landscaping and accompanying cycle lanes. And whereas the first stretch was named after the church in its way that had been unceremoniously demolished, the name of the last was put to the public vote, and duly hijacked by an online campaign. An unignorable 89 per cent of the 27,000 votes cast plumped for the name Lara Croft Way, after the pumped-up heroine of the *Tomb Raider* franchise (there is a local connection, in that she was first created by a Derby software developer). The council had no alternative but to accept it through gritted teeth, and there it is on the map.

There were plenty much larger schemes – motorways even – that either never made it off the drawing board or limped off it half-formed. Look at any road atlas of the age, and there are blue dashes of intent striking out in all directions, in plans that never came to fruition. Spectral remnants of these plans can still be seen today.

NEW COUNTIES, NEW MAPS

It wasn't just the money and dwindling public support that scuppered so many road projects in the 1970s and 80s. There was also the reorganisation of local government, which in April 1974 produced a whole new county map of England and Wales and, a year later, Scotland too.

Responsibility for non-motorway and trunk roads had long lain with the local authority: the county borough for the larger towns and cities, and the county council for everywhere else. In the new system, all counties (called 'regions' in Scotland) were subdivided into districts; matters of road planning were the responsibility of the county authority. For many old county boroughs, inclined towards the Labour party, this meant an abrupt change of political

control, as the predominantly rural – and Conservative – counties were now calling the shots on their roads.

The county councils were much less enamoured of urban ring roads and other such projects than their county borough predecessors, and this was a significant fact in the truncated schemes of Norwich, Worcester, Luton, Carlisle, Leicester, Derby, Nottingham, Ipswich, Plymouth, Grimsby, Gloucester, Southampton and Portsmouth. Budgets were instead tilted towards bypasses and relief roads for smaller towns and the suburbs, places that were much more inclined to vote the right way.

Britain's new counties were never much loved. To many, they were the embodiment of clinical 1970s thinking, with names that only confirmed it: Tyne & Wear, Humberside, Avon, Hereford & Worcester, the Central Region, West Midlands, Mid Glamorgan and Greater Manchester (an improvement nonetheless on the original idea for a county called Selnec, an acronym of South-East Lancashire and North-East Cheshire). Gone entirely were nearly all of the traditional Scottish and Welsh counties, and ancient English divisions such as Westmorland, Huntingdonshire, Rutland and the Ridings of Yorkshire.

As luck would have it for Ordnance Survey, 1974 was also the year they launched the long-awaited metric replacement for their flagship 1 inch to 1 mile map. Initially, the new 1:50,000 maps, couched in their startling pink covers, were little more than slightly expanded versions of their one-inch predecessors, with a few colours changed (for example, blue for motorways and grid lines, pinky-brown for housing). The revamped counties gave Ordnance Survey the perfect opportunity to put something radically new on the maps, and at little extra cost. They went for it wholeheartedly, and removed all trace of the old boundaries, including those of parishes, which hadn't in fact been abolished. To those still smarting from the loss of their beloved old counties, 400 or more years old, it was a betrayal that they never quite overcame, nor forgave.

Above: Thwarted plans are often obvious on the map, as seen in this AA Street by Street example of truncated flyovers at the ghost junction where the M23 crashes to an unscheduled halt in Surrey

Opposite: 1980s land art: the M23/M25 interchange, near Merstham in Surrey

Motorways juddering to an unexpectedly sudden, and often quite chaotic, halt are always a sign that things didn't work out as planned. Perhaps the worst example is the M23 from Crawley, designed to whoosh into London on stilts, but just a mile after its elaborate junction with the M25 it comes crashing to a stop in a tangle of unused flyovers and inexplicable loops. Across the other side of the capital at Woodford, there's the strange intersection with the A406 at the bottom of the M11, with its separated carriageways and abandoned slip roads set in acres of wasteland. This was to be the western end of the M12, in its various incarnations, including one that was to head across the sands (on top of a barrage) and slice through the pier of Southend-on-Sea en route to the never-built airport at Maplin Sands.

Alternatively, travel the distinctly odd M53 up the Wirral, a fine example of a motorway bodged out of an assortment of plans. Just after junction 5, the carriageways kink and flare out around a ghost junction where the original line of the M53 was to head south in order to connect up with roads into north Wales. A flyover was built in 1971 pointing the way and it appeared on all the maps, but then the Vauxhall works road at Ellesmere Port was extended, rebranded as a motorway and eventually became the replacement route for the M53. For nearly 30 years, the

Right: It's hard to believe that just 40 years ago, this was the A625 trunk road on the side of Mam Tor in Derbyshire

flyover upon which no car had ever travelled soared over the motorway, before finally being put out of its misery in 2000.

Most poignant are the truncations – some by the planners, some by Mother Nature – that have blighted connections between Manchester and Sheffield. As the M62 demonstrated, getting across the Pennines has always been a tough call, but the M67 was supposed to be the answer. At the Manchester end, a five-mile stretch was built bypassing Denton and Hyde; as the half-built carriageway (known locally as the Ski Jump) pointing west demonstrates, the intention was for it to reach the city centre. It didn't, and, following protests, nor did the motorway get any further in the other direction.

After its short course, the M67 stops abruptly at the Mottram roundabout, whereupon all Sheffield-bound traffic – up to 25,000 vehicles a day – is squeezed onto the single-track A628 Woodhead Pass. This grinds through juggernaut-choked villages and then climbs in a series of hairy twists and turns up to the top of the pass at 1,483 feet. That this road, frequently beset by fog, snow and high winds, is the designated trunk route between two of the north's biggest cities tells you all you need to know about how poor the alternatives are.

These include the A57 Snake Pass from Glossop, which is just as throttled by hairpin bends and dangerous drops as the Woodhead, only even higher (1,680 feet) and even more prone to closure by bad weather, or, as in early 2008, a landslip. Until 1979 there was a third option, used particularly by traffic to and from the south of Greater Manchester. This was the A625 from Chapel-en-le-Frith to Hathersage, which wound around the slopes of Mam Tor, known as the 'shivering mountain' for the precariousness of its geology. Bits of the carriageway collapsed regularly, and were patched up until the next slip. In February 1977 a huge slip occurred and the road buckled; cracks and steps, some two feet deep, appeared in the asphalt. It was stitched back together once again, but only as a single carriageway controlled by traffic lights; the decision was taken two years later to abandon it altogether. It was an intriguing gap on the map in road atlases of the time: two thick red lines of main road failing to meet in the middle, and with the legend 'No Through Road at present' between them. It's an even more intriguing place to visit now, to see the shattered road drop away in cliffs, its layers of make-do-and-mend tarmac giving it the look of geological strata that have been painstakingly laid down over millennia.

The people of this hard-bitten corner of Derbyshire can feel justifiably aggrieved by how poorly they've been served. The Manchester to Sheffield railway through the Woodhead Pass had been significantly upgraded in the post-war years, with electrification and the building of a new three-mile tunnel under the moor's peak in 1953. Beeching even recommended its further upgrading, but instead the trackbed and new tunnel were seen as a potentially useful route for the planned M67. To that end, the railway was closed to passengers in 1970, whereupon it was found that the tunnel was too narrow anyway for the job. But ideas that it could house one carriageway – the other being sent over the top – persisted, and the line was fully closed in 1981. None of the plans came to fruition, and a relatively modern tunnel through the squelchy morass of the Pennines moulders away. In more recent times the pressure to build at least a bit of the abandoned M67, in order to bypass the choked villages at the Manchester end of the Woodhead Pass, has reached boiling point. Fifty years of innumerable studies, inquiries, plans and protests have left the residents with no railway, no motorway and little patience.

By 1980 there was still no sign of the promised 2,000 miles of motorway. The Department of Transport strongly discouraged any lavish opening ceremonies, lest they attracted protestors and reminded people of the huge sums of money spent on the projects. Not that politicians were queuing up to take part; in 1976, a civil servant archly noted that it was almost impossible to get any cabinet minister to a road-opening photo call, a far cry from the heady days of Spaghetti Junction, just four years earlier.

From the mid-1970s to the early 80s, motorway-building strategy was deliberately low key: to complete existing roads (the M4, M5 and M6 in particular) together with the stitching together of orbital routes around Manchester, Birmingham and London. During this time there were few brand new motorways plugged into the grid, and none of those was especially headline-grabbing: the M69 from Leicester to Coventry, the M11 and M40 from London to Cambridge and Oxford, and, most obscure of them all, the M180 and M181 spur on Humberside. In the latter project, we see some of the loftier – if ultimately thwarted – ambition of the era.

ROUNDABOUT CITY

That Britain is a land of roundabouts is obvious from any map. Although pioneered elsewhere, they have come to define our attempt at managing traffic, so that American-style stacks or massive light-controlled interchanges are still relatively alien to our road network. A roundabout is more polite somehow, more British – after all, you can't plant a floral border on a flyover.

It's no surprise that our new towns have become especially linked with the roundabout. The UK's first (and there are two lovely wooden signs on it to say so) dates from 1909 and is in Letchworth, the pioneering Garden City. Swindon is home to the original Magic Roundabout, a fearsome whirl of five mini-roundabouts around a sixth central one, and in 2002 the 'Roundabouts of Redditch' calendar became an instant cult classic that has since spawned a legion of imitators. None of these, however, can hold a candle to our roundabout capital, Milton Keynes, home to over 300.

Above: The Magic Roundabout signpost at Swindon, Wiltshire

Britain's last, and largest, New Town was officially born on 11 January 1967, with the roads its nursemaid. When the M1 opened in 1959, radical Buckinghamshire county architect Fred Pooley – who'd worked on the post-war redevelopment of Coventry – realised that its trajectory through his patch made this the ideal site for a new Utopia on the grandest scale yet. Even in the car-loving 1960s, however, Pooley was sceptical that the city should be built solely around it. He proposed 50 interlocking housing districts, linked by paths and monorail. Soon the plan was taken out of his hands by national government, and they wanted a quasi-American city built on a grid of roads, but connected by the ubiquitous roundabout. Look at maps from the 1970s and 80s and you can see the grid emerge from the undulating fields and the gaps getting gradually filled in.

Milton Keynes' early days were a soggy, socialist version of the Wild West. New residents were given a £2 tree voucher and encouraged to pool resources

Overleaf: Mark Cain's Harry Beck-style road map of 'Roundabout City', Milton Keynes

Milton Keynes
Road Map

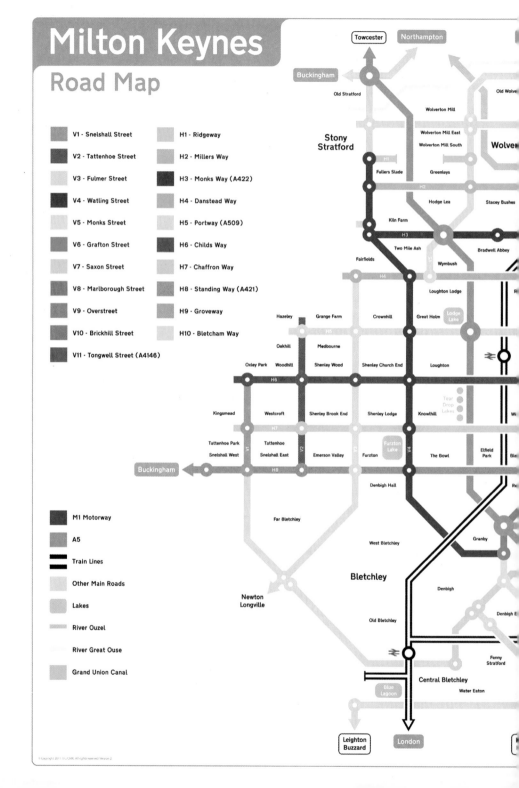

Legend:

- V1 - Snelshall Street
- V2 - Tattenhoe Street
- V3 - Fulmer Street
- V4 - Watling Street
- V5 - Monks Street
- V6 - Grafton Street
- V7 - Saxon Street
- V8 - Marlborough Street
- V9 - Overstreet
- V10 - Brickhill Street
- V11 - Tongwell Street (A4146)

- H1 - Ridgeway
- H2 - Millers Way
- H3 - Monks Way (A422)
- H4 - Danstead Way
- H5 - Portway (A509)
- H6 - Childs Way
- H7 - Chaffron Way
- H8 - Standing Way (A421)
- H9 - Groveway
- H10 - Bletcham Way

- M1 Motorway
- A5
- Train Lines
- Other Main Roads
- Lakes
- River Ouzel
- River Great Ouse
- Grand Union Canal

in a neighbourhood Tree Forum; a magnificent tree cathedral was one result. Instead of the monorail, a dial-a-bus scheme was developed. You rang for one, they radioed the nearest driver and then it took you to where you wanted (it's more usually known as 'a taxi'). Many people didn't have phones at home, so special dial-a-bus phones were mounted on lamp posts in the street. As resident Kathy Sellick remembered: 'You'd press a button and say, "Right, can I have a bus to Bletchley, outside number 21, one adult, two children" and they used to come right outside your house. It was magic.' Sadly, it was also massively expensive and utter chaos, and lasted only 18 months.

Strangely for somewhere incubated as an egalitarian experiment, Milton Keynes took to the Thatcher revolution with gusto. After first decrying it as a 'nest of Marxists', Prime Minister Margaret Thatcher loved it back, and was forever hurtling up the M1 to open a new light industrial unit or give a rabble-rousing speech to local businessmen. After all, there was no post-industrial hangover to be had here, for there was no old industry to mourn. It was never going to be a mining town or steel city, but as a home for banking headquarters, Japanese hi-tech firms or European hypermarkets, or the place to build the first new major railway station of the 20th century (1982), the vast National Bowl concert arena (1980) or the country's first multiplex cinema (1985), it was perfect. It's still surprisingly lovely today, its grid of V (vertical) and H (horizontal) boulevards rarely troubled by congestion. It could be thanks to the roundabouts.

Above: The motorways and dual carriageways feeding the Humber Bridge (and indeed the bridge itself) have never been especially busy

Even after more than 30 years in existence, the M180 is one road that anyone except locals or enthusiasts might struggle to place, for it is among the quietest motorways in the land, out on a limb of what was then the brand new county of Humberside. It was a road into the future, linking the rest of Britain with the massive fishing fleet of Grimsby, the steelworks of the growing town of Scunthorpe, the new Humberside International Airport, a planned new town at Barnetby, the expanding petrochemical works and North Sea oil terminals at Killingholme, the vast container port at Immingham and the shiny new Humber Bridge over to Hull, the largest single-span bridge in the world when it opened in 1981.

All the ingredients were in place, but somehow the motorway – and the area as a whole – never quite achieved lift-off. The fishing fleet, steelworks, oil and port industries are all much reduced now, the new town never happened, numbers using the airport have plummeted and the bridge has long been acknowledged as a beautiful white elephant. Such traffic as there is on the M180 includes a large proportion of container lorries en route from the European mainland to Ireland, for the road is the spirit of Britain-in-Europe, doubling up as route E22 from Dublin, via Holyhead, and thence through Holland, Germany, Sweden, Latvia and Russia. Euro-expansionism and Nimby localism all in one slumbering motorway, for Humberside, the most derided of all the new 1970s counties, was finally killed off in 1996, reverting back to the East Riding of Yorkshire on the north bank and Lincolnshire on the south. There are lots of new signs, but still not much traffic.

If the M180 is the 1970s in motorway form, then unquestionably the totemic motorway of the Thatcher years, the 1980s, is the M25. Margaret Thatcher's government was a great deal keener on roads and road builders; after all, many of them supported her party handsomely with financial donations. The compromised days of the oil crisis and IMF bailouts were a thing of the past; in a 1989 white paper, *Roads for Prosperity*, the government proposed a doubling of the roads budget and 'the biggest road-building programme since the Romans'.

Gone too was the shame of ostentatious opening ceremonies, as the Prime Minister herself cut the ribbon on the completed M25, the long-awaited London Orbital, on 29 October 1986. She was in characteristically bullish mood, berating journalists and other naysayers for their lack of enthusiasm. 'I can't stand those who carp and criticise, when they ought to be congratulating Britain on a magnificent achievement,' she pronounced, before symbolically moving a specially de-weighted cone out of the way and declaring the motorway – and Britain – to be 'open for business'.

The glossy, 60-page booklet published by the Department of Transport to accompany the celebrations sounds in places as if it was written by Mrs Thatcher herself: 'But – for all the carping at occasional congestion – it IS a tremendous achievement. The Victorians would have blown many trumpets; our generation uses the road and, if forced to slow down temporarily to 50mph, grumbles.' Her transport secretary of the day – the long-forgotten John Moore – begins his introduction

Overleaf: The AA's M25 London Orbital Motorway sheet map (1989): even just two years after its completion, the maps of the M25 were using sidebars of colour shading to warn where congestion was likely

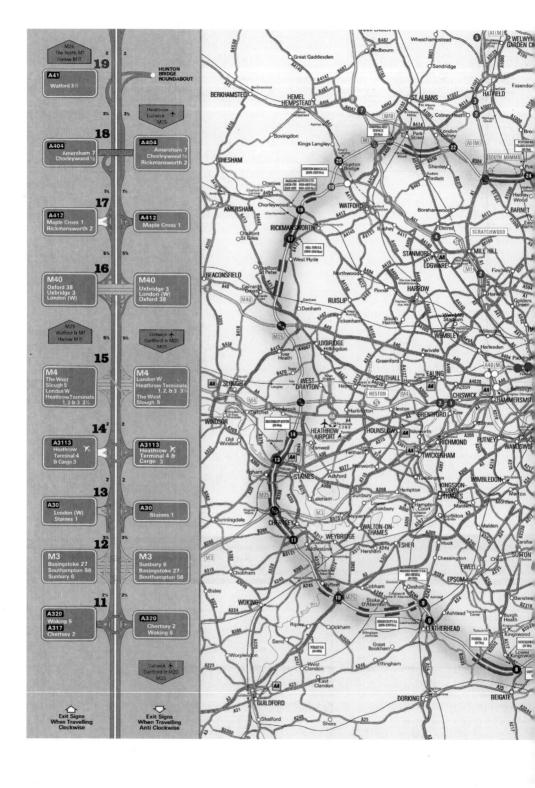

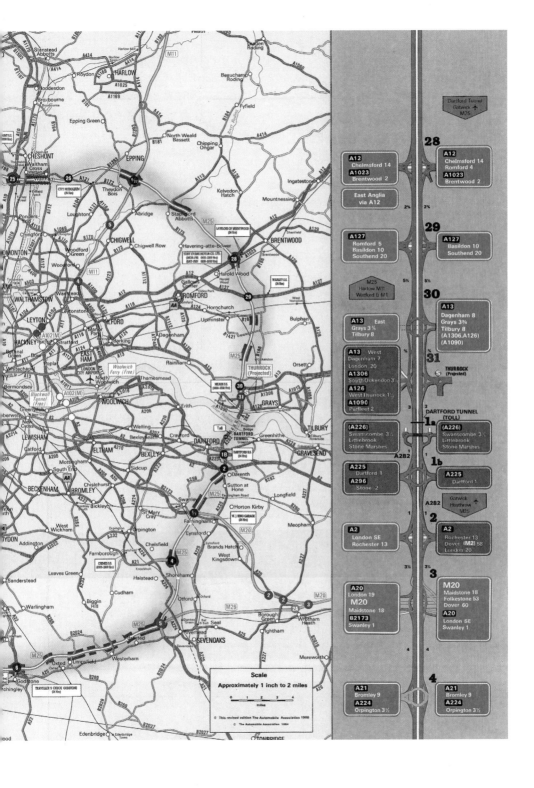

Map legend / junction panels (M25)

Dartford Tunnel
Gatwick ✈
M25

28

A12	A12
Chelmsford 14	Chelmsford 14
A1023	Romford 4
Brentwood 2	A1023
	Brentwood 2

East Anglia
via A12

2¼   2¼

29

A127	A127
Romford 5	Basildon 10
Basildon 10	Southend 20
Southend 20	

5¾   5¾

M25
Harlow M11
Watford & M1

30

	A13
	Dagenham 8
	Grays 3¾
	Tilbury 8
A13 East	(A1306, A126)
Grays 3¾	(A1090)
Tilbury 8	

¾   ¾

A13 West	
Dagenham 7	THURROCK
London 20	S (Projected)
A1306	
South Ockendon 3½	**31**
A126	
West Thurrock 1½	
A1090	
Purfleet 2	

3   DARTFORD TUNNEL (TOLL)

1a

(A226)	(A226)
Swanscombe 3½	Swanscombe 3½
Littlebrook	Littlebrook
Stone Marshes	Stone Marshes

A282

1b

A225	A225
Dartford 1	Dartford 1
A296	
Stone 2	

A282   Gatwick ✈
Heathrow
M25

2

A2	A2
London SE	Rochester 13
Rochester 13	Dover (M2) 58
	London 20

3¼   3¼

3

A20	M20
London 19	Maidstone 18
M20	Folkestone 53
Maidstone 18	Dover 60
B2173	A20
Swanley 1	London SE
	Swanley 1

4   4

4

A21	A21
Bromley 9	Bromley 9
A224	A224
Orpington 3½	Orpington 3½

Map area labels (left panel)

Stanstead Abbotts, Roydon, HARLOW, Hoddesdon, Broxbourne, Epping Green, North Weald Bassett, Chipping Ongar, Fyfield, Beauchamp Roding, Abbess Roding, Ingatestone, Kelvedon Hatch, Mountnessing, CHESHUNT, Waltham Cross, EPPING, Theydon Bois, Loughton, Abridge, Stapleford Abbotts, Shenfield, BRENTWOOD, Ponders End, Chingford, CHIGWELL, Chigwell Row, Havering-atte-Bower, Harold Wood, Hornchurch, Bulphan, Orsett, EDMONTON, Woodford Green, Woodford, Gallows Corner, ROMFORD, Gidea Park, Upminster, WALTHAMSTOW, Wanstead, Leytonstone, ILFORD, Manor Park, Dagenham, Rainham, West Horndon, LEYTON, HACKNEY, Stratford, Bow, EAST HAM, Barking, THURROCK (Projected), Poplar, Bethnal Green, Whitechapel, London City Airport, Woolwich Ferry (Free), Thamesmead, Tockington, Bermondsey, North Woolwich, WOOLWICH, GRAYS, Blackwall Tunnel (Free), Greenwich, New Cross, Erith, TILBURY, Camberwell, Welling, Crayford, DARTFORD, Greenhithe, GRAVESEND, LEWISHAM, Catford, Bexleyheath, BEXLEY, Darenth, ELTHAM, Mottingham, Sidcup, Sutton at Hone, Longfield, South End, Chislehurst, BECKENHAM, BROMLEY, Bickley, Swanley, Horton Kirby, Meopham, West Wickham, Bromley Common, St Mary Cray, Farningham, Eynsford, CROYDON, Addington, Orpington, Chelsfield, Brands Hatch, West Kingsdown, Farnborough, Knockholt, Shoreham, Leaves Green, Halstead, Otford, Wrotham Heath, Sanderstead, Warlingham, Biggin Hill, Cudham, Oxted, Borough Green, Seal, Ightham, Westerham, SEVENOAKS, Mereworth, Godstone, Limpsfield, Edenbridge, Edenbridge Town, TONBRIDGE

Scale

Approximately 1 inch to 2 miles

0 1 2 3 4
miles

© This revised edition The Automobile Association 1988
© The Automobile Association 1994

with a line used repeatedly throughout, that the M25 'is the longest city bypass in the world'. It was, however, running over capacity as soon as it opened, and before long was far better known as 'Britain's largest car park'. It has needed constant upgrading and widening ever since.

Two days before the M25's opening, massive deregulation of the City of London (the 'Big Bang') was enacted. These two events dovetailed together well; among the many who headed to the M25 in order to drive the full circuit were legions of city traders come to race their flashy sports cars. They'd arrange to rendezvous at South Mimms, initially the only services on the M25, very early on a weekend morning, before haring off with only the briefest of pit stops at the Dartford Tunnel. Many completed the 118-mile circuit in around an hour, though CCTV and the eternal tailbacks soon put paid to that. One of the biggest advertisements in the Department of Transport souvenir brochure was by British Telecom for their 'swanky new Cellphones' ('prices start at £899'). 'You know how it is when you see someone on the phone in a car?' it began. Chances are 'he'll be stealing a march on one of his competitors...you, perhaps?' The zeitgeist image of the age is the accompanying cartoon picture of a rosy-cheeked yuppie speeding along as he gabs into his brick-sized mobile, lapping up the covetous stare of his phoneless rival.

The 1980s in a nutshell: the deregulation of the City, the M25, cell phones – and an accompanying property boom. In the year the motorway opened, house prices rocketed by a quarter in the areas within easy commuting distance of its junctions, and the long surge of the southeast as it pulled away economically from the rest of the country had begun. Soon, the flip side of 1980s entrepreneurialism was making its presence felt on the M25, as party organisers used its route as the area in which to put on massive raves, with the service stations as gathering points for thousands of punters. The dance duo Orbital was named in its honour.

The boy racers and the goggle-eyed ravers don't show up on the map, but another face of Thatcherite deregulation sprouting alongside the motorways most certainly did, in the rash of developments for which proximity to a motorway junction was the main criterion. These included

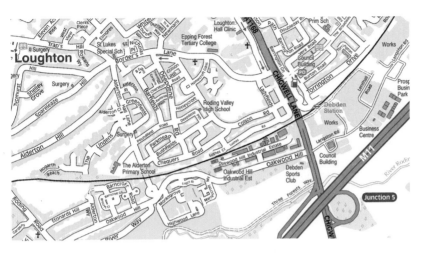

Left: AA Street Level mapping showing a typical 'Motorway Magnet' area

out-of-town retail parks, distribution depots, budget hotels, chain eateries and housing estates, the latter always obvious on an Ordnance Survey from its squiggle of cul-de-sacs hemmed in by distributor roads. As part of their ongoing categorisation of us all, marketing companies began to target the people who moved to such places, christening them 'Motorway Magnets' – typically young, white-collar employees, who commuted by car, and who, when asked where they live, were likely to say something like 'junction 5 of the M11'.

BACK TO THE FUTURE

Ordnance Survey's new metric 1:50,000 series continued very much where the old one-inch maps had left off. The interwar years of fancy pictorial covers had long been forgotten; their maps since 1945 had been packaged in a succession of highly functional covers, the latest design (since 1969) being a very simple outline map of the area portrayed within. The new maps continued this look, with just the background colour changing from red to magenta.

Tourism was becoming an increasingly important market for mapmakers. In 1970 Ordnance Survey launched a new Tourist Map series of some of

Opposite: The 1980s AA and Reader's Digest New Book of the Road attempted to bring a little class and culture back into in-car mapping

the most popular areas, with austere black covers enlivened by positively psychedelic drawings of places within; a far cry from Ellis Martin's eminently sober creations. In 1980 the new 1:50,000 maps were christened the Landranger series, and over the next few years photographic covers were introduced, the first time that the flagship one-inch series (or its successor) had used an illustration since the 1930s. There was no going back. The pictures became ever more dazzling, sometimes almost avant-garde, and seemed perfectly in tune with the heightened design aesthetic of the time. Increasing amounts of tourist information were added to the maps: historic attractions, viewpoints, tourist offices, picnic spots, campsites and car parks, another trend that was set to grow.

Meanwhile, Ordnance Survey's great commercial competitor Bartholomew was slowly disappearing from view. Their USP – the exquisite delineation of relief by colour – had been watered down by also going metric in the 1970s, when the contour interval between shades was significantly increased. Suddenly, the colours looked harsher and the typography old-fashioned, especially compared with the highly modernistic second series of Landranger maps that Ordnance Survey were gradually rolling out. It was the beginning of the end for Barts.

In the early 1980s, the map that seemed to be in everyone's car (and, if not, it was on their bookshelf) was the *New Book of the Road*, a collaboration between the AA and Reader's Digest. It's a fine work, with map pages that fold out and over in flaps, meaning that it's possible to follow a continuous route from east to west, though you still have to resort to the page indicator arrows for north–south roads. Tucked under each flap is a gazetteer of information about the places on that page. The map colours were largely the same as the Ordnance Survey, but more muted, giving it a classily old-fashioned air, with efficient and clear symbolism to pack in all kinds of useful information. It's in the wealth of other information that the book scores so highly; a hybrid of the specialisms of its co-producers. From the AA come 60 or so pages about the rules of the road, breakdowns and emergencies, 109 detailed town plans, and strip maps of motorways and major routes. From the Reader's Digest come prettily illustrated potted guides to everything from river and pond life to inn signs, and from breeds of cattle to types of aircraft.

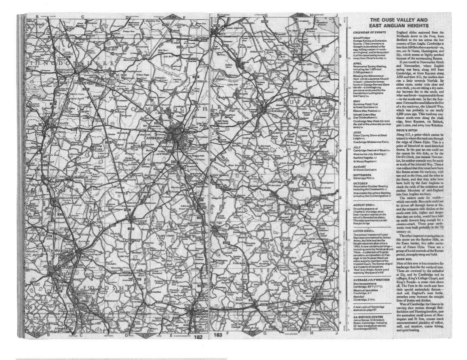

THE OUSE VALLEY AND EAST ANGLIAN HEIGHTS

CALENDAR OF EVENTS

Good Friday
Orange Rolling at Dunstable Downs. This ceremony is thought to be related to the egg-rolling custom in northern England, and to be symbolic of the stone being turned away from Christ's tomb.

APRIL
Newmarket Spring Meeting, including the 1,000 and 2,000 guineas (r)
Bleeding the Silverweave at Ayot. (At St Lawrence Church at Ayot, where the old-time home of George Bernard Shaw stands—a bleeding ceremony service is conducted for the harvest from Luffington Salt Feast) (r)

MAY
Silverweave Flinch Trial at Great Stanmore (r)
Elstow May Festival (r)
Isleof Green May Day Celebrations (r)
Cambridge May Week (r) mark the end of the university summer term) (r)

JUNE
Essex County Show at Great Leighs (r)
Cambridge Midsummer Fairs

JULY
Cambridge Festival of Music to Haverlow fair, July Meeting (r)
Bamford Regatta (r)
St Neots Regatta (r)

AUGUST
St Neots Carnival (r)

SEPTEMBER
Stevenage Peticis

OCTOBER
Newmarket October Meeting including the Cesarewitch (r)
Newmarket Houghton Meeting, including the Cambridgeshire (r)

AUDLEY END (r)
Once the property of Charles II, this large seventeen-mansion stands on the site of a Benedictine abbey. The state apartments contain fine paintings.

LUTON HOO (r)
The palatial mansion of Luton Hoo was constructed by Robert Adam, but later modified by others in 1843. It now contains paintings including those by Rembrandt and Titian—a collection of English porcelain, and jewellery by Fabergé, in the Russian Room are relics worn by members of the Imperial Court. The former chapel is a museum of renovation. 'Hoo' is an Anglo-Saxon word meaning 'the spur of a hill.'

AVERAGE JULY WEATHER
Day temperature
Cambridge, 63°F (17°C)
Hours of sunshine
Cambridge, 6·1
Rainfall
Cambridge, 2·4 in.
A town plan of Cambridge appears on page 97

AA SERVICE CENTRES
Jarrus House, St Andrews Street, Cambridge; including 24-hour breakdown service (Cambridge 63107)

England slides eastward from the Midlands down to the Fens, from Bedford to the sea across the low country of East Anglia. Cambridge is less than 100 feet above sea level—as, too, are St Neots, Huntingdon, and Ely, which seem so highly perched because of the surrounding flatness.

If you travel to Newmarket Heath and Newmarket, where English racing was born, along A45 from Cambridge, or from Royston along A505 and then A11, the surface does rise a little towards Norfolk. By either route, under wide skies and over chalk, you are riding a dry contour between Ivo in the north, and what was flatter—impenetrable forest—to the south-east. In fact the Roman—Newmarket road follows the line of a dry trackway, the Icknield Way, which was probably in use nearly 4,000 years ago. This trackway continues south-west along the chalk edge, Steen Royston, via Baldock, past Luton, and away into Wiltshire.

DEVIL'S DITCH
Along A11, a point which cannot be missed is where the road cuts through the ridge of Fleam Dyke. This is a point of historical or semi-historical drama. In the past no one could cut the reason for this dyke, or for the Devil's Ditch, just outside Newmarket, for neither extends very far north or much of the Icknield Way. Then it was realised that they must have been like fences across the trackway, with one end at the front, and the other at the forest, and that they either have been built by the East Anglians to check the rush of the ambitious and restless Mercians of mid-England into East Anglian territory.

The medium came for wealth—which was certain. Bars-castle could not be driven off through forest or fen, and the conquests with slashes on the south-west side, higher and deeper than they are today, would have held up cattle driven long enough for a counter-attack. These great earthworks were built probably in the 7th century AD.

The other important antiquities in this secure are the Harslow 1520s, the Roman barrier, the miles west of Fleam Dyke. These are a group of burial mounds of the Roman period, strangely steep and bold.

DARK SOIL
Most of this area is less attractive for landscape than for the works of man. These are converted by the cathedral at Ely, and by Cambridge and its colleges, King's College Chapel, and King's Parade—a street vista almost all. The Fens in the north-east have their special melancholy flatness—dark soil, England's most fertile, stretches away between the straight lines of drains and ditches.

West of Cambridge the Ouse in its curving slow motion through Bedfordshire and Huntingdonshire, past the somnolent small towns of Huntingdon and St Ives, crosses much uncommercialised placidity of willow, mill, and meadow, coarse fishing, and quiet boating.

Wild flowers

A. ROADSIDES AND WASTE PLACES

Roadsides are among the richest places for wild flowers, as many different kinds of human activity result in diverse conditions there—bare earth after road widening, piles of road-grit, grass verges that are mown frequently, and verges that are mown hardly at all. Each condition gives rise to a certain group of plants, all with strong powers of survival. The flowers shown are found within two or three feet of the road, where disturbance is regular. On new earth-banks arable weeds thrive, but in time meadow flowers take their place.

See also habitats B, C, D, E, F. Not illustrated: Stinging Nettle, Dandelion, Wild Carrot, Sow-thistle, Burdock

2-6 in.

A B C D E F G H I K L W
1 2 3 4 5 6 7 8 9 10 11 12

COLTSFOOT
After flowers, felted leaves appear

2-3 ft	12-30 in.		1-6 ft
1 WHITE CAMPION 2 BLADDER CAMPION.1-2 ft	GOAT'S-BEARD, JACK-GO-TO-BED-AT-NOON. Blooms shut at noon	1 SILVERWEED. A trailing plant. 2 CREEPING CINQUEFOIL	MULLEIN. Large leaves are woolly on both sides

1-3 ft	1-4 ft	1-3 ft	6-24 in.
BLACK HOREHOUND	WELD. Similar to	EVENING PRIMROSE	COMMON TOADFLAX

(each plant labelled with habitat key) A B C D E F G H I K L W 1 2 3 4 5 6 7 8 9 10 11 12

BODYWORK STYLES

saloon

coupé

estate car

limousine

of modern steel pressing methods, sheet steel replaced the wood panels. Most European and Japanese cars employ a MONOCOQUE type of body, with no separate chassis.

bore
The internal wall of that part of an engine cylinder or a pump barrel within which the piston travels; or the diameter of such a hole, measured in millimetres (inches in U.S.). See STROKE.

bottom dead centre (abbrev. b.d.c.)
The position of a piston when it has reached the bottom of its STROKE.

brake
Means of decreasing a vehicle's speed. By law, a car must have two separate braking systems —one to operate on all four wheels. This system is controlled by the brake pedal; the second, which usually operates on the rear wheels only, is controlled by a hand lever. Most cars employ drum brakes, although on many they are used only on the rear wheels. A pair of semi-circular brake shoes faced with a friction

material (brake linings) is fixed to a stationary plate inside a drum which rotates with the wheel. When the brake is applied, the shoes are forced apart into contact with the inside of the rotating drum, so slowing the road wheels.

Many cars now employ disc brakes in which a calliper holds friction pads on either side of a

---

WASHING THE CAR

The best time to wash a car is when it is raining or just afterwards. Rain softens the dirt, which can then be flooded off with more water.

If the car is dry, soak it with a fine, gentle spray to loosen all the dirt. Never apply a strong jet of water as this can damage the paint surface, nor use a dry duster or mop; fine dust, dirt, or grit particles which settle on the paint surface can cause scratching. Once the car is soaking wet, use a sponge or soft brush and plenty of water to remove the dirt. Leather off to restore a polished finish. The proprietary shampoos help to dissolve traffic film scum and, when followed by a plain water rinse and leathering off, make it easier to achieve a final shine.

Use a powerful jet of water to remove accumulated dirt beneath wings and bumpers and around the suspension and steering units. Never direct a jet on to door windows: water will drain into the doors and rust the panels from the inside. Keep drain holes in the bottoms of the doors and body sub-frames clear of accumulating dirt and mud.

When finishing off the paintwork, dry all crevices, such as those around lamps, along pluted decorative strips and around window frames; damp in these places easily causes corrosion or rust. If rust forms in crevices, clean it away. Remove the first signs of rust from chrome by rubbing gently with a liquid chrome cleaner.

Tar spot stains and petrol stains can readily be removed by a local application of a white spirit soaked rag. Modern paint systems are not improved by frequent applications of polishes; they do not need this attention. Avoid hard rubbing.

Like the arterial roads of a couple of generations earlier, the growing motorway, dual carriageway and bypass network began to alter the shape of our settlements. In the 1980s the most tangible manifestation was the out-of-town shopping centre, often built on brownfield sites but always with easy road access and acres of car parking. The first was Brent Cross in 1976, sandwiched between the beginning of the M1, the A41 Hendon Way and a 10-lane stretch of the North Circular. By 1990 it had been joined by Gateshead's Metro Centre, alongside the A1; the Merry Hill Centre near Dudley, linked by dual carriageway to the M5; Lakeside at Thurrock, a stone's throw from the M25 and A13; Meadowhall near Sheffield, alongside the M1; and the Fosse Shopping Park near Leicester, where the M69 joins the M1.

These were the retail behemoths; the largest, Gateshead's Metro Centre, has grown to encompass 340 shops with over 2 million square feet of retail space, a working population of 7,000 and an annual visitor tally of around 23 million. There were plenty of smaller versions appearing by roundabouts and motorway junctions all over the country, and they all looked like variations on pretty much the same theme. On the map they are as square and boxy as they are on the ground, their borders delineated by tight knots of access roads.

For some areas, the motorways were intravenous drips that boosted their growth. The 'golden triangle' of the M1/M6/M69 between Coventry and Leicester was one of the first examples. It's at the heart of England, and an HGV from here can reach 85 per cent of Britain's population within four hours. In 1988 the Magna Park distribution depot was developed here, on an old RAF airfield part-owned by the Church of England (as is the Metro Centre and many other modern shed developments); it is now the country's largest. Others have sprung up, as has an accompanying service sector of conference centres, flat-pack hotels and retail parks. Compare the Ordnance Survey maps over the past 40 years, and you can see that villages in the golden triangle have also ballooned in size.

As our shopping habits have changed, more and more such places have been developed as distribution nodes, with new clusters forming on brownfield sites in South Yorkshire, around Peterborough and Corby, in the Potteries, around Bristol, Birmingham and Manchester and across the central belt of Scotland. Very few are in the overheated southeast; all are within a mile or two of at least one motorway or dualled trunk road.

Despite the very real fears and reservations, our lives have become ever more dependent on our cars and the roads they travel on. Even those who proudly eschew a vehicle of their own depend on road transport for the distribution of almost everything they buy. Guilty and compromised we may be, but we cannot leave them alone, the true definition of an addict. And for most people, the road network – busy, bustling, often creaking at the seams – is something with which they have a distinctly love–hate relationship.

The target of reaching 2,000 miles of motorway in the UK (including a few dozen in Northern Ireland) was finally achieved in 1992, 12 years late, with the opening of some new stretches of the M74 to Glasgow. The previous year had seen the opening of the last major new motorway in England when the M40 was extended from Oxford to Warwick. It had been one of the most difficult, protracted and expensive motorways of all, largely due to the furious protests that had erupted around the original plans to route the road across Otmoor, a precious pocket of wetland in Oxfordshire. It was an ominous pointer to what was coming next. Remember that government white paper of just two years earlier, and its promise to begin 'the biggest road-building programme since the Romans?' Like so many other hubristic promises of the 1980s, it turned out not to be true.

Above: The motorway network reached 2,009 miles in 1992 (70 of which were in Northern Ireland), twelve years after the government's stated aim

Chapter 7

From Swampy to
Satnav
(1992–now)

On 11 March 1992, Prime Minister John Major announced a general election, having left it almost as late as he could. The Conservatives had been in power for 13 years, the economy was in recession, and he was behind in the opinion polls. The mood seemed to be set for change; or at least it was until Labour leader Neil Kinnock leapt on stage at his party's eve-of-poll rally in Sheffield and acted like a punch-drunk rock star. The nation held its nose, and voted for Major and his trusty soapbox.

In the hubbub of the election campaign, few noticed the small camp of travellers gathering in Hampshire with the express intention of derailing the planned M3 extension through Twyford Down. Labour were committed to scrapping it; the Conservatives to building it. Once the Tories had won the election, the battle lines were drawn and the camp mushroomed in size.

Getting a fast road from London and the Midlands down to Southampton had always been controversial, especially the question of where to take it through the narrow gap in the chalk downs near Winchester. When that city's original bypass (A33) was built in the 1930s, there were angry protests by people who objected to it dividing the Itchen water meadows from St Catherine's Hill, an ancient hill fort between the city and Twyford Down. The bypass, with its tight bends and congested junctions, dated very quickly indeed, and by the 1970s new plans were published to route a motorway across the meadows. The campaign against that was massive and spearheaded by pillars of the community, including the headmaster of Winchester College and the town's Conservative Association. The Ministry of Transport was forced back to the drawing board.

By the end of 1991, the M3 was complete either side of Winchester, but traffic was still funnelled onto the antiquated bypass in between. On busy summer weekends, queues of an hour or more would coagulate along its length, and the accident rate was horrendous. A route to the east of St Catherine's Hill was chosen for the motorway, but this needed to get through the chalkland swell of Twyford Down; a tunnel was ruled out on expense grounds. As the final plans were drawn up, the protests gathered momentum.

Previous page:
Ordnance Survey map of
Buckfastleigh in Devon
– their new 1:25,000
Explorer series has
become the biggest paper
map seller of the 21st
century, almost entirely
driven by their role in
leisure and tourism

Although many of those camped at Twyford Down were the anarchists and crusties of popular imagination, who christened themselves the Donga Tribe after the name of the Iron Age tracks in the area, they were far from the only protestors. As has always been the case, especially in this part of the world, the battle against the road united unlikely bedfellows. The Bishop of Winchester came and conducted a service at the camp, attended by many of the townsfolk who pledged their support. It's a long tradition: there have always been many politically conservative types ready to speak up against such developments. And, after all, many of the pierced and dreadlocked ones were the children of those in Barbour jackets and Hunter wellies.

Sympathy for the camp dwellers was widespread beyond Hampshire. The protestors tapped into not just a latent mistrust of new roads, especially those ripping so graphically through such an obvious beauty spot, but also a growing mood of anger and despair at

Above: Protestors form a human chain on 'the cutting' – the excavated site of the M3 extension through Twyford Down in the early 1990s

the government. Following their close election victory, so much had already gone wrong for the Major administration. On 16 September 1992, Chancellor Norman Lamont had to raise interest rates four times in an ultimately futile attempt to keep the pound crashing out of the European exchange rate mechanism. Various personal scandals, rebellious backbenchers and a growing sense of political sleaze were undermining Major's straight-talking persona. It was not just the Queen having an 'annus horribilis'.

And then, just before dawn on 9 December, a hundred private security guards descended on the camp and started to manhandle the protestors away. It was an ugly scene, with random violence and even assault dished out by the men in the Day-Glo tabards. The following day, with the media in attendance, the police arrived to back them up; the forcible evictions continued into a third day. Conservationist David Bellamy was there, and on camera described them as 'John Major's bully boys'. About 30 of the security guards, sickened by what they'd been told to do, handed in their notice on the spot.

Work began on cutting through the down. More protests flared up the following spring, and the response was just as heavy-handed; a few protestors even ended up in prison. But nonetheless the road was built, even if the lengthy action had significantly delayed it and pushed up the cost. It looks like a raw wound even today; as Joe Moran put it in his lovely book *On Roads* (2009), the spot should be marked on the Ordnance Survey map with the crossed swords symbol for a battlefield.

The battle of Twyford Down changed not just the physical landscape, but the cultural one too. Road protests – at Newbury, Cradlewell near Newcastle, the M11 link road in east London, Fairmile on the A30 in Devon, against the Birmingham northern relief road (the M6 Toll) – became the liveliest shows in town, crystallising within them a whole range of disenfranchised fury. They even spawned their own folk hero, in the shape of a diffident young tunneller known as Swampy.

BYPASSING THE BYPASSES

The fracas of the mid-1990s in Newbury erupted over the building of the town's second bypass. In the 1960s a dual carriageway bypass had been built to the east of the town centre, but it quickly filled up and made the town as much of a bottleneck as before. Less than 30 years later, it was back to the drawing board to find a route for another way of avoiding the town.

Newbury wasn't alone in needing a bypass for its bypass; the same double whammy can be seen in many places, including Shrewsbury, Colchester, Chelmsford, Haddington, Bridgend, Gloucester, Guildford, Silverstone, Exeter, Whitstable and Herne Bay, Lockerbie, Redruth, Broxburn, Billingham, Wetherby and Great Dunmow. Like some chronically ill heart patient, Dartford is on its third bypass.

Some former bypasses sink quietly into suburban torpor, but others are left stranded, like oxbow lakes when the river has changed course. The same has happened to some dual carriageways, leaving telltale curiosities sprinkled around the map. There's a lost bit of the old A48, together with the remnant exits of a service station on each side, in the middle of a field near Skewen, outside Swansea. In Suffolk, the old A12 at Copdock is a rare example of an unclassified dual carriageway, and an even rarer example of one that is now a dead end, as its northern end has been turned into a footpath under the replacement Ipswich bypass.

Even motorways can find themselves usurped by newcomers. The original M4 Severn Bridge, opened with such a fanfare in 1966, was rechristened as part of the tiny M48 when the new M4 crossing was opened downstream after just 30 years. The most poignant reminder of its brief heyday is the old Aust service station, a massive fortress overlooking the bridge and the swirling eddies of the Severn. Named as the largest cafeteria in the land in 1978, its view towards Wales through the huge plate glass windows was a thrilling part of the journey west. With the motorway's 1990s downgrade, the services followed suit and were squeezed instead into the old truckers' cafe on the far side of the site, at the same time being rebranded as Severn View services – ironically, for there's no longer a view of the river, nor the bridge. The old service station proper is now the headquarters of an insurance company, while the M48 burbles quietly by, the motorway equivalent of a country lane.

Above: Protesters block traffic on the Newbury bypass in the mid-1990s

Overleaf: As the 2013 AA Road Atlas graphically demonstrates, the Newbury bypass was the second built for the town

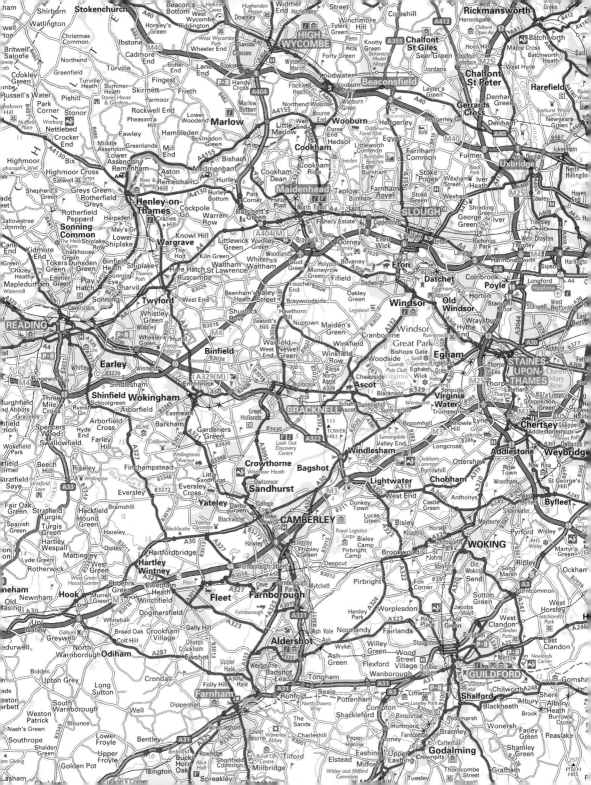

Anger at particular road expansions bubbled up into a wider anti-car movement, Reclaim the Streets, which held flash-mob gatherings in numerous cities from 1995 onwards. I was on two of them in Birmingham, and they were terrific fun. There was something so very liberating in seeing sofas, sandpits, jugglers and dancers in places that were normally just rivers of grumpy traffic. Only when something stops, albeit briefly, do we realise how disruptive it is, and how desensitised to it we have become (something very familiar to people living near airports when the Icelandic volcano Eyjafjallajökull grounded all planes for five days in April 2010). The zenith of Reclaim the Streets came in July 1996, when 8,000 protestors outwitted the police and occupied the M41 in Shepherd's Bush, west London, for a day and a night. Twenty-five-foot puppets of Marie Antoinette danced on the tarmac; unbeknown to the police, protestors were hidden beneath her skirts drilling holes into the carriageway, into which they planted tree saplings.

This upsurge of prelapsarian protest, the last trumpet before the juggernaut of new technology swept all before it, might seem futile or quaint – the roads got built in the end, after all – but it had many far-reaching consequences. The environmental and societal impact of new roads was hardwired into the planning process, and in many different ways. Schemes to offset new roads became the norm, none more impressive than the grassing over of the old Winchester bypass as a direct recompense for the destruction of Twyford Down. I've walked the route; it is delightful and, best of all, it reconnects St Catherine's Hill with the meadows and the city itself.

Another direct effect can be seen 25 miles east of Twyford Down, where the last remaining stretch of single carriageway on the A3, up and around the beautiful Devil's Punch Bowl, was a major headache for both motorists and planners. The intended replacement dual carriageway would have ruined it even further; as it was, environmental impact legislation meant that it was routed instead through a new tunnel at Hindhead, which finally opened to great acclaim in 2011. As with the old Winchester bypass, the former A3 has been returned very successfully to nature.

The same has happened with the A344 that, until 2013, clipped Stonehenge, passing only inches from the monument's 15-foot high Heel Stone. In Tess of the D'Urbervilles' day, Stonehenge lay alongside a dusty turnpike that she and Angel Clare walked from Melchester (Salisbury) under cover of a night 'as dark as a cave'. By the early 20th century, that turnpike had grown into the A303, the main holiday route from London to the West Country. At Stonehenge, the A344 peeled off its bigger sibling, leaving Britain's most celebrated Neolithic monument wedged unceremoniously between two fiercely busy roads.

Things only worsened in the 1960s with the construction of a dingy underpass to take visitors from the car park, under the A344, and to the stones. It was more reminiscent of a shopping precinct in a 1960s new town than a World Heritage Site on the wide open spaces of Salisbury Plain. Through the 1990s and into the new millennium, the debate raged as to how to improve poor Stonehenge's standing.

Initially, the government opted to build a tunnel to take the busier A303, though costs and controversies escalated, and the plan was abandoned in 2007. Instead, the A344 was closed and, where it brushes the stones, grassed over. Its remaining tarmac section is now used only by the park-and-ride vehicles that shuttle people from the new car park and visitor centre at Airman's Corner two miles to the west. Many visitors choose instead to walk from there to the stones, either along the closed road itself or through the fields on ancient trackways that converge on the monument. Even if the problem of the A303, still roaring unceasingly by just 100 yards away from the stones, remains unsolved, the new arrangement is a huge improvement, and seems to let Stonehenge breathe far more deeply in its dramatic setting. It was well worth consigning the two-mile A344 to history.

After 18 long years, the Conservative government finally collapsed under the weight of Tony Blair's landslide in May 1997. The Labour manifesto had said little about road policy, except that they would continue to use the Conservative policy known as the private finance initiative (PFI) to 'improve road maintenance'. It was widely expected though that the new government would be far less pro-road than the previous one; a month after the election Deputy Prime Minister John Prescott (whose super-department now included transport) said, 'I will have failed if in five years time there are not many more people using public transport and far fewer journeys by car. It's a tall order but I urge you to hold me to it'. Five years later, car traffic was up by 7 per cent. The Deputy Prime Minister himself swiftly earned the soubriquet of 'Two Jags' for the fact that he owned a Jaguar on top of his ministerial limousine. He remained in post until 2007.

It was largely all spin. With the sleight-of-hand boost of PFI, a kind of institutionalised hire purchase scheme, the Labour government quietly doubled the road-building budget of the Major years, while somehow managing not to invoke the wrath of the protestors to any great degree. The explanation for this may be that much of the money went on relatively low-key projects, such as the hugely expensive widening of the M25 and other already existing motorways. The government's strategy,

A New Deal for Transport (1998), cancelled many of the ongoing plans outlined at the tail end of the Thatcher years; some of them were junked in their already half-built state.

By the turn of the century, there was little point updating your in-car road atlas every year, for the number of absolutely brand new routes was tiny. A bypass here, a bridge or tunnel there, a few miles of dualling somewhere else, but nothing that would take you to whole new destinations in the way that the motorways of the 1960s, 70s and even 80s had done. Between October 2000 and December 2003, there was not a single mile of new motorway opened anywhere in Britain, the first such gap since the Preston bypass was opened in 1958.

THE TURNPIKE'S RETURN

The motorway opening that broke the long drought in December 2003 was the M6 Toll, Britain's first turnpike road for well over a century. For years the M6 through Birmingham was one of the most dreaded sections of motorway for any driver; the 27-mile loop to the north its supposed solution. Transport Secretary Alistair Darling opened it, saying that: 'At £2 a car, I think many drivers may decide that, for the journey time, it would be something worth doing – I certainly would.' Calling it 'an early Christmas present for motorists', Tom Fanning, managing director of Midland Expressway Ltd, the road's operator, described it as 'exceptional value for money – £2 is the price of a cup of coffee'.

Britain's first – and, to date, only – toll motorway was intended to help revive the romance of the road, perhaps more literally than we realised, for the carriageway included 2.5 million Mills & Boon novels pulped into the tarmac in order to aid absorbency. Unlike a slushy chick-lit, though, the motorway hasn't had a fairy-tale existence. The projected numbers of vehicles never materialised, a situation made considerably worse by the economic downturn since 2008; it's currently used by fewer than half of the anticipated 74,000 cars a day. In a bid to make up the shortfall, tolls have risen almost every year, to £5.50 on a weekday at the time of writing – considerably more than a cup of coffee, even at motorway service station prices.

The very limited success of the M6 Toll has made the government hold back from using it as a model for other new motorways. Investors are nervous too, for if a smooth, easy ride bypassing one of the most notorious sections of the motorway network cannot provide a return, what chance anywhere else? Other prospective toll motorways, mooted when the M6 Toll opened, have been quietly put aside – for now, anyway.

Congestion charging in cities has been the other great plank of revenue-raising road policy, but that's had only marginally more success. The city of Durham was the first to pilot a scheme, in 2002, though this covered only a tiny part of the city centre. All eyes were on London, whose central congestion charge zone began in February 2003 under the city's former mayor, Ken Livingstone. In the 10 years of its existence it has become thoroughly normalised, but how effective it has been in combatting congestion – or pollution – is another matter. Yes, journeys by private cars in central London are down, but so are they in most other big British cities, none of which have a charge (Edinburgh and Manchester tried to bring one in, but both were heavily defeated in local referenda). The number of taxis, buses and delivery vans has rocketed, but so has the number of bicycles.

Technological advances in surveillance mean that the London charge is now largely policed by automatic number plate recognition (ANPR), and that is where many politicians are looking to go next on a wider scale. It will not be popular. In 2007, more than 1.8 million people signed an anti-road-pricing petition on the Downing Street website; there are many – and not just on the libertarian right of the political spectrum, though they of course are incandescent – who feel deeply uneasy about this as a potential development. And like the M6 Toll, the London charge has escalated substantially. When it was introduced, Ken Livingstone said 'I can't conceive of any circumstances in the foreseeable future where we would want to change the charge, although perhaps 10 years down the line it may be necessary'. Nine years later, it had already doubled to £10 per car.

The road atlas has been by far the biggest seller of all maps over the last few decades. Despite that, and perhaps unfairly, they have always been the maps that people have treated with the least regard, especially

Congestion charging

Central ZONE

Above left to right: The quieter-than-expected M6 Toll motorway: entering the London congestion charge zone

the floppy versions, condemned to spend eternity gradually shedding pages in the footwell of the passenger seat. In fact, their cartography is often excellent, even if the emphasis on motorways and trunk roads at the expense of all else has promoted a rather reductive view of the landscape, but that's been the case since the very first road atlas at the beginning of the 20th century.

There was little to choose between the road atlases available; you tended to find the one whose style of mapping you liked the most, and stick with it. Lorry drivers, sales reps and petrolheads often preferred the A–Z road atlases, with their forensic depiction of each swirl and slip road of every motorway junction. As in the street atlases that made their name and reputation, it is the roads that matter above all else, and the main roads at that. These are not maps for people who want to go off the beaten track.

At the other end of the spectrum, Ordnance Survey's efforts appealed to those who were already devotees of their larger-scale map series.

*Opposite: A–Z road
atlases emphasise the
main roads more than any
other; they would be a
mile or more wide if they
were to scale*

They sold in handsome quantity throughout the 1980s and 90s; many editions of their annual *Motoring Atlas of Great Britain* went to eight or nine reprints. They very much played to their traditional market, their covers often emblazoned with the logos of the National Trust and English Heritage, flagging up the fact that the maps not only showed such sites but included directories of them too (the inherent Anglocentricism of this goes apparently unnoticed). As if to confirm that this was the chosen atlas of Middle England, later editions also included directories of gardens open to members of the Royal Horticultural Society and a list of publicly open 'Historic Royal Palaces'.

Between these extremes, Collins, RAC and AA atlases share a certain aesthetic. The mapping is clean and functional; it will get you to where you want to go and even show you a few interesting back road alternatives if you have time on your hands or hit an unexpected hold-up. On occasion, companies have produced sponsored maps and atlases, for those more interested in locating their nearest supermarket or burger bar than National Trust property. There have been supermarket tie-ins too; for many years, the AA co-produced maps with the Morrisons supermarket chain – the fact that both had yellow and black as their signature colours made for harmonious packaging, at least.

In some ways, the supermarkets took up where the oil companies had left off in the 1970s, selling branded, smaller-scale atlases at rock-bottom prices. Sainsbury's worked with Ordnance Survey and then the Oxford Cartographers; true to form, Tesco chopped and changed its suppliers between the RAC, Geographers' A-Z, Collins and the Oxford Cartographers. You could even pick up free mini-atlases, though these were christened *Tesco Storefinders*, with every store prominently marked (although in 2005 they had to remove the smaller Tesco Extra stores from the map, as there were now so many of them and the map had become prohibitively cluttered).

While the sponsored atlases shrank, there was a movement at the paying end of the market towards giganticism. In 1996 the *Philip's Navigator Road Atlas* hit the shops, described on the cover as 'Britain's most detailed road atlas'. Indeed it was; the predominant scale of

1:100,000, roughly 1 inch to 1.5 miles, was at least twice that of any of its rivals. Most of Scotland was relegated to a far smaller scale – no surprise perhaps in the sparsely populated areas of the Highlands and Islands, but slightly random in according the same demotion to the Dumfries and Galloway area of the southwest. It's a handy tool for those of us who like to explore away from the main roads, although it's a bulky old beast, and following a long journey does necessitate an awful lot of page changing. Other cartographers briefly followed suit, for example the AA with their *Close-up Trucker's Atlas* that included a 'Bashed Bridges Hit List' and locations of truck stops and caffs, but this market is all Philip's now, and although it has dwindled, they still sell a decent number today.

MAPPING NOISE

Modern life is loud. It is a rare treat to find yourself these days in a place with little or no noise pollution, and prolonged exposure to noise is now increasingly being thought of as a significant health factor. When the European parliament drew up its Environmental Noise Directive (END) in 2002, it was said that exposure to noise was directly accountable for 10,000 deaths across the continent each year.

The END instructed member governments to draw up noise maps of their major conurbations and strategic transport routes. These maps are good examples of how the digital age has revolutionised cartography, for they mash up a variety of data to produce the end combined result. The geographical layer comes first, broken in to small tiles that are individually processed to give a highly localised level of precision. On that is overlain the different noise levels of roads, rail and air travel according to recognised parameters that take into account factors such as speed and number of vehicles. These are further filtered through digital terrain models that identify natural sound barriers or bafflers such as hills and forests. Once the map has been produced, it is tested by taking measurements on the ground. The strike rate of accuracy is extremely high.

Noise maps are an invaluable tool for planners, whether of new housing or infrastructure. They are useful too for countryside campaigners, the tourism

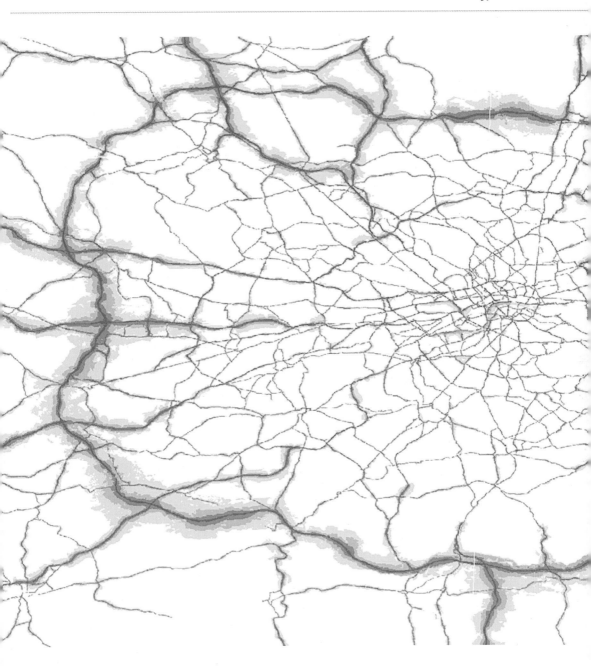

Above: The return of the cyclists' map: Ordnance Survey's 1990s series of Cycle Tour atlases was a symbol of the rebirth of cycling cool

industry and people looking to buy houses. Peace and quiet, an all too elusive commodity for many, has a financial value, and it is one that is increasingly being mapped.

The road atlas market peaked in the years following the turn of the millennium, with many variations on the theme to tempt prospective punters. Harking back to maps of a century earlier, Ordnance Survey produced a series of A5, spiral-bound regional road atlases for cyclists, each with a few dozen recommended day-ride routes from railway stations. New mountain bikes were making off-road and rough terrain cycling a fast-growing sport, though there were precious few dedicated cycle routes at the time. Using their 1:50,000 Landranger mapping as the base, Ordnance Survey highlighted in Day-Glo yellow quiet lanes as the main recommended routes, even when there were excellent alternative options in the canal towpaths. For these, cyclists were supposed to have a permit from British Waterways, although few ever bothered; Ordnance Survey played it safe, even telling cyclists to get off and walk when they hit a towpath. Tea shops and pubs en route, and that necessary old favourite of cycling maps, the gradient profile diagram, were included.

Perhaps the most startling addition to the stable was the *Upside Down Atlas of Great Britain* (2000), which grew from a map first produced in 1997 by a young inventor, Ashley Sims. The cover strapline – 'For Easier and Safer Travelling from North to South' – gave some hint of its genesis, when his dad John, a trucker, had returned home to Derby from a trip to Scotland and had become increasingly exasperated at trying to follow the route in a conventional atlas. 'If you turn the map upside down, the place names are unreadable and if you read the map backwards in the direction you are driving, right-hand turns and places are on the left and vice versa,' he explained.

Most people thought it was a joke – including the cartography companies and booksellers that Ashley approached with the idea. But after an unsuccessful meeting with an all-male panel of executives at W H Smith, one of the company's female bosses who hadn't been there heard about the idea and backed it. They received massive publicity:

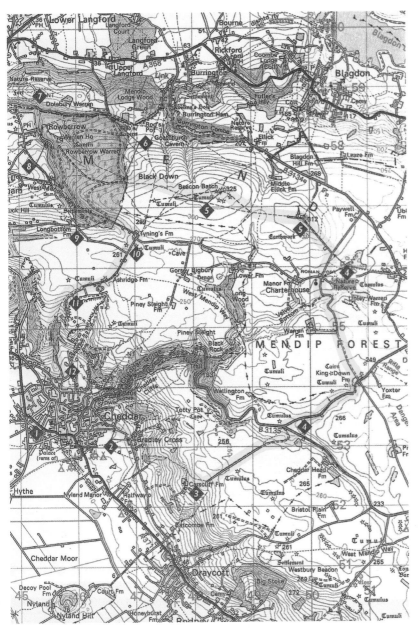

Left: Detail from
Ordnance Survey Cycle
Tours Avon, Somerset
& Wiltshire *(1995).*
Slightly bizarrely, the
designated route ignores
the most spectacular
option of cycling through
the Cheddar Gorge

Right: John and Ashley Sims's early Upside Down Map of Great Britain *(1997)*

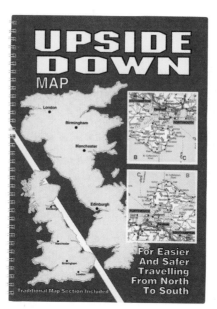

a few 'and finally...' TV news pieces and similarly wry press coverage. *The Daily Mail* ran a story about the map and offered a free copy to the first hundred people to write in. They had 15,000 requests, all but a tiny handful from women. It seems that there was some truth in the old cliché about women turning the map upside down to navigate – though why not? To do so has been the recommended course of action in the British Army map-reading handbook since 1906, and as an Outward Bound leader once said to me, 'it's a lot easier to move the map than move the mountain'. Ashley and his father went on to publish 'Upside Down' maps of other places; the series sold over 300,000 copies.

All of these, and indeed the full spectrum of printed paper maps, were about to be engulfed in a cartographic revolution. Digital technology was sweeping all before it, and in the world of maps its effects were revolutionary. For many of those steering their way around Britain's increasingly crowded road network, the satellite navigation device – or satnav, as it quickly became known – was a godsend. Until the arrival of

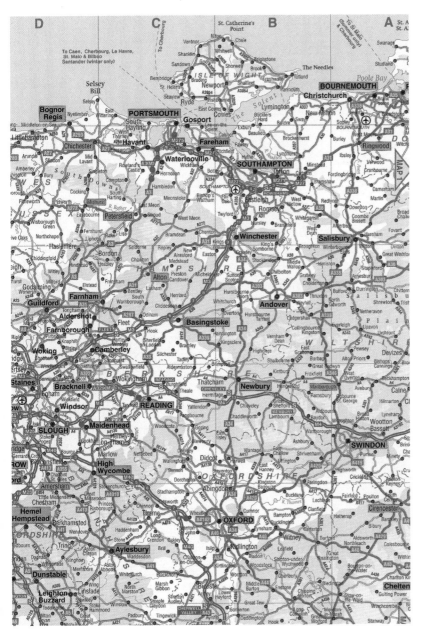

Left: Detail and index map from the Upside Down Map of Great Britain *(1997)*

Opposite: M74 plan:
Perhaps the last major
new motorway project of
all, the M74 south
of Glasgow finally
opened in 2011

the smartphone in the following decade, satnavs were the fastest-adopted piece of new gadgetry in British history; most new cars now include one built in as standard. Paper maps and road atlases were jettisoned with gusto, as millions took to their TomToms and headed for the hills.

GOING OUR SEPARATE WAYS

Since the establishment of the Scottish Parliament and Welsh Assembly in 1999, many aspects of life have diverged in the three constituent countries of Britain. Transport policy has been one of the more obvious, especially in Scotland. Old railway lines have been brought back into service, and most of the new motorways of the last decade have been north of the border. If it wasn't for the almighty cock-up of the Edinburgh tram scheme, you'd almost believe that the Scots have found answers to questions that the rest of Britain are still struggling to decipher.

The M77 to Kilmarnock, thence via dual carriageway to Ayr and Prestwick Airport, was finished in 2005. That was nothing, though, compared with the mighty achievement of the M74 finally getting to snake its way through the southern reaches of Glasgow and connect up with the M8 just to the south of Kingston Bridge. Not that you can directly access the bridge from the M74: such is the congestion on the M8 as it winds its tight little way around the city centre that it was decided to allow the new motorway to disgorge only onto the westbound M8, meaning that the famous ski jump, where the original plans had the southern motorway joining, remains gloriously intact and redundant still.

The M74 is a staggering project all the same. It's not quite the Glasgow motorway box as envisaged in the 1960s, but it does complete a bigger, baggier circuit around the city, and in its boldness does hark back to long-gone days when urban motorways were thought of as the panacea to all transport ills. It is likely to be the last of its kind. Due mainly to the large elevated sections needed, the five-mile Rutherglen and Glasgow extension to the M74 is one of the most expensive pieces of road ever built, its total cost of £692 million working out at £78,000 per yard. £200 million of the bill was swallowed up in the compulsory purchase of land and buildings alone.

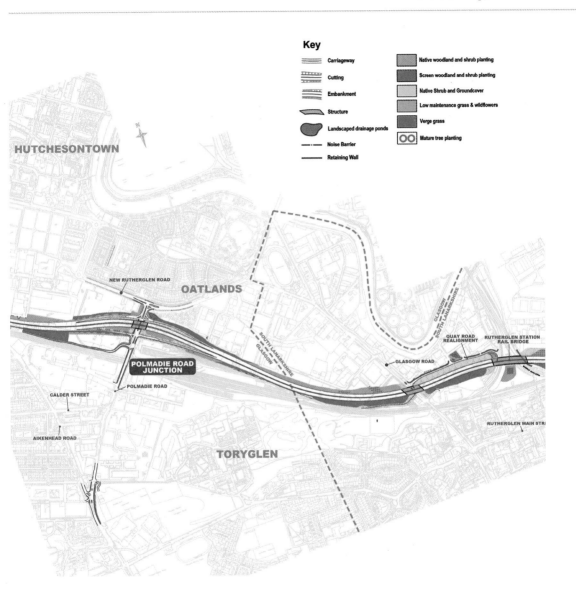

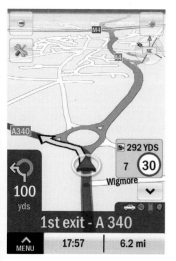

Above: Screenshot from AA Satnav UK & Ireland iPhone® app

Only the A3 Hindhead tunnel and the Limehouse link in east London have proved more costly.

The M74 extension was opened in June 2011. Just beyond its other end, by the Scottish–English border at Gretna, the last gap in the London to Glasgow motorway (M6/M74) was filled in a couple of years earlier with the completion of the section north of Carlisle. Neatly, it was opened on 5 December 2008, 50 years to the day since the opening of the Preston bypass, the first part of the M6 and the first motorway in Britain. Once this, the M74 and a new bit of the A1(M) had been built, however, there were – for the first time since those heady days – no motorways under construction anywhere in Britain. The era may well have drawn to a close – as indeed may the era of the United Kingdom.

Like so many advances in cartography, the satnav is a spin-off from military development. The Global Positioning System (or GPS) that powers it is not a generic term, as many suppose; it is the name of the network of satellites first launched by the Pentagon in the 1970s. It was fully operational by 1994, but only allowed into the civilian sphere in 2000. This gave birth to the commercial satnav, but the Pentagon's tight hold on GPS has meant that some use the equivalent Russian GLONASS system. China and the EU are both also developing satellite systems, though these are not yet fully functional.

Since the earliest days of the car, inventors have dreamed of something like the satnav, and finally technology has allowed the dream to come true. Over the years there were numerous analogue prototypes of an in-car navigation system; a US patent was filed in 1909 for the Jones Live Map, which relied on prescribed paper routes mounted on a turntable and mechanically powered by the car's odometer. An early advertisement for the device promised that drivers can 'take all the puzzling corners and forks with never a pause. You never stop to inquire' – the holy grail indeed for the driver.

Even in little more than a decade, the GPS-driven satnav has developed at a staggering pace. Early examples were prone to all kinds of mishaps; combined with inevitable human fallibility, the catalogue of

satnav woes built up almost daily. Cars, lorries and especially delivery trucks were getting wedged in medieval gatehouses, plunged into rivers, stuck in muddy farmyards and left teetering on cliff edges as drivers preferred to trust a gizmo from Halfords over the evidence of their own two eyes.

To satnav refuseniks like me, every such story offered a smug dose of *Schadenfreude*. My suspicions were based entirely on years of loving and studying maps, and the consequent love of travelling and exploring that this passion had nurtured in me. I couldn't see how a satnav would ever ignite such a sense of wonder, for their blocky, angular mapping and truncated topography seemed to boil down the infinite variety of our landscape into a grey nothing: just the next mile or so of traffic lights, speed cameras, gyratories and petrol stations. You could drive from Aberdeen to Aberdare and barely notice where you'd passed through en route.

None of this made me warm much to the satnav, though there is of course another side to the story. The explosion in digital cartography – not just satnavs, but the GPS systems on our phones and the phenomenal range on the internet – has meant that few people get through a day now without looking at a map or two. Although there is a danger of over-reliance on our gadgetry, this upsurge of easy familiarity with cartography is surely a good thing, and perhaps thanks to this, our sense of topographic context has not suffered as much as I feared; indeed, for many people, it may well have improved.

In 2010, I did a series for Radio 4 called *On the Map*, and wanted to test my cold (and, if I'm honest, snobbish) certainty that satnav devotees drive through a limbo landscape, knowing little of where they are en route, and caring even less. The series producer and I spent a chilly winter's afternoon at a service station on the M40 in Oxfordshire, pouncing on new arrivals and asking them to mark, on a blank outline map of Britain, where we were. The punters had come from all over the country (a disproportionate number were heading south from Scotland), but almost everyone was able to do it to a remarkable degree of accuracy. I was wrong.

I do still wonder about the mapping on satnavs though, and how it affects people's perception of the country. As we've seen throughout history, road maps emphasise roads, and as the roads have got bigger, their representation on the map has ballooned even further out of proportion. Satnavs take this to a logical conclusion, where the road – and you on the road – are the centre of everything. Little else exists. It's not beyond reason to see the psychological effects that this might have – everything from extreme selfishness and impatience, through intolerance of other road users, to a sour, curdled certainty that the country seems to be bursting at the seams.

THE MAP IS DEAD – LONG LIVE THE MAP!

If you read a report about maps these days, it will almost inevitably contain something about 'the death of the traditional paper map'. So often has it been said that it has become a truism all of its own, without actually being true. In just the same way that books, newspapers, magazines and vinyl records have been prematurely written off as casualties of the digital revolution, so it seems are paper maps refusing to follow the script and quietly die.

i	Information centre, all year/seasonal Office de tourisme, ouvert toute l'année/en saison Informationsbüro, ganzjährig/saisonal	**cycle**	Cycle trail Piste cyclable Radfahrweg
V	Visitor centre Centre pour visiteurs Besucherzentrum		Mountain bike trail Chemin pour VTT Mountainbike-Strecke
	Forestry Commission visitor centre Commission Forestière: Centre de visiteurs Staatsforst Besucherzentrum		Cycle hire Location de vélos Fahrradverleih
PC	Public convenience Toilettes Öffentliche Toilette	**U**	Horse riding Equitation Reitstall
	Telephone, public/roadside assistance/emergency Téléphone, public/borne d'appel d'urgence/urgence Telefon, öffentlich/Notrufsäule/Notruf		Viewpoint Point de vue Aussichtspunkt
	Camp site/caravan site Terrain de camping/Terrain pour caravanes Campingplatz/Wohnwagenplatz		Picnic site Emplacement de pique-nique Picknickplatz
	Recreation/leisure/sports centre Centre de détente/loisirs/sports Erholungs-/Freizeit-/Sportzentrum		Country park Parc naturel Landschaftspark
	Golf course or links Terrain de golf Golfplatz		Garden/arboretum Jardin/Arboretum Garten/Baumgarten
	Theme/pleasure park Parc à thèmes/Parc d'agrément Vergnügungs-/Freizeitpark		Water activities Jeux aquatiques Wassersport

Left: Tourism and leisure are the main drivers of sales for Ordnance Survey's beautiful, and spectacularly successful, new 1:25,000 Explorer series, as the ever-increasing array of blue symbols testifies

Although sales of hard-copy Ordnance Survey maps have dropped by about a quarter in the last decade, they actually recorded a noticeable spike in 2008–09, the first upsurge of the 'staycation', especially for their 1:25,000 Explorer series in its bright orange livery. This is a relatively new kid on the block, for Ordnance Survey mapping at this scale had hitherto been quite patchy and always a very poor relation to the flagship one-inch series and its metric replacement, the 1:50,000 Landranger. The Explorer series only finally covered the whole country in 2003.

Its success says much about why people still buy paper maps, and will continue to do so. Their covers say it all; most are highly posed shots of people walking, cycling, climbing, riding horses or sailing – this is very much pitched as the map for folk who want to get outdoors and explore. Walkers in particular find the Explorer maps essential, for this is the smallest scale at which all field boundaries can be shown, a godsend on the occasions when the dotted green line on the map fails to translate into an easy or obvious path on the ground.

This is very much a pointer to why and how we use maps these days, for the purposes of tourism. Day-to-day navigational needs, especially in vehicles, are increasingly left to the satnav and the smartphone, but it is when we relax that we often prefer to return to the map. You can see it in the cartography, as a welter of little blue tourist symbols, denoting anything from a country pub to a craft centre, proliferates across the paper. Licensing of Ordnance Survey's extensive database means that you can now buy their mapping but interpreted and published by other companies, most notably the AA and A–Z.

Of course, for every happy hiker setting off with their trusty Ordnance Survey, there are the requisite numpties trying to get up Snowdon or Scafell in flip-flops and armed with only the TomTom from their dashboard. As Ruth Crosbie, from the Loch Lomond and the Trossachs National Park, put it: 'We get asked a lot for the postcode of the top of Ben Lomond (3,196 feet). These are from people who are actually going to walk up it without any maps but armed with a satnav.' If it weren't for the inconvenience to mountain rescue teams, my hunch would be to let them go for it. There's a lot to be said for natural selection.

Selfishness is an almost inevitable by-product of car culture. Like many people, I become a far less patient person as a driver than I am in the rest of life, and it's not a very appealing trait. It's a long-standing one, though. In 1931, C E M Joad wrote about suddenly coming upon a busy road on a day's walking:

> *The procession moves, now faster now slower, and every now and then two cars in it change places; but always it goes on. The faces of the motorists are strained and angry; upon them there is an air of tense expectancy, and in the intervals between their spasmodic bursts of activity they glower at one another.*

Also in this same dark corner is a thoroughly questionable sense of victimhood, and that's been there since the beginning too. Way back in 1926, *Autocar* wrote that a driver's 'sense of injustice is very developed, and it is inborn in us to revolt at injustice'. This was written in defence of someone who had killed a pedestrian and driven away from the scene, for 'motorists run away after causing accidents because they know their case will not be tried free of prejudice and they feel they will not obtain justice'. Six years later, in another fatal accident when a car mowed down an 86-year-old pedestrian, the coroner commented that 'old ladies who go about like this may cause any amount of danger to other people'.

We drivers are not a persecuted minority. We may well be the victims of many years of poor government decisions, dithering and a fair scattering of utter incompetence, but exactly the same could be said for train passengers, cyclists or pedestrians. But still the grievances persist. In recent years the exponential growth in speed cameras on roads has been one of the major flashpoints, and has often been cited as proof that successive governments are 'waging war' on the motorist.

The controversy leaked onto our maps too. From the early days of satnavs, many included the capacity to warn drivers of impending speed cameras, which was undoubtedly one of the main reasons for their swift uptake. When that information was first placed on paper maps, in the 2006 *AA Road Atlas*, all hell broke loose. A spokesman for pressure group Transport 2000 described it as 'irresponsible in the extreme' and 'encouraging illegal behaviour'. In truth, the information was already out there – on police forces' own websites for starters – and all the cartographers did was collate and display it. And as the AA pointed out at the time, if the first thing you knew of a speed camera was when the fine landed on your doormat, then it hadn't done its job of slowing traffic down very well, a point supported by the Association of Chief Police Officers.

Showing the sites of speed cameras is now standard practice in nearly all road atlases, for commercial reasons as much as anything. After all, it's hard work persuading satnav devotees that they should also invest in a proper map, and any feature that might encourage that is gratefully employed. As ever, the latest crop of road atlases reflects the mood of the moment, including regular locations of mobile speed cameras as well as the static ones, hospital A&E units, new 'jam busting' maps of good alternative routes, and, in something of a return to the mapping of old, 'wide minor roads (more than 4m)', many of them former A roads that have been demoted. Perhaps the best reason why you should have

a paper map in your car was put to me by someone from Google Maps, no less: 'You have to remember that power fails. Technology fails. And it's all in the hands of the US military.'

Opposite: Controversy was sparked in 2006 when the AA first put speed camera locations in its road atlases, though by 2013 this was common practice

ROADS AS CULTURAL ICONS

A decade or two ago, if you'd gone into your local bookshop to search out works on roads, it would have been a thin – and decidedly dry – range that confronted you. Things have changed. Roads are now so ingrained in our national psyche that they have leapt from the dusty corners of transport academia to become iconic subjects of books, websites, online forums, even pop songs, films, radio and TV programmes.

In his *Notes from a Small Island* (1995), American writer and humorist Bill Bryson writes of his bewilderment at the typical small talk of a British party, where guests describe in detail their routes along the A-this and the M-that, mentally reliving the journey to an appreciative audience. A querulous one too; Bryson describes the inevitable ensuing arguments as guests tell of their own secret back roads, short cuts and rat runs. To Bryson, such pernickety subject matter is ripe for his sardonic observations. I remember reading this section of his book and thinking, 'what's his problem? I love those conversations…'

And not just for their content. If someone is detailing their journey along the B4022 or round the Nether Twinkle by-pass, and is copiously acting it out with their hand gestures as they mentally roam around the map, I know that they are, quite literally, a fellow traveller, and that I may well have an interesting chat with them before the night is through.

Murders in cold Nordic climes aside, one of the most successful series ever shown on BBC4 was the surprise and much-repeated hit *The Secret Life of the Motorway* (2007), which told the story of how we fell in, and then out of, love with the motorway system. They are beautiful, elegiac films, with a soundtrack, inevitably, that includes not just Kraftwerk's groundbreaking electronica *Autobahn* from 1974, but Black Box Recorder's bittersweet *English Motorway System* from 2000.

The Secret Life of the Motorway mined the seam of social and cultural context to the roads, one that has been cropping up too on the bookshelf.

Joe Moran's *On Roads* (2009) is peerless for a thorough – and deeply charming – overview, while others chose to dig deep into the myth and mediocrity of individual roads: Edward Platt's dystopian history of London's A40 Western Avenue in *Leadville* (2000); Pieter and Rita Boogaart's quest for the hidden pilgrim route in *A272: An Ode to a Road* (2000); Tom Fort's cheerful and nostalgic *The A303: Highway to the Sun* (2012), which he also turned into an hour-long documentary on BBC4. This, too, has been one of the channel's greatest hits.

As the digital revolution roars on, our mapping options have become seemingly limitless. Spend a few seconds online and you can now call up bespoke recommended routes for any journey possible, a far cry from writing politely to the AA or RAC and waiting a week or so for their typewritten response. The AA's online route-planner service, launched in 1999, delivers over 4 million routes a week, with Gatwick Airport being the most regularly requested destination. As well as showing a selection of routes, including if chosen those that avoid motorways or tolls/congestion charges, the AA Route Planner also offers overlays of reported accidents, roadworks and closures, or hotels en route – AA-approved, of course. It is the classic 1960s members' handbook come to digital life.

Cartography is one of the areas of existence that has undergone the greatest change in the digital revolution. Click on any location in GeoHack and you're presented with a bewildering array of available mapping options: fully zoomable and up-to-date cartography from Ordnance Survey, Bing, Michelin, Yahoo! and others, databases of old, out-of-copyright maps, and bespoke interactive plans of roadworks, flood warnings, traffic conditions, petrol prices, cycling options and pretty much anything else that combines a depiction of the lie of the land with fast-changing information.

Particularly noteworthy are Open Street Map (OSM), often referred to as the Wikipedia of cartography, and the all-conquering Google Maps. OSM is a vast and growing database whose aim is to map the entire world, free of charge and for infinite re-use. Using freely available

'Delightful, nostalgic, slyly witty, perceptive . . .
a wonderfully charming book' SPECTATOR

TOM FORT

THE A303

HIGHWAY TO THE SUN

aerial photography, old maps and GPS data crowd-sourced from its volunteers, it is editable by any of its million registered contributors. Inevitably, the mapping is patchier in some parts of the world than others, but it is growing steadily, its cartographic interface is clean and quite traditional (the colours used are largely the same as found on an Ordnance Survey map), and the level of detail in the best-mapped towns and cities is phenomenal.

The comparison of OSM with Wikipedia is perhaps even more striking than at first it seems. In the early days of the online encyclopedia, it was frequently criticised for the hyper-subjectivity, and hence inaccuracy, of its entries. As more people, in all corners of the world, have become involved, these have been steadily ironed out, and although some enduring howlers and short-lived pranks can and do spike its accuracy, there were mistakes aplenty too in the printed heyday of the *Encyclopaedia Britannica* and its ilk, and some of those lasted for decades. As the breadth of data used to update OSM or Wikipedia increases, so too do their depth and reliability.

The concept of free, crowd-sourced mapping has been extended into the world of interactive data collection, too, telling us not just where we are travelling, but how well we are likely to get there. The best known example is Waze, founded as an Israeli community project in 2006 and which took off so speedily, it was bought by Google for $1 billion in 2013. Downloadable as an app for mobile devices, Waze deploys its users' real-time flow of GPS information to keep tabs on average road speeds so as to warn others of especially slow routes or sudden hold-ups. As well as providing a passive, constant supply of information this way, users can also input specific alerts about road closures, hold-ups, accidents and police speed traps, and even use it to point them to today's lowest petrol prices in a particular area. The UK is one of Waze's best-covered countries, and has been downloaded by half a million drivers in London alone.

As in so many other areas of life, it is Google that has created most of the headlines in the digital mapping market, and it's hard to remember that their service has only existed in Britain since 2006, so swiftly has it taken all before it. In the early days, Google Maps were

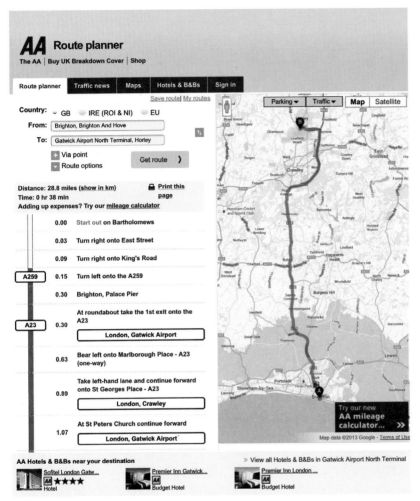

Left: The AA Route Planner: Online cartography creates bespoke route plans that can be seen at every different scale, or overlaid with whatever information the viewer wants

quite rudimentary and caused much caustic comment – in 2008, a spat erupted between them and the British Cartographic Society, whose president called their mapping 'corporate blankwash' that was 'diluting the quality of the graphic image that we call a map'. Since then, they have improved exponentially, and with the addition of superb satellite imagery, together with the incredible Google Street View captured by

Above: A Google Street View car collects its information by taking a constant stream of 360° photographs

360° cameras mounted on cars, it is now possible to look in minute detail at almost every road, street, lane and close in the land without leaving your armchair.

The mapping is so instinctive that it is easy to forget what mammoth and specialised cartographic input has created it – a salutary reminder of that came in 2012, when the previously untouchable Apple corporation launched their rival mapping service to a well-deserved chorus of derision. Thanks to judicious acquisitions, Google has now become by far the biggest player in digital mapping – indeed, some of their most expensive takeovers have been to expand specifically in this area of their operation. Waze (see earlier) is well within their top ten takeovers, as was Skybox Imaging, a company that specialised in producing high-resolution satellite imagery, high-definition video and analytics services now used to augment Google Street View. They search amongst the small fry too. A further Street View boost was provided in Google's 2015 buyout of Digisfera, a small Portuguese start-up company that specialises in 360° panoramic photography.

It is Google, too, at the forefront of the race to pioneer the driverless car, surely the next big revolution on the road. Google's supremo behind their efforts, Sebastian Thrun, was also one of the chief designers of Street View; they have been showing off the results since 2012, but only in certain prescribed areas of the USA. In the UK, the government granted permission in 2015 for driverless vehicles to be tested on Britain's roads. Pilot schemes are operating in Milton Keynes, Greenwich, Coventry and Bristol, principally using the Lutz Pathfinder prototype vehicle, designed and built in the old motor manufacturing city of Coventry. The Lutz contains 22 sensors, including panoramic cameras, laser imaging, and radar, which are used to build a virtual image of the world around it. While it may seem counter-intuitive, much of the impetus for developing driverless cars has come from the imperative of improving road safety. The early driverless vehicles have had a few scrapes, but most have occurred when the system was over-ridden for manual control, or due to the fault of other drivers on the road.

If the future is driverless, it is also potentially mapless, although there is a certain irony that the ever-enjoyable sport of idly following a map on your knee may well be the one to survive, and available to everyone – the 'driver' included – in the car of 2030. Until then, though, what does the future hold for road mapping? As our phones become ever smarter (and used less as phones and more as mobile computers), even the apparently all-conquering satnav is threatened with extinction, let alone the paper maps that it so unceremoniously swept aside only a decade ago. Yet paper maps still exist, and still sell – admittedly in smaller quantities than before, but not as diminished as might perhaps be expected. We have entered the age of the entirely bespoke map, created for precisely the journey you want to make and containing precisely the levels of information that you wish to include.

This is perhaps the world that the space-age dreamers of the post-war years imagined they were creating when they bulldozed our motorway network into place. Had all their plans succeeded, we would no doubt have a much more streamlined network, rather than the sometimes cramped and compromised one that we have ended up with. Yet, for all the sophistication of modern cars and the technology that now guides them, what we actually want to do with those cars, and where we want to go, remains as obdurately timeless as it did a century ago. We want to go shopping, to visit interesting places, see exciting things and catch up with far-flung friends and family. Although few of us would choose now to go out just for the sake of a drive on a Sunday afternoon, the thrill of the open road is still there for the taking, especially if you're prepared to ditch the monotonous diktat of the satnav and head for the smaller roads. Thanks mainly to the car, we all know our beautiful little island a great deal better than did our ancestors, and for that we should be truly grateful.

BECAUSE THE NIGHT

Of all the satellite views to which we have now become so used, the one that never fails to take my breath away is the one showing our world at night. Zoom in on Britain, and you can read so much from the brightly lit clusters and streaks that fill it.

London dominates, of course, a massive pulsing star firing its beams out in all directions. The Birmingham–Leeds–Liverpool triangle would be one big shield of light were it not for the dark sump of the Peak District at its heart. Pitch-black Scotland wears a thick neon belt across its narrow waist. The valleys of south Wales look like a fiery comb with its tines pointing down to Cardiff. And far off, in the inky gloom of the North Sea, blazing pinpricks mark where men wrestle oil and gas from the hostile depths.

Between the flares big and small of our towns, cities and expanding conurbations, lines of light thread their way across the murk: our motorways and trunk roads like a finely spun cobweb. They seem drunkenly erratic. The choke chain of the M25 is the brightest of them all, its job of restraining our hungry capital apparently doomed to failure. The area around Manchester and Liverpool is ablaze with lines criss-crossing each other and back again, as if drawn by a hyperactive toddler. The M5 and M4 are dot-to-dot puzzles straggling west.

'Light pollution' is a phrase much heard lately. To those allergic to any kind of green thinking, it gets lumped in with all the other things they hate to be reminded of: recycling, wind farms, road pricing, bus lanes, park and rides, conservation, the catch-all political correctness *gone mad!* But the realisation that many people barely ever see a proper night sky has made us pause for thought. 'Dark sky reserves', such as Galloway in Scotland, Exmoor in England and the Brecon Beacons in Wales, are using their very lightlessness as a marketing tool, and it's working.

We can't escape the roads' impact here. One of the most poignant and poetic sections of Meera Syal's fictionalised memoir *Anita and Me* deals with the aftermath of the new motorway near her village. Gone was the view from her bedroom window of the Milky Way, the Pole Star and Venus. Gone too was the ability to distinguish between the 'midnight blue black on the horizon', the 'pearly opaque black encircling the moon' and the 'heavy wet green-black of a stormy night sky' – all obliterated by the glare of the motorway which 'stitched up the horizon like a cheap seaside necklace'. Black 'was no longer a colour in its own right, but simply an absence of light'. We really don't know what we have until it's gone.

Opposite: Looking north up the spine of the Malvern Hills, the light pollution of the Herefordshire side to the left literally pales in comparison with that being pumped out to the right by Worcester and the distant conurbation of the West Midlands

Overleaf: Cobwebs of light mark out our towns, cities and the roads that connect them, none brighter than the M25 encircling London

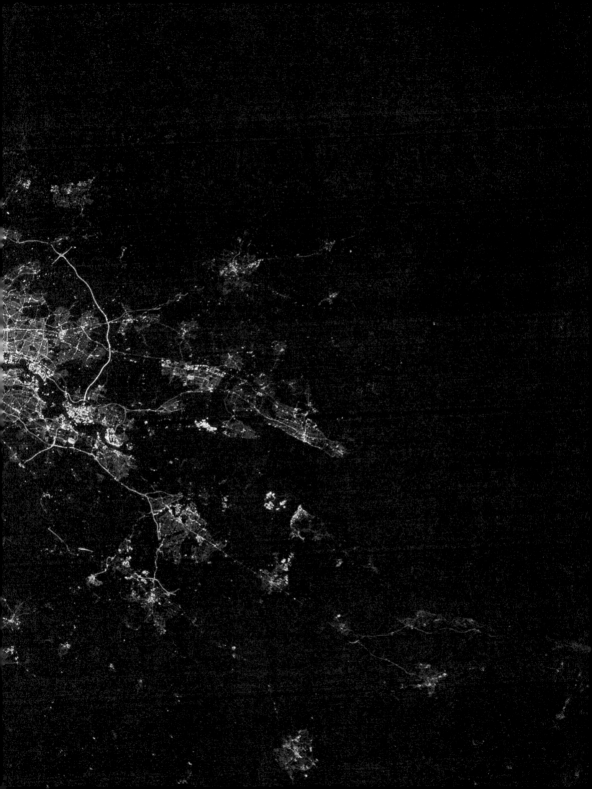

Further Reading

If, fellow map addicts, you've enjoyed *Mapping the Roads*, there's still an entire internet out there. This is just a small selection of my favourite blogs, websites, Twitter accounts and Pinterest boards. Perhaps they'll be of interest to you too. Perhaps you'll want to start up your own. Watch this space...

Blogs

The Map Room, www.maproomblog.com: USA-based, but with maps, including some highly unusual examples, from all over the world, and from all eras.

Jones the Planner, www.jonestheplanner.co.uk: incisive, erudite and fascinating essays on architecture, urban design and planning issues.

The Bodleian's Map Room Blog, blogs.bodleian.ox.ac.uk/maps/: always illuminating blog picking over some of the treasures of Oxford's Bodleian map library and placing them into a wider context.

Ordnance Survey, www.ordnancesurvey.co.uk/blog/: keep up to speed with the latest developments at the UK's national mapping agency.

Maps Mania, googlemapsmania.blogspot.co.uk: interesting overview of new developments in online and digital mapping, with comprehensive links.

Stanfords, www.stanfords.co.uk/blog: a lively blog about maps and voyaging, ideal for the armchair traveller.

Websites

National Library of Scotland, maps.nls.uk: a dazzlingly good resource for maps not just of Scotland, but England and Wales too. Side-by-side comparison of old and new, paper and digital, plus 3D realisation, estate and military maps, and all presented with crisp clarity.

Society for All British Road Enthusiasts (SABRE), www.sabre-roads.org.uk: huge historical resource of maps, pictures and write-ups of Britain's road network, including some real oddities. Lively forums too about a bewildering array of road-related matters.

Chris' British Road Directory (CBRD), www.cbrd.co.uk: comprehensive and fun road resource, including sections on sign fonts, notoriously bad junctions and a host of oddball facts and figures.

Pathetic Motorways, www.pathetic.org.uk: specializing in the lost, unbuilt and unfinished sections of the motorway network, this is full of great maps and pictures.

Motorway Services Online, motorwayservicesonline.co.uk: a comprehensive history site of the places we all love to hate. Full of strange facts and includes forums for the seriously interested.

The Motorway Archive, www.ukmotorwayarchive.org: a comprehensive history of the creation of Britain's motorway network, including documentation and photography from its creation.

Mapping London, mappinglondon.co.uk: from art to transport, planning to tourism, this is the best jumping-off point for an eye-watering variety of maps of the capital.

Glasgow Motorway Archive, www.glasgows-motorways.co.uk: a phenomenal collection of historical features, photos and maps of the motorways that Glasgow did build, and the many it did not.

Open Street Map, www.openstreetmap.org: the 'Wikipedia of mapping' – open source cartography of the world, always looking for new volunteers to help fill in the blanks.

AA Route Planner, www.theaa.com/route-planner/index.jsp: comprehensive and easy-to-use route planning site, with customarily excellent mapping.

Charles Close Society for the study of Ordnance Survey maps, www.charlesclosesociety.org: the venerable OS map 'fan club', with an ever-expanding repertoire of all things connected to our national cartographers.

Twitter
@BLMaps: regular updates from the British Library's Map Library.

@BritishSigns: dedicated to cataloguing the esoteric and unusual road signs of the land.

@carltonreid: American historian and author of the excellent and fascinating book, *Roads Were Not Built for Cars*.

@jackthurston: writer, broadcaster and photographer about transport and geography, specializing in cycling.

@joemoransblog: keen-eyed author of the lovely *On Roads* and other works of modern social history.

@onlmaps: News on maps from around the world, together with regular examples of some of the more interesting.

@worldmapper: hundreds of different maps of the world, distorted to show relative information (such as income, health, transport etc) between countries in an instantly visual way. Fascinating, and sometimes shocking.

Pinterest
Road Maps, uk.pinterest.com/lfwilson/road-maps/: From decoupage to drawer liners, coasters to jigsaws, this is a fun collection of ways to decorate your life with road maps.

UK Maps, uk.pinterest.com/dave_in_lincs/uk-maps/: a hugely varied collection of British maps, from the historic to the purely whimsical.

Maps & Illustrations – UK, uk.pinterest.com/globopato/maps-and-illustrations-uk/: some lovely hand-drawn maps of towns and regions of Britain, in art, advertising and travel guides.

Bibliography

Books

Baldwin, Sir Peter; Baldwin, Robert and Evans, Dewi Ieuan,
The Motorway Achievement: Building the Network in Southern and Eastern England

Barber, Peter, *The Map Book*

Barty-King, Hugh, *The AA: A History of the First 75 Years of the Automobile Association*

Black, Jeremy, *Maps and Politics*

Brown, Lloyd A, *The Story of Maps*

Browne, John Paddy, *Map Cover Art: A pictorial history of Ordnance Survey cover illustrations*

Carrington, John, *The Motorway Achievement: Building the Network in The Midlands*

Charlesworth, Dr. George, *A History of British Motorways*

Emmerson, Andrew and Bancroft, Peter, *A, B, C and M: Road Numbering Revealed*

Farley, Paul and Symmons Roberts, Michael, *Edgelands*

Fleet, Christopher; Wilkes, Margaret and Withers, Charles W J, *Scotland: Mapping the Nation*

Fort, Tom, *The A303: Highway to the Sun*

Gardiner, Leslie, *Bartholomew, 150 Years*

Gascoigne, Bamber, *Encyclopaedia of Britain*

Gilbert, Nigel, *A History of Kidderminster*

Grigson, Jeffrey, *The Shell Country Alphabet*

Hadfield, John (Ed.), *The Shell Guide to England*

Hawker, Brian and Stevens, Howard, *The Motorway Achievement: Building the Network in Wales*

Headicar, Peter, *Transport Policy and Planning in Great Britain*

Hewitt, Rachel, *Map of a Nation: A Biography of the Ordnance Survey*

Higley, Chris, *Old Series to Explorer, a field guide to the Ordnance map*

Hill, Marion, *Memories of Milton Keynes*

Hindle, Paul, *Maps for Historians*

Hindle, Paul, *Medieval Roads and Tracks*

Llewellyn, Alun, *The Shell Guide to Wales*

McLaren, Moray, *The Shell Guide to Scotland*

Merriman, Peter, *Driving Spaces: A Cultural-Historical Geography of England's M1 Motorway*

Millea, Nick, *The Gough Map*

Milner, David, *The Highways and Byways of Britain*

Moore-Colyer, Richard, *Roads & Trackways of Wales*

Moran, Joe, *On Roads*

Moule, Thomas, *The County Maps of Old England*

Nicholson, Jon, *A1: Portrait of a Road*

Nicholson, T R, *Wheels on the Road, Road Maps of Britain 1870–1940*

O'Connell, Sean, *The Car and British society: Class, Gender and Motoring 1896–1939*

Oliver, Richard, *Ordnance Survey Maps, a concise guide for historians*

Perkins, Chris and Dodge, Martin, *Mapping the Imagined Future: The Roles of Visual Representation in the 1945 City of Manchester Plan*

Platt, Edward, *Leadville: A Biography of the A40*

Rackham, Oliver, *The Illustrated History of the Countryside*

Rickards, Maurice, *The Encyclopaedia of Ephemera*

Rowley, Trevor, *The English Landscape in the Twentieth Century*

Sillitoe, Alan *Down from the Hill*

Sims, F A, *The Motorway Achievement: Building the Network in the North-East of England*

Speed, John, *The Counties of Britain: A Tudor Atlas*

Syal, Meera, *Anita and Me*

Wacher, John, *Roman Britain*

Yeadon, Harry L, *The Motorway Achievement: Building the Network in the North-West of England*

Websites

A1; The Great North Road – www.biffvernon.freeserve.co.uk/contents.htm

A Vision of Britain Through Time – www.visionofbritain.org.uk/maps/

Automotive Timeline – www.gracesguide.co.uk/Timeline:_Automotive

Cartography Unchained – www.cartographyunchained.com/tp1.html

Chris's British Road Directory – www.cbrd.co.uk/

Commercial Motor Archive – archive.commercialmotor.com

Glasgow Motorway Archive – www.glasgows-motorways.co.uk

Hipkiss' Scanned Old Maps – www.hipkiss.org/data/maps.html

(Adrian) Jones the Planner – www.jonestheplanner.co.uk

M1 Motorway – The Age of Innocence – aipetcher.wordpress.com/tag/m1-motorway/

The Motorway Archive – www.ciht.org.uk/motorway/page1.htm

Motorway Services Online – motorwayservicesonline.co.uk

Motorway Services Trivia Site – www.msatrivia.co.uk

Old Maps Online – www.oldmapsonline.org

Old Roads of Scotland – www.oldroadsofscotland.com/index.html

Ordnance Survey New Popular Edition maps – www.npemap.org.uk

Pathetic Motorways – www.pathetic.org.uk

Petrol Maps from Europe – www.ianbyrne.free-online.co.uk/index.htm

Roads UK – www.roadsuk.com/website/about/

Roads Were Not Built for Cars – www.roadswerenotbuiltforcars.com/

Rural Roads – www.rural-roads.co.uk/index.shtml

SABRE (Society for All British Road Enthusiasts) – www.sabre-roads.org.uk

Thanks

Karla Baker, Alan Rosevear, Richard Oliver, Margaret Wilkes, Rodney Leary, David Archer, Steven Jukes, Frank Prest, Peredur Tomos, members of the Charles Close Society, Helen Brocklehurst and colleagues at the AA. Most of all, thanks to the endlessly helpful members of the Society for All British Road Enthusiasts (SABRE), without doubt the best – and most entertaining – place to find out anything about roads and their strange history. You can lose whole days on those forums…

Index

Picture Credits

The AA wishes to thank the following photographers and organisations for their assistance in the preparation of this book. Every effort has been made to trace the copyright holders, and we apologise in advance for any unintentional omissions or errors. We would be pleased to apply any corrections in a following edition of this publication. Abbreviations for the picture credits are as follows – (t) top: (b) bottom: (l) left; (r) right; (c) centre; (AA) Automobile Association.

4 The British Library Board/Cotton Claudius D. VI, f.12v; 7 European Space Agency–ESA; 8–9 The Bodleian Library, University of Oxford, MS.Gough Gen.Top.16;.11l Filippini Graziano; 11r Atlantide Phototravel/Corbis; 12 Brian Kerr Photography/www.briankerrphotography.com; 13 Anna Stowe Landscapes UK/Alamy; 15 Adrian Warren/www.lastrefuge.co.uk; 16 The British Library Board/Cotton MS. Nero d.I.fol.187.v.; 18 AA; 20–1 ONB/Vienna Cod.324, segm.1r.; 24 The British Library Board/Royal 14 C. VII f.2; 26–7 The Bodleian Library, University of Oxford, MS.Gough Gen.Top.16; 31 National Library of Scotland; 32 Courtesy of The Warden and Scholars of New College, Oxford/The Bridgeman Art Library; 34 The British Library Board/Crace Port. 1.33; 37 The British Library Board/G.15961; 38 National Library of Wales; 40–1 The Bodleian Library, University of Oxford, Laxton Map 1635 MS.C17:48(9); 42–3 Alexander Duckham & Co. Ltd/Britannia by John Ogilby 1675; 45 Private Collection/The Bridgeman Art Library; 47 Alexander Duckham & Co. Ltd/Britannia by John Ogilby 1675; 48–9 Alexander Duckham & Co. Ltd/ Britannia by John Ogilby 1675; 51 The British Library Board/Maps C.24.aa.11; 53 Science and Society/SuperStock; 56–7 The British Library Board/ Maps C.9.b.17; 58 The British Library Board/Maps c.24.a.13; 60 National Library of Scotland; 63 The British Library Board/Maps c.24.f.1; 66 The British Library Board/Maps c.24.c.4; 64–5 The British Library Board/Maps C.24.C.4; 68 Private Collection/The Bridgeman Art Library; 71 The British Library Board/Maps c.10.d8; 74 BL/Robana – www.agefotostock.com; 76–7 The British Library Board/Maps 6020.(5.); 80 The Syndics of Cambridge University Library; 82–3 The British Library Board/Maps 7338(1); 87 Poop! Poop! 1998 (oil on canvas), Barry, Jonathan (Contemporary Artist)/Private Collection/The Bridgeman Art Library; 88 The British Library Board/Maps 14a72; 89 AA Archive; 90 AA Archive; 91 AA Archive; 92 The British Library Board/Maps 2.aa.62; 93 The British Library Board/Maps 1.aa.67; 94–5 The British Library Board/Maps 1.aa.67; 97 The British Library Board/Maps 2.aa.47; 99 The British Library Board/Maps 2.aa.47; 100 The British Library Board/Maps 7338(1); 101 The British Library Board/Maps 7338(1); 102–3 AA/1921 Ordnance Survey; 106 Brooklands Museum Archive; 107 Topical Press Agency/Getty Images; 108 National Motor Museum/The Car; 109 National Motor Museum; 112 The British Library Board/ Maps 14a72; 113 The British Library Board/ Maps 14a72; 114 The British Library Board/Maps 14a72; 115 William Earle; 116 Collins Bartholomew Ltd/National Library of Scotland; 118–9 William Earle; 120–1 The British Library Board/Maps 1205.(72.); 123 AA Archive; 124 Michelin/The British Library Board/Maps 10359.b.29; 125 Michelin/The British Library Board/Maps 10359.b.29; 128–9 National Library of Scotland; 130 AA/Ordnance Survey; 131 AA Archive; 132 Mary Evans Picture Library/Ordnance Survey; 134 City of London, London Metropolitan Archives; 135 English Heritage. Aerofilms collection; 136 TfL from the London Transport Museum collection; 137 City of London, London Metropolitan Archives; 139 Rhondda Cynon Taf Libraries; 140–1 The British Library Board/Maps 1175(264)/Ordnance Survey 1947; 144 © Historic Environment Scotland (Aerofilms Collection) Licensor canmore.org.uk; 148–9 Lancashire Archives; 150 Town & Country Planning Association, 2005. Drawing granted to the Association by Dr Tom Osborn and Margaret Fenton; 152 AA Archive; 155 Daily Herald Archive/National Media Museum/Science & Society Picture Library; 156 AA Archive; 157 AA Archive; 158 Fox Photos/Getty Images; 160–1 The British Library Board/Maps 1205.(72.); 162 AA Archive; 164–5 The National Archives UK/Travers Morgan/Capita; 167 German Air Force photographer/IWM via Getty Images; 168 AA Archive; 170 Coventry History Centre, Coventry Heritage & Arts Trust Ltd; 171 a-plus image bank/Alamy Stock Photo; 173 Press Association Images; 174 Lancashire County Council; 177 AA Archive; 178–9 Amey/Sir Owen Williams & Partners/Northamptonshire Record Office; 180 AA Archive; 183 English Heritage/John Laing Charitable Trust; 184 PA/S&G Barratts/Empics Archive; 186–7 The Syndics of Cambridge University Library; 189 AA; 192 The National Archives UK; 193l Amey/Sir Owen Williams & Partners/Institution of Civil Engineers; 193r Amey/Sir Owen Williams & Partners/Northamptonshire Record Office; 194 The National Archives UK; 196 AECOM/Mitchell Library, Glasgow City Council; 198 Steve Lindridge/Alamy Stock Photo; 200–1 Peter Trulock/Fox Photos/Getty Images; 204 Original Source from within the Civic Survey & Plan publication from 1949; 206 Press Association Images; 207 Amey (Owen Williams & Partners)/Institution of Civil Engineers; 208–9 AA; 210 AA Archive; 211 Valentines Postcards/collection David Lawrence; 213t AA; 213b AA; 214l I Spy, Polystyle Publications Ltd; 214r I Spy, Polystyle Publications Ltd; 215 Cymrupix/Alamy Stock Photo; 218 Worcestershire Archive and Archaeology Service. Reference 705:1010 BA9306 parcel 129 section iv.; 219 William Mitchell; 221 City of Norwich Corporation. Crown Copyright and database right 2016. Ordnance Survey 100019747; 222 Archant CM Ltd – Norfolk; 224 Skyscan.co.uk/I Hay; 225 AA; 226 David Lauberts; 229 Nick Hawkes/Alamy; 230–1 Mark Cain www.cmk.net; 232 David Lee Photography; 234–5 AA; 237 AA; 239t AA/Readers Digest; 239bl AA/Readers Digest; 239br AA/Readers Digest; 241 Peter Hewitt/Motorway Archive Trust; 242–3 Ordnance Survey; 245 Nigel Dickenson; 247 Adrian Arbib/Corbis; 248–9 AA; 251 James Kerr/Alamy; 255l Rex/Shutterstock; 255r Stu/Alamy; 257 Geographers' A–Z Map Company Limited; 259 DEFRA; 260 Ordnance Survey; 261 Ordnance Survey; 262l Ashley Sims, Inventor; 262r Ashley Sims, Inventor; 263 Ashley Sims, Inventor; 265 Crown Copyright. Transport Scotland 100046668 2013; 266 AA; 267 Jim Holden/Alamy; 269 Ordnance Survey; 272 AA/ Ordnance Survey/RoadPilot © 2013 RoadPilot® Driving Technology; 273 © SIMON & SCHUSTER UK Ltd, Cover Illustration © Garry Walton represented by Meiklejohn; 277 AA Route Planner routing data ©2006–13 TomTom, Map Data ©2013 Google; 278 David Cruickshanks/Alamy; 280 Ian Butler Landscapes/Alamy Stock Photo; 282–3 ESA/NASA